WHEN WORDS
Waver

SANA KHATRI

CARINA
Ribeiro

MYLES
Reyes

ALSO BY SANA KHATRI

Those Chance Encounters

Can We Pretend?

Presuming You

Unturned Rubbles

For those who are brave enough to wish upon a star.

Search for 'When Words Waver' on Spotify!

ABOUT THE AUTHOR

Sana Khatri is an International Bestselling author, an IT (Information Technology) graduate, a bunny momma, and a makeup junkie. She resides with her aunts, mother, and her younger brother in Mumbai, India. Because her dad is the one who initially motivated her to keep writing, she makes sure to ask him for book-related opinions and suggestions whenever she needs them. She is an unwavering reader, dreamer, and believer, and prefers to have a speck of reality in her fictitious stories.

Twitter & Instagram:
@isanakhatri

PROLOGUE

Her scream – it was so achingly guttural that it stunned him in place. It was a sound so foreign that he could do nothing, *feel* nothing but its echo in his ears as he looked at her.

And, when their eyes met, when her tears slid down her flushed cheeks, he saw the fear, affliction, struggle, and slight confusion on her face, that not only made him stumble forward a bit, but also made him want to tear through everything he was enduring – deep inside his clawing chest.

But it was when her lips shook as she tried to signal something to him through her trembling hands, that he snapped out of his brief numb-fest; that he actually realized what had happened.

And, when a sob hitched out of her and reverberated across the low-lit room, did his stomach begin to clench; his palms begin to sweat.

And his heart – it might as well have stopped beating; his lungs may as well have stopped drawing in air. But it wasn't like he cared anymore, not when *she* was suffering…

1.

Myles

'The Snowed-in Crotch'.

That'd be the name of my autobiography – if I ever decided to write one. Because really, I was *freezing*, from head-to-cock-to-toe, and my client just wouldn't open his damn door.

Chicago, with everything that it has to offer, is an *amazing* city, don't get me wrong. But the *winters* here in November…

I shuddered a little as I blew out puffs of air through my mouth, and then knocked on the slightly chipped wooden Dutch door *again* before quickly shoving my gloved hands deep into the pockets of my dark jeans.

It was 9a.m., and being that it was a Monday, the vibe around me was…well, *glum*, to put it mildly.

Maplewood Ave was a very scenic area in Chicago. Every house, including my client's, was stunning, with snow-coated roofs and stairs, brick-made exteriors, and picturesque windows and doors. Despite the chill and gloomy atmosphere, everything around me was…eye-soothing.

As I waited for my client to open his door, just like I had been for almost ten minutes, I turned around and looked at the brown van parked right in front of his house, next to a set of polished stone stairs.

I scowled. "Remind me again," I said to the man in the driver's seat, "why *I'm* the one standing here and freezing my balls off, while *you*," I pointed a finger at him, "get to sit in the van and keep your ass warm?"

Taron, my ridiculously smug elder brother, and also the creature responsible for my occasional bout of annoyance, smirked at me. "Because

2

you're the one who signs our clients, not *me*. I'm the beast, and you're the beauty; toughen up a bit."

Our caramel-brown hair and grey eyes – both a courtesy of our mom – were the only things that were common between us. Where Taron looked like a combination of an axe murderer from the hills (mostly when he smiled at someone), and a lumberjack (because of his build, and, well, his beard), I looked like a chewed-out version of Chase Crawford. Please don't ask me why, because even if I tried, I wouldn't be able to tell you. It was something an ex of mine had posted on her Facebook wall. Just *two* minutes after our breakup. 3 years ago.

I ruffled the snow out of my hair and deepened my scowl when Taron arched a brow at me. "Fuck you, man," I told him.

He chuckled and shook his head. "I'm being serious, Myles."

"As am I." I took a step forward, but cursed and moved back when I almost tripped off the topmost stair.

Taron chuckled harder. "Careful, bro. We don't want that face of yours to get a scar, now do we? We both know it's the moneymaker in the business." When I flipped him off, he snorted and leaned back in his seat. "I love you, Myles," he all but sang.

When our dad had decided to call it quits on his job four years ago, he'd asked Taron and I to take over our company, *Reyes Constructions*. Not the most dramatically unique name for an enterprise, I know, but our dad is a simple man, who prefers to live an even simpler life. Our mom, God bless her, loves every single thing about him, and in my twenty-nine years of existence, I have *never* seen them disagree or argue about anything. Inhuman? Maybe. Impossible? Unlikely.

I opened my mouth, ready to ask Taron to go fuck himself yet again, but the door behind me *finally* opened, making me pivot on my feet immediately.

"Mr. Ribeiro!" I said in greeting, and flashed a broad smile at the man before me.

3

"It's *Monday*, Myles; show some respect to it and stop being so damn chirpy. It puts a major damper on the day's reputation, in case you didn't know." When I laughed, he tapped the worn-out tip of his wooden cane on the snow-covered '*Welcome*' carpet. "Did you swallow a living bird or something this morning?"

"Hey, Miguel! What's cookin', buddy?" Taron hollered from the van.

I wanted to turn around and glare at him, but decided not to, because really, there was no point in it.

Mr. Ribeiro looked over my shoulder. "You seen your commonsense around this morning, kid?" he asked Taron. "No? How would you? It's because I've got it all, and I currently have it on grill in my kitchen. *That's* what I've been cookin', *buddy*."

I wasn't sure whether to double over and cackle, or hide my face behind my coat in utter embarrassment.

For my *brother*, of course.

Either way, I chose to keep a poker face and not give into my urges.

"So, Myles," Mr. Ribeiro began as he brought his attention back to me, "will you be starting today, or do you want to see the rooms and get the measurements and materials written down first?"

He'd hired me to redecorate a couple of rooms in his massive 5BHK Cape Cod. It was a fun project to undertake, because Mr. Ribeiro's house was a pretty dated one, especially for this part of Chicago.

Before I agreed to take on the renovation, he'd shown me pictures of the rooms that needed rework: the kitchen, and a storage room next to his granddaughter's bedroom that he wanted me to turn into a mini library for her. The latter would be a challenge, but it wasn't something Taron, I, and our team couldn't handle.

"I'll have to ask you a few questions about what exactly it is that you want changed or added," I told Mr. Ribeiro, "and according to that, Taron and I can give you design and material options, along with suitable themes and color schemes."

4

He raised an amused brow. For a 65-something year old dude, he was pretty sassy. "Your brother will help with the logistics?"

I chuckled. "I'll have you know that he *does* come up with creative ideas, however fleeting they may be."

Mr. Ribeiro laughed, but stopped when we heard footsteps. He turned and looked behind him – at the stairs that led to the bedrooms – and then shifted on his feet before smiling an open smile at the person walking down them.

He said something in Portuguese, his voice soft and loving, and as the person – the *woman* – came to stand next to him, he wrapped an arm around her shoulders and faced me.

"Myles, this is my granddaughter, Carina." He then looked at her. "Carina, this is Myles. He's here to fix our fucked-up kitchen and give you your in-home library."

Carina chuckled, and so did I.

The early morning light hit her features as she gazed up at me and grinned, gave me a side-salute, flattened one hand, palm up, slid the other one over it once, and made the #1 gesture with both forefingers before touching the left fist to the right.

I stood there like an idiot, looking at her, and then realized that she was using Sign. Dumbfounded, I glanced at her short dark hair, bright sable eyes, arched cheeks, rich golden skin, and still-grinning lips. She was wearing a lime-colored puff blouse and an emerald-green skirt with a cherry branch on each side. There was a thin black strap on her right shoulder, which was attached to a small black purse. She blinked at me, and I just...couldn't take my eyes off her.

A gush of ice-cold wind hit me in the back, and I shivered a little under its force.

"She says it's nice to meet you," Mr. Ribeiro finally translated Carina's gestures.

I licked my cold lips and took half a step forward. "Yeah." I swallowed and smiled at Carina. "Yeah, it's nice to meet you as well." I extended a hand, and she shook it briefly before letting it go.

Maybe it was because I'd never met someone like her in my life so far, or maybe it was my inability to act rationally in that moment, but God, I...I couldn't stop looking at her.

I just... Fuck, why *couldn't* I stop looking at her?

2.

Carina

He was staring at me, but not in a way that made me uncomfortable. Most strangers, when they meet me, have the exact same reaction: drooped eyebrows, a persistent frown; sympathetic gazes, words of pity on their mouths.

I guess it *is* rare to meet a person who is a mute – a selective mute, in my case – especially when it's something one doesn't exactly expect while going about their day-to-day life.

I chose this for myself at a very young age, and it's now become a vital part of my life. Part of *me*. I *chose* silence for myself, and I did it because I knew it was the only thing that could save me. It's my comfort and source of confidence, and I'm so damn proud of who I am today.

I hugged myself and stepped back when *Avô* invited Myles into the house.

I wasn't always like this – unable and unwilling to speak, I mean. I do remember reciting nursery rhymes and Christmas carols with my *mãe* and *pai* at the age of five. But things changed a year later. Broke. Tarnished.

Faded.

And with them, so did my drive for a lot of things. I lost so much at the age of six, and every time I think about that Tuesday afternoon of March 2000, about what happened that day, I find it hard to see, breathe, or even remember who I am. I shut down completely, in a way, and I know *Avô* feels the same; goes through the reflection of thoughts and memories that I, too, go through. But he never really shows any of it to anyone. He's good at masking himself with neutrality and humor, but I know he hurts, too.

More than me, if I were being honest.

I swallowed and briefly touched his left shoulder, and when he faced me, I smiled and pointed a thumb behind me, indicating that I was leaving, and then signed, *Shop.*

Avô tilted his head to the side. "*Você não quer ficar? Afinal, é um pouco cedo para abrir a loja,*" he said. Do you not want to stay? It is, after all, a bit early to be opening shop.

I shook my head, and he raised a brow in return.

"*Você tem certeza, pequena?*" he asked. Are you sure, little one?

I smiled and rose on my tiptoes so that I could give him a quick peck on his cheek. When I stepped back, I placed my left index finger against my lips, and then quickly moved it forward a few inches in a sign to say, *Sure.*

He sighed, but nodded and pressed a kiss on my hairline. "*Ok, então. Eu te amo. Fique segura, e me ligue quando chegar no do Açaí.*" Okay, then. I love you. Stay safe on the way, and call me once you've reached *do Açaí*.

Vila do Açaí was our Açaí shop, where we not only sold Açaí in its true form, but also with desserts, baked goods, and, of course, ice cream. Ours was the only Açaí shop in Chicago, and being that it was both unique *and* wildly popular among Chicagoans, the crowd we saw daily was crazy. In a *good* way, obviously.

Because Myles would most definitely be working at the house for weeks, *Avô* and I had decided to take turns in going to the shop each day. One of us had to stay back, after all, in case Myles needed anything, or wanted our consent over something.

I felt his eyes snap to me as I turned to go, and then I heard him say, "She's leaving?"

Avô quickly told him about *Vila do Açaí*, and the daily routine we'd be following until the construction was completed.

I looked at Myles then, and as our eyes met, he slowly dragged his greys over my face. Again, the way his gaze traveled over me made me feel the opposite of uncomfortable. It made me feel…important, I think. Like I was the center of his immediate focus, but also something that made him curious.

8

When he blinked at me, I jerked my head upwards with a *"Huh?"* expression on my face. As he clearly didn't know Sign, I thought using an obvious gesture would make my question clear to him.

"Uh." He scratched the side of his neck. "I'm going to need your input on the library's theme, etcetera," he said, and then took off his gloves when the living room got toastier due to the ongoing heater next to the entrance.

There were random wet and matted-down spots on his caramel hair because of ice having melted on them, and his face was a clear shade of pink – due to the heat or the outside weather, I couldn't tell. The tan-and-beige winter coat he had on stood out against his complexion, but complemented him perfectly.

"Maybe we can discuss things once you're back from the shop?" he suggested, but it came across as a hesitant question.

I shifted on my feet, and again, our eyes met. God, when was the last time I'd had such an experience? I honestly couldn't remember.

There was an unknown warmth in my chest; a tingling flush coursing through my skin. I let go of a short breath and smiled, and then gave Myles a thumbs up.

He glanced at it first, then my face, and then broke into a sudden chuckle before mirroring my gesture.

I laughed, and began stepping backwards as I waved at both him and *Avô*.

When I finally turned and headed for the door, I hastily opened my purse and pulled my car keys out from inside it.

Contain yourself, woman. Get a damn grip, I told myself. *You're being ridiculously weird for a twenty-seven-year-old.*

I shook my head, pushed open the door, and exhaled against the chilly morning air.

Good fucking morning to you, Carina Ribeiro.

3.

"This used to be a haven to *minha nora*," Mr. Ribeiro said as we entered the kitchen. His cane made stark *click* and *clack* noises as he moved around the space with eased familiarity.

I followed him inside, then stood next to the well-used counter on the left. "Nora?"

Mr. Ribeiro turned, and blinked as if ridding himself of a daze before giving me a faint smile. "*Minha nora*, meaning my daughter-in-law," he said with a tinge of pain on his face. "The kitchen was where you'd always find her. She never gave up a single chance of making a feast for us, and would drive my son, João, mad with her endless grocery lists." He chuckled to himself with a slow shake of his head. "She was so enthusiastic to learn our ways and language when he'd first introduced her to me and my wife, Irene. So enthusiastic, that it sometimes drove him insane." He pursed his lips in contemplation. "Madison was something else entirely, and was, in truth, the life of our family." His features turned crestfallen for a moment, but then he quickly recovered before taking a seat on one of the silver stools next to the pantry shelf.

I looked around the kitchen – at the periwinkle mosaic wallpaper, white countertops, silver appliances and furniture, and then at Mr. Ribeiro, who laughed airily.

"I told you she was different," he stated.

The rest of the house was warmly mellow – all shades of brown, yellow, and the slightest bit of red – which made the kitchen stand out quite massively.

"So, you'd like me to renovate this area to match the rest of the house?" I asked.

"Not really, no." He placed his cane sideways between his legs. "I do want the periwinkle and silver incorporated somehow into the mix, because those were Madison's colors, but mostly I just want everything new. Carina and I have been facing leakage and other issues for the past few months, and, as you can tell, the countertops have clearly seen better days. She likes it here, but she's been having pest and water problems that I just won't stand to bear."

I inclined my head in agreement. "I can call in the pest control once I've cleared the space out for the makeover, and I can do ivory tiles on the walls instead of a wallpaper. Those work well, and you won't have to worry about replacing them time and again. The flooring can be the same, or I can use a darker shade to add a contrast element." I pointed at the white cabinets. "I can have Taron build completely new ones with a beige fiber coating on 'em to avoid roaches." I then patted the counter. "I can do periwinkle marble on top, with the same beige drawers as the cabinets. The appliances and furniture can have silver accents. That way, we'll be able to balance the theme and keep the colors you want."

Mr. Ribeiro nodded. "I like the idea, and I'm sure Carina will, too. But do discuss this with her today, if possible."

"Of course. Um," I scratched my jaw. "I could give you a reference catalog for the tiles."

Mr. Ribeiro waved a dismissive hand. "I'm sure you'll pick something appropriate. I'm too old for this sorta thing."

I smiled. "You got it." I then slid my gloves into the back pocket of my jeans before leaning my hip gently against the refrigerator behind me. "If you don't mind me asking: what...what happened to Carina's mom?"

Mr. Ribeiro looked at me, a bit startled by my question, of course, to which I quickly added, "I'm sorry if I'm overstepping. I know it's not my place to inquire about something so sensitive."

"Then why did you?" There was no anger on his face, or his voice.

11

I dropped my eyes to the floor, and realized that a lot of it was cracked and uneven, clearly due to the constant presence of people bustling around in the kitchen.

"I guess...I just wanna *know*," I said, and then glanced at Mr. Ribeiro. "I feel like I *have* to know, for some reason."

He said nothing, and only kept looking at me for a long, contemplative moment. Or maybe it was an uncertainty about my intentions of wanting to know. I honestly couldn't tell.

"Have you heard of the March 2000 *Laura. M. Boutique* fire?" he asked.

The hair on the back of my neck rose at the leveled calm he exuded in that moment. "Yes," I managed to say.

He looked at me – *really* looked – and I saw a glimmer of unshed tears in his brown eyes.

"Ours was a case of 'In the wrong place at the wrong time', I'll say," he began, and then swallowed once. "Carina didn't wanna go to school that day, because on her way back home a week ago, she'd seen a dress at the boutique that she really wanted. And, when you're six years old and an only child, you get what you want. So, we decided to make it a family trip and get some absolutely unnecessary shopping done." He sighed and wiped a hand over his jaw. "We'd just made it out of the boutique when Madison found a fault in the bill. Apparently, the cashier had added a couple of items to our list that weren't ours. Her and João decided to head in again and get the money back, so my wife, Irene, and I decided to take Carina to the McDonald's just opposite *Laura's* for a quick ice cream." He sniffed. "We heard the outer glass explode while we were waiting for our ice creams, and then, right before my eyes – before I could even comprehend what was happening – the entire boutique went up in flames." He shuddered, so I turned and grabbed a bottle of water from the refrigerator.

"Here." I handed him the bottle, and then knelt beside him. I watched helplessly as he continued to shiver under the weight of the dreadful memory, and felt something in my gut twist so hard that I flinched a little at the pain.

12

"Carina screamed for them as soon as we ran out of McDonald's – over, and over, and *over*…" Mr. Ribeiro closed his eyes and shook his head. "But it was useless. They were *gone*. They were gone, and there was *nothing* I could do, no one I could turn to for help." He took a long swig from the water bottle. "There were 64 casualties that day, including João and Madison. The fire department said it was arson – some sort of rivalry at play, which was later revealed fully through news and the media. But…" He looked at me – a man so broken I was scared he'd crumble before me. "I keep asking myself: What if Carina had decided to go to school that day? What if we hadn't decided to go out shopping when Madison suggested it? What if I'd asked her not to go back in after reading the bill? What if I'd asked João to convince her not to? What if…" He let go of an unsteady breath and shook his head again. "That's all I'm left with: what ifs, maybes, if onlys. All of them baseless against the significance of my loss, really."

He was right; nothing mattered. What was taken from him would never come back to him, and thinking about it constantly would only empower agonizing and unwarranted guilt to take over him.

Life really was a bitch, wasn't she?

I placed a hand on his left knee. "I'm so sorry for your loss, Mr. Ribeiro."

He sighed again and gave me a faint nod. "That day – it was the last I ever heard my Carina's voice. All those speech therapy sessions and meetings with her doctors over the years did nothing, *meant* nothing. She can hear just fine, but she can't speak. I don't want to say she's lost her voice, because really, she hasn't. I guess…I guess she never really *tried* to put it to use after the accident. It's like she forgot about it; forgot to speak, and what it means in general.

It took us a couple of years, but when the three of us found a rhythm and began living our lives normally, I thought the darkness that'd surrounded us was gone, that it had decided to finally leave our doorstep, but…" He laughed then, a haunting gesture that made my heart race. "I guess God wasn't done punishing this family, because in 2017, I lost my Irene to metastatic melanoma." When I squeezed his knee in assurance, because I really didn't have words to salve the pain I knew he was feeling just by revisiting the past, he gently patted my hand and gave me a glum smile. "But she fought, Myles; my wife didn't give up till the very end. She was brave, willing to grab a chance at life, no matter how slim it was. But, in the end, she lost. The strongest pillar in the foundation of my existence just…collapsed. Her death wasn't sudden, sure, but that doesn't mean I wasn't hoping against hope, that I didn't pray that she'd break the cycle of inevitability for me and Carina."

We were quiet for a while, with only the occasional jeering of a flock of blue jays as they moved around the neighborhood, keeping us indirect company.

I glanced at Mr. Ribeiro, and found him staring blankly at the glass window in the living room. I followed his direction, and watched as thin sheets of snow fell peacefully on the hoods of trucks and cars alike.

He'd seen, felt, and recovered from so much, and yet, he knew how to balance himself, knew how to look the part for others; how to mask what was really on the inside. It may not always be necessary, but it was important, especially when it felt like the walls around you were close to falling apart. Everyone had to act or pretend in this world. The range of it, though, depended on the level of one's struggles and bruises. And also their conveniences, perhaps.

Mr. Ribeiro threw the half-empty water bottle into the bin to his right, and made to stand. I rose quickly, and then helped him to his feet before handing him his cane. He briefly placed a hand over my head, and gave me another smile – a clear one this time – before saying, "Let me show you the storeroom so that you can get an estimate, huh, son?"

I could see it on his face – that soundless plea of wanting a distraction from the fresh wave of agony he was experiencing. And, because it was the least I could do for him, given that he'd entrusted me with such crucial memories of his past, I nodded and followed him out of the kitchen.

4.

Carina

T he electronic cuckoo chimed beautifully as I opened the shop's glass door and walked in. *Avô* hated, and I mean *hated*, the cuckoo bell I'd gotten installed last year, but I absolutely loved it. Every time the door opened and closed, and the cuckoo chirped, he'd glare at it as if he wanted nothing more than to strangle it. He couldn't, obviously, but it was quite a hilarious tradition between us and our employees.

I shivered as I settled into the plush chair behind the main counter. I'd forgotten to grab my coat on the way out – distracted as I was by a certain constructor – and now every inch of me was cold as fucking ice.

Just great.

The toasty air inside the shop was working a little too slowly to my liking as I dusted the slightly melted snow off of me, switched on the multi-colored fairy lights that adorned the front of the counter, turned on the laptop, placed my purse next to it, and smiled at Simran and Remi when they greeted me good morning.

As I looked around the shop, I couldn't help but be in awe of what we had – *Avô* and I, I mean. We never took our shop, or its success, for granted, because we knew what it stood for, and what it meant to our family name.

VILA DO AÇAÍ

· RIBEIRO & CO ·

The shop was my *Bisavô's* vision brought to life. He'd moved to Chicago with his family at a very young age, and by the time he turned twenty-three, he'd decided to contribute to the society by bringing an essence of our culture to life for the people and city he'd come to love and appreciate so much. It's only because of his vision and determination that *Vila do Açaí* is as successful as it is among Chicagoans of all ages, and I couldn't thank him more for the legacy he's left behind for the family.

Açaí is well-loved and used in Brazil. It could even be called as a staple of sorts, if I did say so myself. It's one of the top match-up picks for dessert and baked goods for us Brazilians, which is why *Bisavô* had decided to introduce it to the American culture.

I leaned back in my chair and drummed my long nails over the stack of papers next to the laptop.

The décor at *Vila do Açaí* was a pleasant combination of purple and white, and everything in the shop sang of elegance and simplicity. Lavender walls and ceilings, with massive frames of Açaí desserts hung candidly on the former. White-tiled flooring, glass display cases, along with warm lighting throughout the area that kinda contrasted, but also complemented, the shop.

The parcel/purchase counter, which Remi handled, was opposite mine, while the cute little desk next to it was for taking (from customers) and giving out (to our dealers) both retail and bulk inventory orders. Simran took care of all that good stuff, along with the ice cream station, because Lord knows Remi would be a mess by the end of the day if he were to do any of that.

We had a small baking kitchen to my left – exactly opposite to the shop's entrance – where our bakers, Cruz and Daniel, made fresh Açaí-stuffed muffins, cupcakes, pastries, breads, etc. for everyday customers, grocery stores, and online platforms.

Simran was a couple years younger than Remi and I, and had decided to become a permanent employee at *Vila do Açaí* last year, after announcing that she'd quit her other job as an assistant HR at a restaurant due to the constant disrespect of work ethics by both her colleagues and seniors. Remi, however, has been working at the shop since he was eighteen. Our families go way back, and our grandfathers have a friendship that movies are made and books are written about.

"Hey, kid."

I blinked and looked up, and found Cruz grinning down at me. His hair, which was always in a bun, and his beard, which he liked to braid because it was so long, were both hidden behind lavender bouffant caps. His purple apron was splattered with flour, along with some Açaí as well, and when I quirked a brow at him, he placed a small tray with three cupcakes in it, in front of me.

"Had these out of the oven and cooled just for you. Hope you like em'," he said, still grinning. The guy looked like Seth Rogen on steroids, but he had a personality of a friendly, next-door puppy. I swear.

"And, in case you *don't* like them, you can always shove them in his eyeballs!" Daniel hollered from the kitchen.

I laughed, just as Cruz scowled and turned to glare at Daniel. "I wonder, every night I go to bed, why I haven't shoved your smug face into the hearth by now. For the amount of times you get on my nerves on a daily basis, I've already burned you in at least two-hundred different ways in my head. I just need Carina's permission to do it in real life."

I placed a hand over my mouth and laughed harder. Those two were the Laurel and Hardy in the modern slapstick that was my life.

Daniel leaned against the kitchen's threshold and folded his long arms in front of himself. He was lanky, fair, with a head full of unruly salt-and-pepper hair, and blue eyes that were mostly always glimmering in amusement. "You think about me when you're in bed with your *wife*? Jesus Christ, Cruz, does Valeria *know* that?" he quipped.

Cruz's scowl deepened – if that were even possible. "Why are you like this? WHY?!"

Remi and Simran snickered, whereas Daniel flashed his teeth at his partner.

"Because it's *fun*, Cruz; you should try that sometime. It'll change your whole world, I promise."

Cruz placed his hands on his wide hips. "I have fun by scorching your ass in my imagination. There's nothing more satisfying than that, *I promise*."

Both Laurel and Hardy – I mean Daniel and Cruz – have been working at the shop since I was twelve. They're not just crazy-talented when it comes to baking, but they also never disappoint when they decide to cook savories for everyone.

In the years I've known them, I've come to consider them as part of my family. Their wives, too, treat me with the same kinda love they do their children.

Daniel chuckled at Cruz's retort. "Come back to the kitchen, big guy. I miss the smell of your anger mixed with dough as you constantly breathe down my neck."

"Does *your* wife know this about you?" Cruz sassed. "Jesus Christ, Daniel, what must Brianna think of you?"

Daniel opened his mouth, ready to missile another one of his snarky comments at Cruz, but I slapped the counter twice to stop him. When the two of them looked at me, I jerked my head toward the kitchen, fisted my hands, and knocked the left one on top of the right in a sign to say, *Work*.

Cruz sighed. "Fine, fine; we're goin'." He then pointed at the tray. "Do try these, though. I've added primary flavors in them in an effort to mix and match the taste. We don't have to make these a thing, of course, but if you do like em', I can make more for you and Miguel."

I nodded as I smiled, and touched my fingers to my chin before bringing them forward to say, *Thank you.*

Cruz gave me a soft wink. "You're welcome, kid." He turned and headed back to the kitchen. When he reached it, Daniel gave me a two-finger salute and flung an arm around Cruz's shoulders. The latter didn't push him off, and if I wasn't mistaken, I saw his posture slack a bit as if giving up against Daniel's persistent nature.

With a shake of my head, I grabbed my phone from my purse and picked up the first cupcake, which Cruz had labelled: *Vanilla + Açaí.*

I opened the message app and shot a quick text to my best friend, Ashleigh.

Me: *My construction guy is a total cutie :'(*

Her response came in just as I finished the impossibly yummy cupcake and moved onto the next.

Banana + Açaí

Ash: *And that's a sad thing because…?*

Me: *Because he's so disgustingly gorgeous and I'm an absolute macaca.*

Ash: *Uh, excuse you? You do NOT look like a monkey.*

I chuckled and began typing a response.

Me: *I do. You know, there are people out there who find monkeys sexually attractive, but for the sake of the early hour, let's not dive into that factoid just yet.*

Ash: *Be honest: are you on something this morning?*

Me: *Snow fumes – they've damaged my brain. I'm addicted and can't get enough.*

Ash: *I don't know why I even try with you, seriously.*

I laughed.

Ashleigh and I became friends when we were ten. She'd come to the shop with her parents every evening for flavored breads and pastries, and we just…clicked.

Because I was homeschooled, I didn't exactly have anyone my age to be around at the time – except for Remi, I guess – so Ash and I quickly got attached to the hip. She'd spend hours at the shop, either completing her homework, talking about the people at her school, and, as we grew up, about the hot boys she knew and had kissed. Our sleepovers were just as colorful, if not less.

She's the one who'd helped me score my first date and boyfriend when I was nineteen, and when things went downhill six months later, she was there to kick my ex right where the sun hates to shine.

She was the one who'd held me in her arms outside the ICU during my *vovó's* final days, and she's the one who pulled me out of the darkness after *Vovó's* passing. In a way, Ash has shown me how to live life at different angles, ones that lead to just as many outcomes.

She's never had an issue interacting with me, and as I learnt Sign over the years, so did she. Once she decided to be there for me, she didn't ever think of leaving my side. And thank God for that, because I'd be an utter disaster without her in my life.

It isn't always your family that makes you who you are, or strengthens your empire to make you a better person. Sometimes it's a friend, someone who just randomly walks into your shop one evening and decides to hold your hand for as long as you'll let her.

I sniffed and let go of a long breath, and then realized I hadn't replied to Ash's last message.

Me: *AnyWHO. So, speaking of gorgeous… I can't exactly call his brother that. The dude looks like a freight train with teeth. Almost freaked me out with his smile when I walked out the door.*

Ash: *OMG! Hahahahaha, really?*

I licked my fingers after shoving the last of the second cupcake into my mouth. Christ, these were *good*. I had to let Cruz know, and also ask him for samples so that I could get them approved by *Avô* before adding them to our daily list.

Me: *Yeah, really. I did wave at him, though.*

Ash: *Why the hell would you wave at him?!?!*

Ash worked as a checkout manager at *Trader Joe's*, and her schedule was just as hectic as mine, so the fact that she was indulging me with this conversation clearly showed her investment in me. I have, after all, been known to be a bad influence.

Only *occasionally*, of course.

Me: *Because he has kind of a friendly face???*

Ash: *You literally JUST called him a freight train with teeth, Rina. Get your act together.*

I grinned and grabbed the third cupcake.

Butterscotch + Açaí

Me: *I didn't wanna come across as rude…*

Ash: *So you waved at a potential axe murderer.*

It wasn't a question, but a statement, which made me giggle.

Me: *He has Myles's eyes. And hair. And face. Almost. I couldn't ignore that :'(*

Ash: *Myles, huh?*

I felt my neck and cheek flush at that.

Me: *Yeah :')*

Ash: *God, you're smitten, aren't you?*

Me: *Maybe… But it's not like he's into me or anything. It's a one-sided, bound-to-end-in-snots-and-tears-if-I-let-it-affect-me-too-much kinda thing.*

Ash: *Then why tell me about it at all?*

I wiped my fingers with the tissue Cruz had set on the tray for me.

Me: *Because you're my best friend? And also because he'll be working at the house for weeks and I need someone to talk to about it.*

Ash: *Talk about how he uses his hammer to nail things, you mean?*

I slapped a palm against my forehead.

Me: *My eyes are burning from reading that. That pun just gave me a virtual-contact conjunctivitis.*

Ash: *Oh hush. We both know you want in his pants.*

Me: …………

I liked to live my life by grasping onto any and every opportunity I could get. After losing my parents, and then my *vovó*, I've realized that if you restrain yourself, that if you keep long-term goals, then you may end up not fulfilling them at all. Piling up dreams and desires could leave you with disappointment and regret in the future, so why not do what you want to, in the *moment*?

Ash: *Well, then what are you waiting for, babe? Grab him by the collar, pull him close, and fucking maul him. Life's too short for those who don't take risks. Live your extra life, girl. You've got my blessing and support.*

She was right, wasn't she? But sometimes, things weren't as simple as that, because not every factor that led up to an ultimate decision was one that had a valid ground to stand on. And when it came to Myles, I really didn't know how fast or slow I'd have to throw my dice, if *at all*, to learn of the kind of pace he liked. But I'd find out soon enough, wouldn't I?

5.

D o I throw the dice, or do I let her take the lead?

Do I even have a choice in the matter? If yes, then what *is* that choice?

I righted the pile of catalogs next to me – *again*. Was it the seventh or the eighth time? I genuinely couldn't remember.

I was nervous, if I was being honest with myself. I guess it was natural for me, given the circumstance, because I was terrified of what I might say, or do, or *not* say, perhaps. I've never conversed with someone who couldn't speak, especially one who'd left me speechless, and had so effortlessly pulled at the most vulnerable string of my very being just by looking at me. I didn't wanna offend or hurt her, or make her feel uncomfortable.

I shifted on the couch as I waited for her, and felt a lump forming in my throat, which I quickly pushed down by swallowing a few times.

I'd spent the day fixing some minor issues that Mr. Ribeiro had pointed out while showing me around. Pro bono, of course. He'd insisted on adding the charges to my final payment, but Taron and I ended up refusing the offer.

I think Mr. Ribeiro mainly let us off the hook easy over the small charges because Taron kept pissing him off every two seconds, and he prolly just wanted him to shut up and get busy with work so he'd stop annoying him.

Relatable.

The relief on his face when my brother left two hours ago had been utterly comical. Not that I blamed him, given Taron's eccentric nature and talent for random word-vomit.

I tapped my bare feet on the carpet, one after the other, and fought the urge to move the catalog pile again. I was sitting in front of the massive living-room fireplace, and as the ember flames crackled and rose higher, so did the rate of my heartbeats.

I stretched my fingers and tried to distract myself by thinking of the storeroom. When I'd seen it earlier, it'd become clear, by the cluster of dirt and boxes in it, that it'd take Taron and our guys at least 2 days just to get everything out so we could clear out the space for further assessment. Mr. Ribeiro had told us that him and Carina had already gone through everything in there, and that there wasn't anything in the room they wanted to keep. At least there was that, huh?

I turned my head in the direction of the door when it opened, and in walked – more like *waddled* – Carina. She was shivering as she put the locks in, took off her shoes at the threshold, and then padded over to me.

I stood and grabbed the blanket Mr. Ribeiro had given me before retiring to his room an hour ago, and as Carina set her purse on the small wooden table next to the sofa before stopping in front of me, I completely lost my train of thought.

Fantastic.

She waved at me with a wide grin on her face, and so, I did the same. Just…wow; I'd really lost it.

"Uh…hi," I then said, like the dumb sloth that I was, and unfolded the blanket before offering it to her.

Something in Carina's eyes flared, like the fire in front of us, and she stepped closer to me instead of taking the blanket from me.

So, I guess it was *her* who'd made the first move, then.

Should I be relieved, or should I be frustrated?

The answer was a gamble on my mind.

I moved even closer to her, and when she blinked up at me with wet, snow-sprinkled lashes, I smiled and wrapped the golden cashmere around her.

She hastily grabbed the hems and pulled the blanket snug against her body, and then plopped – *actually* plopped – onto the sofa. She canted her head, silently asking me to join her.

I did, obviously.

"Hi," I said again, then scratched the back of my head when Carina chuckled softly.

"Sorry," I muttered, and grabbed the catalogs from next to me before placing them on my lap. "So, what do you wanna start with? We can pick a basic theme first, and I can then coordinate it with appropriate shades, materials, any special item or style request, etc."

She brought a hand up, asking me to wait, and then grabbed her purse before pulling out her phone, a notebook, and a pen from inside it. She then tapped around on her phone, and after a few seconds, turned it so that I could see the screen.

I looked down at the picture, at the rustic library. The floor was most definitely Elm – sanded and polished to give it a textured feel. There were wide shelves on either side of the library, with the center bare, save for a dark, wooden study table at the very end – right above a tiny, namesake window. There were period frames on either side of the window, and the roof was an upside-down V – with a tainted glass in the middle and Oakwood plies on either of its side. It was simple, yet intricate. It was…

"Gorgeous," I whispered, and then looked at Carina. "You want it exactly like this?"

She nodded excitedly, and I don't think she did it on purpose, but she shifted closer to me, and our knees bumped.

"Can you send me this picture?" I asked her. "I'll need it for reference."

She nodded again, pointed at me, and then pinched the fingers of both her hands before touching them together and twisting them once.

I shook my head, and my brows furrowed. "I'm sorry, I don't understand."

25

She gave me a thumbs up, then picked up her pen and notebook, and it's the first time I *actually* saw the two items properly. Her pen was shaped in the form of a watermelon slice, and her notebook...

It took me a moment to realize what it meant. Both the front and back of the book had Makkari from *Marvel's Eternals*, the movie, on them. Makkari was portrayed as a deaf character in it, and I'd seen her signing her words in the movie's multiple trailers. Her condition was different from Carina's, yet their manner of communication was exactly the same.

"Nice notebook," I remarked.

She smiled and signed, *Thank you.*

I knew how that was done; I wasn't completely stupid.

She flipped open said notebook and wrote something in it before showing it to me.

Give me your number so that I can send you the photo.

"Oh yeah, of course," I said.

We quickly exchanged numbers, and a few seconds later, my phone *pinged* back-to-back with two new messages from her.

Carina: *Hi :')*

Carina: *sent a photo*

I saved the picture on my camera roll, and then showed her the layout and color scheme Mr. Ribeiro had decided on for the kitchen. Carina consented to everything, and once we were done, I jerked my head at her notebook.

"You going to watch the movie?" I asked her. I told myself that I was curious, but the truth was: I didn't wanna go home. Not yet.

Carina nodded, and then started writing something in her book.

I'm going to watch it with my best friend, Ashleigh. You?

"I'm going with my family," I said. "What about your grandfather?"

What about him? she wrote.

"Isn't he going with you?"

She shook her head, and then wrote, *Shop.*

"Ah, gotcha." I nodded. Mr. Ribeiro had told me all about the shop's popularity and origin over a delicious spread of homemade *Farofa* and *Arroz Carreteiro* at lunch earlier. It was a surprise that I'd never visited, or even heard of, *Vila do Açaí* before. When I'd asked Taron about it, he'd told me that he ordered their baked stuff to his apartment every other day, but he didn't know about the shop being owned by Carina and her grandfather until I'd told him so. It's weird how the world can be such a small place, and then not so small at the same time.

Carina patted me on the arm to get my attention. When I looked at her, she showed me her open notebook. She'd written something new.

Do you have a nickname?

I raised a brow at her, to which she shrugged.

"I don't know if it's a nickname, to be exact, but my elder brother calls me Beauty," I told her. "He says I'm the face, and he's the muscle of the family."

Carina laughed, an action so airy and breathless that I just couldn't look away from her. Her face was partially illuminated by the raging fire before us, accentuating her mellow features drastically, and her eyes – they seemed to glow like orbs of timber under the warm ambience around us.

"God, you're *stunning*." The words escaped me before I even realized I'd spoken them out loud.

Carina inhaled sharply, and I reached out – I *dared*, more like – to push the curtain of her soft hair behind her right ear.

Fuck, was that too much, too forward?

Had I crossed the line?

She smiled that magnetic smile at me then, and gently wrapped her fingers around my wrist before erasing a little more of the distance between us.

"*Rina…*" I whispered, and then swallowed. "Can I call you that?"

She nodded, still smiling, and our noses brushed.

She smelled so good – like lilacs and almonds and vanilla, all mixed together. I wanted to pull her to me, feel every inch of her pressed against me, but I also didn't wanna push my luck too hard.

27

"I wanna kiss you so bad right now," I confessed. My heart was thrashing in my chest – literally – and as our breaths mingled, I tilted my head to the side.

Rina fisted the collar of my t-shirt and leaned in further, an indication that she wanted a taste just as eagerly as I did.

I sighed, and our lips brushed. Fuck, I was going to lose it. I was hard; I was burning up.

"Rina." I parted my lips slightly, just as she did hers, but sucked in a breath and moved back when I heard the sound of Mr. Ribeiro's cane against the stairs behind me.

Shit.

Rina clicked her tongue and frowned, but then pulled me to her before pressing a sound kiss on the left side of my mouth.

Damn tease.

I chuckled, and nuzzled my nose against her cheek for a lingering moment before getting to my feet.

She followed suit, and then began shoving her things inside her purse just as Mr. Ribeiro reached the last of the stairs.

"I thought I heard you two down here," he said with a grin, and then looked at Rina. "Had a good day, hon?"

She gave him a thumbs up, and I pursed my lips to hide a smile when I noticed her flushed face and neck.

Mr. Ribeiro nodded, and Rina glanced at me. When our eyes met, she gave me a subtle wink, followed by a wave, and then jogged up to her room, but not before kissing Mr. Ribeiro on the cheek.

That woman was an apocalypse waiting to happen.

I gently cleared my throat, put on my coat, grabbed the catalogs from the sofa, and pointed a thumb over my shoulder. "I should go. I'll, uh, see you in the morning. I can start with the kitchen walls tomorrow, if that's okay with you."

"Sure," Mr. Ribeiro stated.

"Great, then. Well, good night, sir." I turned and made my way to the door. I'd only just touched its knob, though, when I halted, my heart in my throat, after I heard a sharp *tap* of Mr. Ribeiro's cane against the wooden railing.

"Myles?"

I didn't face him; I couldn't. The steel in his voice was enough to turn me immobile, for a bout of shame and guilt to wash over my pathetic conscience. "Yeah?"

"You've disappointed me, son," he said stoically, right before he headed back upstairs.

I gritted my teeth as I closed my eyes and pressed my forehead against the door.

Fuck.

6.

Carina

I woke to the elegant singing of blue jays outside my window, which made me smile. I say "singing" because they're basically called songbirds, and I'll forever prefer waking up to *their* voice than that of a blaring alarm siren.

I like what I like.

They'd started coming outside my room more and more over the last three years – since I'd had someone come in and attach a large food tray to the wall next to my window. It's hard as it is for these birds to feed themselves properly, so I thought doing this little thing for them might help them in some way. Also, I just wanted an excuse to visit a pet store and buy fancy bird food for them. *And*, also because I really love their singing.

It's mostly because of the latter, I promise.

I stretched and turned in bed, and groaned at the pressing pain in my lower back. Sleeping in the same position for too long was not something I did intentionally; it just happened sometimes.

I looked to my left, and smiled even bigger when I found my teal vacuum mug on the nightstand, with a small note placed under it. I sat up and quickly grabbed the former, and when I twisted open its cap, I sighed as the heady aroma of coffee hit me right in the face.

Heaven.

As I took a large swig of it, I grabbed the note and read it.

Eu te amo, minha Carina.

I love you, my Carina.

I touched the note to my chest for a brief moment, and then carefully put it in the 2nd drawer of my nightstand, where it joined more of *Avô's* little notes to me over the years. I then grabbed my phone before sending him a text.

Me: *Bom dia, Avô. Thank you for the coffee :') Love you.*

He responded a few minutes later, just as I was about to swallow another mouthful of coffee. Don't judge.

Avô: *You're up. I figured I'd make coffee before Myles and his guys revoked kitchen access. They're already at the house and working on the walls, by the way. Might be a while before we can use the area for cooking. You good for the afternoon? You can order takeout, or have lunch with Ashleigh during her work break.*

Just the mention of Myles's name made my breaths come in faster. God, why was I being like this, especially towards a guy who was a complete stranger?

31

I cleared my throat and typed a response.

Me: *Yeah, I'm good. And yeah, you're right; I'll take lunch with Ash.*

Me: *Also, you always give me shit for going to the shop early, but look at you. It's only 9 and you're already there.*

Avô: *How do you know I'm at the shop and not somewhere else?*

I rolled my eyes as I drank more of the delicious coffee.

Me: *Where else would you be, Avô?*

Avô: *Come now, at least give me the benefit of the doubt, pequena.*

I chuckled.

Me: *Never change, Avô. Never change.*

Avô: *It's already a little too late for that, don't you think?*

I shook my head as I laughed, just as my phone *beeped* with another text from him.

Avô: *Also, I'm at the shop this early because Cruz called and asked if I could come in before opening time. He said he wants me to sample a few things, and that he had your approval on them?*

Me: *Yeah. It's these yummy cupcake flavors he's come up with. They're so good, Avô; I really think we should add them to our menu.*

I placed the empty mug on the nightstand and hid a yawn behind a hand.

Avô: *I'll try them, then, but I'm sure they're great. It's about time we introduced new things to the customers.*

Me: *I agree! Okay, I gotta go freshen up and look for something to eat. I love you, Avô. Text me after you've tried the cupcakes.*

Avô: *Will do, hon. Eu te amo.*

I got to my feet and headed to the window. I slowly slid its small glass door to the side, and leaned my head out so that I could look at the blue jays' food tray. The sunflower seeds were hidden under a thick blanket of snow, and I could already tell that a lot of them had frozen over. I liked to clean and fill the tray late at night so that the birds had food in the morning, but ever since it had started snowing, I'd been having issues keeping the tray safe from the stupid snowflakes. I had, however, thought about getting a roof added over it

32

to avoid the snow from falling directly inside it. The guy who'd installed the tray wasn't free to come in and do it for me, and I, of course, couldn't do it myself. But...maybe *Myles* could do it.

I shivered at the cold outside and moved back to avoid getting hit by strong waves of chilly air. I then shut the window and stepped to the side, and tapped my nails on the back of my phone, which was still in my hand.

It wasn't like I was going to be candid with Myles if I did decide to text him. It would be a work-related thing, and even if I *did* send him a random message, it wasn't like I'd commit a crime against humanity or anything. We'd exchanged numbers for a reason.

We'd almost *kissed* last night for a reason, too.

Ugh, why was it so hard being a fifteen-year-old in the body of a twenty-seven-year-old? The struggle was *real*, let me tell you.

I glanced at my phone, then at the food tray, and then at my phone again. Deciding that the birds mattered more than my silly procrastination, and also that it'd be nice to simply *hear* from Myles after almost getting caught by *Avô* last night, I unlocked my phone and sent out a text.

Me: *Morning, Beauty :') I need a quick favor.*

I then explained everything in the message, making it look more like a movie's monologue than an actual request. I think I waited for a little over ten minutes for him to reply, and when he didn't – even after reading the message within the first minute itself – I sighed, threw my phone on the bed, and decided to go downstairs.

What? I was at home for a reason, okay? Examining the work progress was *part* of that very reason. And, if I wanted to check in on a certain constructor as well, then I would.

Why?

Because I damn well could, that's why.

7.

"**F**ucking *fantastic*, Paul; why don't you go ahead and break the damn door while you're at it, huh?" I said to one of my guys, and sniffed against the dryness in my nose.

"Sorry, boss," he mumbled before carefully placing the box he was holding, at the entrance.

It was *freezing* outside, and I was helping Paul and Greg haul the tile boxes, marble counter-tops, and wood plies from the mover's truck to the house.

When Mr. Ribeiro had opened the door for me an hour or so ago, he'd only given me a quick nod before going about his business. I'd seen him go up to Carina's room with a mug and a note in hand, and then watched him leave for the shop a few minutes later with another curt nod in my direction.

It was *awkward*, almost *painfully*.

And I don't know why, but it made me angrier at myself. Probably because I'd genuinely hurt the man by almost making out with his granddaughter in his house.

I was an A-grade tool, pun definitely intended.

I'd had half a mind to ask my brother to go in early instead of me, but I knew he'd throw the "*You're the one who approaches clients, not me*" bullshit at me, so I'd decided to face the music myself. I would have to anyway, one way or another. It's not like I could avoid Mr. Ribeiro for weeks on end. Shit didn't work like that in real life, did it?

"Jesus, Greg, *what the fuck?!*" I all but exploded when he almost dropped the marble-tops he was carrying. "We need these in the kitchen, not on the damn pavement!"

He opened and closed his mouth, and then apologized before slowly climbing up the stairs.

Paul and Greg are twin brothers, aka Ed Sheeran doppelgängers, and have been working for Taron and I ever since we took over *Reyes Constructions.* They're outstanding at what they do, don't get me wrong. But sometimes, even accomplished people held the power of getting on my nerves, especially when I was in a *very* particular kind of mood.

"Whoa, whoa; what is *up* with you this morning, man?" Taron came to stand to my left, and when I glared at him, he folded his arms across his chest.

"Stop fucking looming over me like that," I told him, and then slightly pulled my blue beanie forward.

Taron put his tongue to his cheek. "You do realize that you've used that word at least four times in the last minute, right?"

I huffed. "I don't fu–" I stopped myself, and cleared my throat before looking away from him. Just then, my phone *pinged* in my back pocket. With a grunt, I pulled it out, and sucked in a breath when I saw her name flashing on the screen.

I quickly scanned the message, and then shoved my phone into my coat's side-pocket.

Focus, Reyes, I told myself. *You're here to work, and work* only. Investing emotions into something that'll never be an actual thing is pointless. I had to work more on that little fact, however hard it may be for me.

"Hey."

I felt Taron's hand on my shoulder. When I looked at him again, his brows were furrowed in clear concern.

"What's wrong, Beauty?" he asked. "Is it a girl problem? If it is, you can tell me, and I'll help you out no matter the magnitude of the issue."

35

And here I thought, just for a moment, that he'd suddenly turned into a sage. Oh, how *wrong* I was.

Even though we were both covered from top to bottom in winter wear, my brother somehow looked more at ease with all the layers on him than I did. Frustrating, I know.

"You're married to your *high school girlfriend*, Taron," I told him. "The *only* girlfriend you've ever had, need I remind you. So no, you won't be able to help me with my girl problems, not by a long shot."

He grinned. "So it *is* what I thought it was. I guessed it right, didn't I?"

"I know you have a teenage daughter, but you don't have to act like her all the time."

He laughed and wrapped an arm around me. "Ah, Myles, but it's a very refreshing feeling to be a fifteen-year-old girl. I've actually been learning so much from Sienna these days. All those social apps and TikTok trends and whatnot. It's like my eyes were closed until my daughter opened them with her vast knowledge and intelligence."

I rolled my eyes and shook my head. "Dear Lord," I muttered. God forbid if I saw him doing one of those TikTok dances with multiple transitions and shit. I'd prolly have a coronary right there and then.

Great, now I couldn't get the visual of Taron doing the *Renegade* out of my head. The day just keeps getting better and better for me.

"Myles?"

"Yeah?"

Taron let go of my shoulders and crossed his arms again. "Tell me what's wrong, because I know something is."

I shoved my hands into my coat pockets and gave him a faint smirk. "I was just imagining you doing the TikTok dances. Almost gave myself a headache because of all the vivid visuals my mind kept conjuring up."

He scoffed. "I'm being serious, man, come on."

I scanned his face for a moment. There was no amusement on it, or even an ounce of his usual smugness.

36

I sighed, and felt the snow crunch under my boots as I shifted a little.

Greg and Paul were working together now, moving the boxes and plies at a much-relaxed pace than before.

I swallowed and looked at my brother again, and when I saw the softness in his gaze, I relented and told him about yesterday.

"I really like her, man," I said. "I hardly even know her, but it's like she's become the center of something worth looking forward to for me, and yet, she's also something I can't have."

Taron's eyebrows almost reached his hairline, and his beard started moving in kind of an uncomfortable manner as he worked his jaw left and right.

"Yo, boss, can you come here, please? We need your help with somethin'," said Paul.

"Coming," I told him, and then shrugged at Taron. "So, there's that. Back to work for us. You good to grab our equipment from the office?"

Taron nodded. "Yeah, I'll get them and be back in fifteen."

"Perfect." I turned and began jogging over to Paul and Greg.

"Myles?"

I stopped and faced my brother. "Yeah."

He smiled at me. "Just wanted to tell you that if you start living your life under someone else's expectation meter – someone who you barely know, despite their trust in you – then you're not exactly living your life like it's supposed to be lived. I'm not asking you to disrespect or disregard Miguel and his tragic past, but know that you're just as much entitled to doing what you want as he is. Carina, too, to be honest. She didn't choose to take a step forward just to have you backing out; that's not how things work, bro. If she's willing to take the risk, then so should you. That's all."

I swallowed as I mulled over his words. He was right, of course, but he didn't have the same perspective on things as I did. We both thought things through very differently. It's why he's always been so carefree, and I've always functioned under the fear of screwing shit up.

37

I smiled back at him. "Thanks, Taron," I told him honestly. Because I really was thankful for everything he'd said. At least he understood where I was coming from, even if his approach at resolving the issue was a spontaneous one.

He shrugged. "No problem. Oh hey, you want an espresso macchiato or somethin'? I'm feeling really hollow after only a single cup of coffee since I woke up."

I chuckled. "That'd be great, yeah."

Taron grinned. "Cool. I'll grab a few on the way back. See ya in a bit."

I nodded. "Love ya, man."

His eyes lit up at that. "Love you."

With a nod, I turned and followed the guys inside the house. I'd only just crossed the threshold, though, when Carina came down the stairs wearing nothing but a thin, blue t-shirt dress with pink roses all over it. Her hair was a wavy mess; her feet were bare. And, as she touched them to the carpet, she looked up and smiled at me.

With everything inside me, I wanted to grab her and kiss her waiting lips.

With everything inside me, I wanted to fucking burst into flames for this woman, and that's a scary notion because I'd only met her yesterday.

And, with everything inside me, I wanted to stay glued to the same spot so that I wouldn't end up accidentally doing either of the above things. So, I did just that, and saw as Carina's expression morphed to one of confusion.

She jerked her head upwards when she reached me, and instinctively, I took a step back.

This close, the hurt on her face was clearly visible, and so was the silver that immediately lined her eyes upon my action.

"I can't," I told her. "I really can't, I'm sorry."

She blinked, and I watched as a single tear slid onto her right upper cheek and stayed there.

She bent and grabbed a discarded marker from the coffee table, and then looked around for something to write on.

I snatched a little diary out of my coat and handed it to her, and as she took it from me – anger riding her beautiful features – I waited for her to jot down every possible curse under my name, but what she instead wrote was:

Why?

Such a simple question, which would most definitely have an even simpler answer. For anyone but me, that is.

But if I looked at it practically, the answer *was* indeed very simple. It's just that, for some reason, it felt inadequate now that I'd seen Carina's reaction to my decision.

So, instead of being rational and telling her why we couldn't do what we both wanted to, I took another step back and repeated myself. "I can't."

She swallowed, and her chest rose and fell as she took even breaths. I could tell that she was struggling to understand my sudden change of behavior, and I really wish I could explain it to her; wish I *knew* how to do it in the first place.

After a short while, she pushed her hair behind her left ear and began writing something. Then, once she was done, she flipped the diary in my direction, but kept her gaze turned sideways, like she couldn't even look at me anymore.

It hurts.

My eyes burned as I read those two words, again and again. As if she hadn't already been through enough hell in her life, now *I* was acting like a damn punisher to her.

"*Rina…*" I let her name fall from my lips; let it brush against the suffocating air I was breathing in.

She inhaled sharply, threw the diary and marker on the couch, and then turned around before heading up the stairs and back into her bedroom.

As I watched her go, I let the throbbing pain in my gut multiply. I let it take over every thought, every reason in my muddled head. I did, after all, deserve every bit of it.

8.

Carina

They're so annoyingly abstract, these emotions. And yet, they see no rhyme or reason; they just attack. They claw at you so deep – their talons sharp and piercing – that you have no choice but to surrender.

I'll never fully know why I can't let certain things go. Why I can't stop thinking about the different outcomes they'd lead to if only I could just...*ask*. If only I could put a proper voice to the things I wanted to know and learn about.

Things I simply wanted to say. *Out loud.*

His rejection had slammed against me like a wrecking ball, even though it shouldn't have.

His sympathy towards my naivety had been embarrassing, to say the least.

And the way he'd said my name after I'd told him that he'd hurt me – it'd been just as painful to hear as the words he'd uttered just before it.

I can't. I really can't, I'm sorry.

Well, *I* couldn't, either.

I couldn't stand the idea of him having affected me so much. We were strangers, after all, and he was here only temporarily, to fix something that actually needed fixing. You know, the walls, the floors, the cabinets.

Not *me.*

9.

They're so damn conceptual, these feelings. And yet, they don't give an inch's worth of shit; they just strike. They cut through you so fast – their blades true and sharp – that you have no option but to give in.

I'll never fully understand why I care so much about what others think – of me and my choices. Why I can't brave brushing aside outside scrutiny and do what matters the most to *me*. If only I could put the right amount of emphasis on the idea of *going with the flow*.

On the things I simply wanted to *have*.

Her anger had slammed against me like a bolt of lightning.

The pain on her face towards my cowardice had been torturous, to say the least.

And those two words she'd written in my diary before walking away from me – they'd been just as painful to read as the question she'd asked before them.

It hurts.

God, it really *did* hurt. Knowing that I'd put tears in her eyes, distrust on her mind, and maybe even hatred in her heart, wasn't exactly a comforting feeling.

No wonder she'd left me alone in the living room in the wake of a fresh wave of disgust towards myself. She didn't owe me anything, not after what I'd said to her.

Her time was rightfully reserved for the people in her life who actually understood the importance of her presence. *They* are the ones who deserve her smiles, her laughter, her touches.

Not *me*.

10.

Carina

I pressed my lips together to make sure my lipstick was in place as I reached the living room, careful not to let my eyes wander. It was a new day, and if I allowed it, it'd be one full of opportunities, more happy customers, and even some laughter with friends along the way.

I could hear him, and even smell that spicy aftershave of his – one I'd first smelt when I'd almost kissed him the day before yesterday.

I took another step forward, and he turned. I told myself not to – oh, how I fought the urge – but I still looked up. Our eyes met. He ran his gaze over me, slow and thorough, so I did the same.

Eyes clashed.

He licked his lips. I parted mine – just barely.

We looked. We stared. We held back.

And then, when I realized that all of this'd go nowhere, I rushed past him to the door and out into the street in the next heartbeat.

I did the same thing the next day.

And the next.

And the one after that.

11.

Myles

I dusted the wood shavings off my jeans before rising. I then asked Paul to grab a sheet of fiber and a bottle of adhesive from the kitchen so that we could be done with the fourth cabinet before moving onto the drawers.

I sensed her first, and then, the smell of her perfume wafted over to me – the one I'd first smelt when I'd ran the tip of my nose over her cheek the day before yesterday.

I turned, just as she took a step forward. I yelled at myself not to – oh, how I strained against the urge – but I still looked up. Our eyes met. She stopped in her tracks, so I took that as an opportunity to slowly drag my gaze over her. She mirrored my assessment.

Eyes clashed.

I licked my lips. She parted hers – just enough to throw my coherency out the back door.

We looked. We stared. We held back.

And then, as if realizing something, she rushed past me to the door and out into the street, and reluctantly, I got back to work.

I did the same thing the next day.

And the next.

And the one after that.

12.

Is that a knock? A tap of *Avô's* cane? An alpaca banging its head against my headboard?

I groaned and managed to half-open my eyes. It was still a little dark in my room, and a quick glance at my bedside clock confirmed my suspicion of it being too early for my lazy ass to be waking up.

7:03a.m.

Another tap, followed by a scraping sound.

I sat up and looked around, and when I found nothing out of the ordinary – not even the alpaca I'd wished for, which is a shame – I glanced to the left. I shouldn't have done that, because right outside my damn window, standing on a silver ladder wearing a Blackhawks beanie and an ivory fisherman's sweater, was Myles.

Why in the *hell* did he have to look so fucking cute at such an ungodly hour?! This wasn't fair to me. AT ALL.

There was a screw pressed between his teeth, and a marker tucked behind his right ear. He had a wireless drill machine in one hand, and it took me a few long seconds to realize what it is exactly that he was doing.

I stood, grabbed a spare notebook and pen from my nightstand, and marched over to the window before opening it with a resounding *bang*.

Myles looked up, a bit startled, and then pulled the screw out of his mouth. "I'm sorry I woke you," he said casually – like he couldn't see the warring emotions on my face. "I was trying to be as quiet as I could, but aluminum can be a bit tricky to work with, so it got a bit noisy."

45

Almost *two* weeks of absolutely *nothing*, and now he wanted to talk *metal* to me?! Was he serious?

I clicked open my pen and began writing in the notebook.

What're you doing?

He read it, and then shifted his weight on the ladder. This close, I could see the stark flush on his cheeks and nose, and tiny flakes of snow on both his day-old stubble and dark lashes. He was *beautiful*, there was no doubt about that, but that very thing was frustrating me beyond measure because I couldn't just reach out and touch him, nor ask him to touch me.

"You wanted my help with the food tray, remember?" His voice pulled me out of my train of thought. When I blinked at him, he continued. "It took me a while to come up with the idea, but I think this'll do just fine." He jerked his head forward, and I noticed, for the first time, that he had attached a roof a few inches above the tray, along with two aluminum sections on either side of it.

"I thought that covering the tray from three sides would not only help keep the food safe, but also turn the area into a refuge for birds who need a place to sleep in," he said. "Aluminum can get very cold during winters, though, so I was thinking maybe I could screw pieces of wood plies over or under them." He scratched his jaw. "But wood might not do well against the brick wall. It prolly won't give a neat finish, but I'm still working on the whole thing, so we'll see." He knocked on the roof then. "This has a door as well." He flipped said door upwards. "See? You can easily clean the tray this way, and also replace food and water without a hassle."

The whole time he was talking – *explaining* – I kept staring at him in awe.

He'd thought of *everything*, and had even come in *hours* before his daily schedule just to work on the food area.

I swallowed when he exhaled a long puff of air, and then quickly scribbled a few words in the notebook as the snow outside grew thicker.

You shouldn't be out for so long. It's freezing like the devil's balls outside.

His lips twitched as he read what I'd written. "I'm heading over to the office in a few. Taron and I have a client coming over in about forty minutes."

Okay.

What else could I say to that? It was awkward small-talk at its best, and it was making me itchy all over.

Myles sighed, and I saw the struggle on his face as he looked at me.

Stop resisting, I wanted to tell him. *Just stop, and fucking* tell *me what's making you pull back so earnestly.*

But instead, I put the tip of my pen on the almost-full page and wrote:

How much will the whole roof thing cost? I'll make a note of it now so that I don't forget about it later.

He shook his head after reading that. "I'm not going to charge you for this; it's for a good cause."

You have to.

"I don't want to."

Don't do this.

He shook his head again. "I'm not going to take money for this, Carina, and that's final."

Carina, not *Rina*.

I tried not to let that little change affect me, but God, it did. It *really* did.

I closed the notebook and moved away from the window. I had to create some distance between us, otherwise he'd see the mist forming over my blurring gaze, or even sense the pain before I could hide it.

I wasn't sure if I could, but I'd try.

I also wasn't sure why I was still this affected by him, when nothing had even happened between us to begin with. I guess it was my stubbornness that was making things difficult for me. He'd clearly moved on from that slight slipup two weeks ago. It was *I* who had to do the same now.

I sniffed to rid myself of the tingling in my nose, and then dropped the pen and notebook on top of one of my bookshelves.

Thank you, I quickly signed at him, and then turned around before making a beeline for the shower.

He was made of dreams, and made of meadows. He looked so sweet, and yet he hurt so deep.

13.

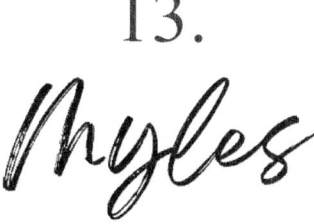

She was still hurting.

Should I be relieved over the fact that she still cared, or should I be worried because I, too, cared just as much, if not more?

All it had taken was her close proximity for me to lose my rationality. What did that say about me?

There was no point in it – in staying away, I mean. I'd tried to follow the routine of doing my job, minding my own business, and avoiding her at all costs, but what had that done for me?

Absolutely *nothing*.

I was done – *so* fucking done with playing the dud.

Then why the fuck wasn't I doing something about it and living my life the way I *should* be living?

I may or may not know the correct answer to that question, but at least I knew what I had to do *next*.

Thank Christ for small miracles.

14.

Myles

Three short chirps rang out as I opened the shop's door and stepped in. "Cute," I muttered, and then shook myself a little – like a freaking puppy on a wet day – to get rid of the excess snow on my clothes.

A short guy with glasses smiled at me in greeting, and so did the woman next to him – who was on the phone talking a bit too rapidly for it to be comprehensible to me.

Crash.

Everyone, myself included, turned towards the main counter, where Rina – shell-shocked and a little pale – was staring at me with wide, possibly wild eyes. She was wearing another one of her puff blouses, and this one was crimson, with two white buttons beneath a cute, lacy collar.

"What the hell just happened?" asked a guy who could give Taron a run for his money in terms of his physical appearance. He walked out of what looked like a kitchen, and frowned as he approached Rina.

I watched as she began signing something to him – so fast I had no idea what any of it meant – and after a while, the two of them chuckled.

"Daniel can clean it up for you," the man said to Rina.

She pressed her lips together and shook her head at him. She must've then realized that I was still standing at the store's entrance, because she briefly glanced at me, grabbed a pencil from the holder on the counter, and started writing something. She then snatched the paper and showed it to me, her expression unreadable.

What are you doing here?

I saw a flash of curiosity, and maybe even hope, in her eyes as she looked at me. I could tell that she was holding her breath, and somehow, that made mine come in faster.

I took a few steps in her direction. "I thought I'd check out the store, and buy a few things while I'm at it. I'm really curious to try some of the stuff I read on the menu outside."

Rina visibly deflated at my answer, and her gaze hardened again, just like it had earlier today, right before she'd walked away from me after I'd refused to charge her for the birds' food tray.

"Oh dear, you're the asshole who hurt Rina, aren't you?" said a voice from behind me.

I turned towards its owner, and saw a tall guy standing just outside the kitchen, his arms crossed in front of him, and his brows raised in surprise.

"He *is*?" asked the big dude, and then gave me a once over. "You *are*?"

I opened my mouth, but didn't know what to say. I wasn't sure what I could say in that moment, to be honest. Everyone was looking at me like I was a sacrificial lamb or something. I just wanted to put a paper-bag over my head and call it a day.

"Wait, *you're* Myles?" asked the guy with glasses. "Dude, you've got some balls coming in here. In case you didn't know, the four of us are *Team Anti-Myles*. We basically despise your ass."

Jesus Christ.

"Yikes, man; thanks," I mumbled.

Rina really did tell them all about my stupidity. Mr. Ribeiro wasn't wrong when he'd told me that these people loved Rina something fierce.

The guy shrugged. "I'm Remi, by the way. I've known Rina since we were kids," he then introduced himself, which was savage, because he'd literally just told me that he didn't like me. At *all*.

"This," Remi pointed at the big guy, "is Cruz. He's probably thinking of squashing you to a pulp right now, but the verdict's still out on that, so let's not jump to conclusions."

51

Cruz scowled at me, and I gave him a wobbly wave. I really didn't wanna know what it'd feel like being sandwiched between that man's hands.

Nope, not at all.

Rina kept glancing at us all like a deer caught in headlights. She looked like she wanted to blend into the wall with the way she was grimacing at everyone.

"I'm Daniel," said the man who'd called me out on hurting Rina.

The woman on the small desk placed the phone down and rolled her eyes. "I can't believe you people are doing this…" She half-heartedly wiggled her fingers at me. "I guess I should introduce myself. Well, I'm Simran, and I'm pissed at you for hurting my friend, but I'm willing to let it go if you do end up redeeming yourself somehow. Good luck." She picked the phone back up and continued on with her task.

Wow.

"Okay, so now that the painful introductions are out of the way, let's get to the serious question," Daniel said to no one in particular. "Who mentioned my name a few minutes ago? I heard it, so you better not lie to me. Have you all started gossiping about me after all?"

"You wish, knucklehead," Remi mused, and I pursed my lips to suppress a grin.

"Oh yeah, we were just talking about how fabulous you'd look mopping Rina's broken mug off the floor," Cruz said to Daniel.

Rina snorted, and then placed a hand over her mouth before laughing fitfully.

Unable to hold it in, I chuckled.

She glanced at me, so I gave her a faint smile. She averted her gaze in return. I didn't blame her for that.

The shop's door opened, and a few people walked in, chatting animatedly. They all greeted Remi with excited hellos, and then proceeded to place their orders.

Daniel rolled his eyes. "You really know how to make me feel special, don't you, Cruz?"

Cruz smirked. "You deserve nothing but the best, partner."

"I'll make a believer out of you one day, just you wait," Daniel told him, and then looked at me. "Your Instagram pictures don't do you justice. You're fucking hot, and if I wasn't married to my wife, I'd   definitely bend you over the baking station and go to town on your pretty ass. But that doesn't mean I'm not angry over the fact that you upset Rina. You should be ashamed of yourself for doing that. She's a treasure, and the four of us love her like family." And with that, he winked at me before disappearing into the kitchen.

Rina's mouth formed an 'O' as she stared at him. Cruz coughed into a fist, just as Simran snickered, and Remi whistled.

And I? Well, I took it all in with a brave face; let every bit of what Daniel had said, seep into my pores. It wasn't like I hadn't earned any of that.

I've always believed that it takes courage to own up to one's faults, and it's true that I haven't exactly treated Rina with the level of respect she deserves to be treated with. I accept that, and I'm ready to make amends for it, too.

Just not by letting Daniel *go to town on my ass*. That was so far out of the question that I couldn't emphasize it enough.

Someone cleared their throat.

I glanced to the side, and found Cruz looking down at me. "If you're here for a second chance," he said low enough so that Rina couldn't hear, "then you're in luck, because Rina is the kind of person who doesn't hold grudges. She may be upset or angry with you, but she'll never resent you for what you did. You're also lucky that you didn't do much of anything, otherwise you'd be rocking a nice shiner on that pretty little face of yours right about now." When I awkwardly cleared my throat, he continued by saying, "I'm not going to act like an overbearing asshole, but I care about that girl like I do my own daughter. She's already been through so much, and the last thing she needs is to get her hopes wounded by someone she genuinely wants to get to know. I'm pretty sure you can do better than that, Myles, for her sake, if nothing else."

"You think I haven't thought about any of that?" I told him. "You don't know me, sure, but Cruz, I'm not dense. I've taken every consequence of my decision to heart and considered it seriously. There's a part of me that's so disappointed in myself right now, especially after seeing all you guys' support towards her, but if I keep dwelling on that, then I'll never be able to rectify my mistake. And I *will* rectify it, I promise. I wanna do this for myself just as much as I wanna do it for Rina."

Cruz scanned my face for a moment, and then slightly inclined his head at me. "That remains to be seen, doesn't it? But I'm glad you're at least *willing* to step up and do the right thing." He slapped my back good-naturedly, and then walked away from me and towards the kitchen.

Alone, I shoved my hands into the pockets of my jeans and looked at Rina. She was standing behind the counter, looking back at me with curiosity on her face.

I rocked on my feet for a second, and then made my way over to her.

"Hey," I said.

Someone please applaud me on my conversation-starter skills. Where was my medal? My trophy? A damn hole so that I could fall into it?

Rina showed me a piece of paper with two words written on it.

Fuck you.

I put my tongue to my cheek. I didn't know when she'd written that, but she clearly wanted to say it to me for a while because she had that paper right on top of the stack – ready to shove it in my mouth if she could.

"I deserve that," I told to her. "That, and so much more."

You hurt me.

I flinched a little. "Believe me, I know, and I'm really, *really*, sorry for behaving that way, Rina. There is an explanation for it, but at this point, it'll only be an excuse to mask my error."

So now I'm Rina again.

54

"You've been Rina since the moment I asked to call you that," I said honestly.

Her eyes flashed.

Am I?

"I wouldn't lie about something like this."

Why aren't you at home working on the kitchen?

"Because I wanted to see you and talk to you, so I asked Taron to take over today," I told her.

I'd come straight to *Vila do Açaí* after my client meeting. I'd hardly paid any attention to it, because for more than half of it, I'd been busy thinking of the things I'd tell Rina, all of which I ended up forgetting the moment I saw her, of course.

I know why you did what you did, but it still doesn't make it right. You shouldn't have kept it from me. As much as I love my avô, he isn't the one who dictates my life, Myles. He shouldn't dictate yours, either, directly or otherwise.

"Wait, how did you know?" Her and I hadn't exactly spoken much since my fuckup, so how would she know?

She rolled her eyes and began writing something.

You aren't as smooth as you might think yourself to be. You've been acting like a scared hyena in front of my avô for the last two weeks. It'd be clear to anyone with eyes that you were trying not to get on his bad side, or piss him off by even breathing the wrong way.

"Hey, now." I arched a brow. "A *hyena*, seriously?"

She scowled at me.

I'm being serious, Myles.

I sighed. "Right, sorry." I scratched my jaw. "Look, you're right about everything; I did push you away because of your grandfather. But I also did it because I thought I owed it to him, especially since he'd trusted me enough to tell me about your parents and grandma, and I just…disregarded that and gave into my impulse. I thought that maybe I was disrespecting him somehow, and I

55

was right." I placed both my hands on the counter and leaned in a bit. "That first night, after you went up to your room, your avô told me that I'd disappointed him. He knew, Rina, and he was hurt."

I noticed that some of the color had drained from Rina's face.

He told you about the fire? And my vovó?

I nodded. "I asked him about your mom, actually, and he told me everything." I put a subtle emphasis on the word 'everything' so that she'd know that I was also aware of the reason behind her loss of speech.

She swallowed.

When did he tell you?

"The first day," I answered.

Her shoulders slumped, and she looked so small and broken that I reached out and cupped her face between my hands. "Rina, hey."

She gazed up at me, and then wrapped her fingers around my wrists.

"I'm so sorry for your loss," I told her. "And I'm so fucking sorry for hurting you like this. I am ashamed, just like Daniel said I should be, and I'm willing to do anything to fix what I've fractured."

She sniffed before nodding at me. I gave her a gentle smile, and then let go of her face.

You're still an asshole, even though you've apologized.

"Of course," I said.

She bit the inside of her cheek as she studied me for a moment.

And I still think that you made the wrong decision by letting my grandfather affect your choices.

"I agree."

She took a fresh page and continued writing.

You pronounced Avô incorrectly, by the way.

I cleared my throat. "Okay, I'm sorry."

Rina pressed her lips together to hide a grin, but I could still see it pushing through. Well, at least she was having fun at my expense.

Her expression, though, soon turned solemn as she wrote something new before showing it to me.

So, what changed, then? What made you defy Avô?

"What, you don't think your friends insulting the hell outta me just now was reason enough for me to change my mind?"

She gave me a *'Really?'* look, so I just...told her the truth.

"I was miserable, Rina," I began, and then swallowed. "Not being able to look at you without feeling guilty, not being able to touch you, talk to you, or even think of you – it was all starting to get too much for me. I kept telling myself that I'd be okay; that I'd get over it. But the truth is: I wanna learn everything there is to learn about you, and I wanna do it without feeling like a damn criminal. I've decided to live for *me*, and live life the way that fits my comfort more than anything else."

Her eyes darkened; my pulse quickened. She slowly pulled a new paper out of the stack and scribbled something on it.

I want hot chocolate.

I did a double-take just to make sure I'd read that right.

"You want hot chocolate?"

She shrugged.

I snorted. "I just poured my heart out to you, Rina, and you want *hot chocolate*?"

She smirked as she nodded. *An expensive one*, she then wrote with a flourish.

"Expensive, right..." I muttered to myself. "Well, there's a really great chocolate shop on Armitage Ave that has both yummy *and* pricey hot chocolate options. We could go there right now. I mean, only if you want to."

Her smirk turned kinda sinister, which scared me a little, but also enticed me at the same time.

Remi can look after the shop in my absence.

I chuckled as I shook my head at her. "Come on, then. Let's go."

15.

"I can't believe you broke your coffee mug when you saw me walk into your shop," I told Rina. "Talk about a knee-jerk reaction. I'm *honored.*"

She rolled her eyes at me, and then touched her forefinger to her thumb, stretched her other fingers up, and then moved her wrist slightly forward to say: *Asshole.*

This was the most decent out of the three ways the word could be signed. The other two were…slightly on the vulgar side, to put it mildly, but that didn't mean Rina hadn't already used them on me on our walk over to the chocolate shop. It was for *"demonstration purposes"*, she'd written in her notebook when I'd stared at her with horror on my face.

What a beautiful liar.

We'd decided to leave our cars back at *Vila do Açaí* and walk to *Katherine Anne Confections* – you know, the shop with the *expensive* hot chocolate. It was only a few blocks from *do Açaí* anyway, and the weather was bearable enough that I'd suggested we not go by car.

And also because I wanted Rina with me for as long as I could have her. Selfish intentions and all.

She didn't mind the walk, actually. If anything, she seemed excited about it. She'd perk up every time we came across a store or building with Christmas lights and decorations already hung up, and I found that super fucking cute.

It was mid-November, but I guess fellow Chicagoans wanted to get into the holiday spirit early this year. Can't say I blamed them.

Rina loves Christmas; it's her favorite time of the year. She wrote an entire paragraph – *while walking* – about how much she adored fairy lights, hollies, hot chocolate with marshmallows, the idea of Santa Claus and Elves, and Christmas carols.

Especially the Christmas carols.

I'd refrained from asking her about mistletoes, because let's face it, that shit's just flat-out corny, and she'd probably stomp me in the dick if I even mentioned it to her indirectly.

So I didn't. Simple.

Rina stopped in front of *Katherine Anne's*, and then looked up at me with a wide grin on her flushed face.

She was wearing a crimson, white-faux-fur collared pea coat with pink embroidered roses on it, and her white beanie had a Havana bunny painted on its center.

When she'd stepped out from behind the counter back at her shop, I'd expected to see her in another one of her quirky skirts, but nope, she was wearing dark, skintight jeans and Joan of Arctic boots, both of which made her appear sexier than she already is.

I blew out a puff of air, and watched as Rina wiped snow off her face with a gloved hand.

I think it was the way she looked in that moment – so uncontrived and at peace – or maybe it was just an instinct, but I decided to *show* her how gorgeous I thought she was, instead of using words I knew would hardly do her justice. And, because I didn't need a damn quartet playing in the background, or even doves flying over our heads to do what I wanted to, I quickly stepped closer to her, placed both my hands on either side of her waist, and pulled her to me before leaning in and pressing my lips to hers.

It was sublime; it was hypnotic. Kissing Rina for the very first time was like finding home under a neon sky.

She was made of roses, and made of silence. She felt like bliss, and a little bit of snow.

I was so lost in her, that I ended up finding a piece of myself that was new, thrilling.

Addictive.

She smiled against my lips before opening them for me, and as soon as I got my first real taste of her mouth, I forgot where I was, or *why* I was. It was only us, our warm, stumbling breaths, the gently falling snow, and the insistent sounds of our lips as they came together again and again.

I brushed my tongue over the roof of her mouth, and she sucked in a breath. She pushed herself against me, so I tightened my hold on her. She bit my lower lip, and I groaned. Back and forth we went, and even earned a few whistles and suggestions about getting a room from the unintentional audience we'd earned. Not that I paid much attention to any of that.

Rina slowly, reluctantly, broke the kiss, and then fanned herself. I chuckled, and pressed two short, sound kisses on her lips before letting go of her waist. She started walking backwards, and then gave me a thorough once-over before pushing open the shop's door and disappearing inside.

I chuckled again as I followed her, and all but moaned when I entered the shop. The potent smell of chocolate, paired with the lingering taste of Rina's mouth – they were making me dizzy with exhilaration.

By the time I joined her at the ordering counter, she was already browsing the menu with a look of concentration on her face. When she saw me, she shifted on her feet and tapped a nail over the seventh item on the menu.

I looked at the woman behind the counter. "We'll have two Hot Chocolate and Truffle Flights, please."

She smiled. "Sure thing. Anything else?"

Rina pulled at the sleeve of my sweater, and when I looked at her, she pointed at something in the display case to her right.

I raised a brow. "*Rum Cake Balls*?"

She grinned and nodded excitedly.

"It's 10:30 in the morning, Rina."

She gave me a thumbs up, that grin of hers still in place.

60

"Are you trying to intoxicate me as an act of revenge?" I mused.

She wiggled her brows and lifted a shoulder.

I laughed. "Fine. You're lucky you're too fucking adorable for me to say no to."

She clapped her hands, and I asked for six Rum Balls before handing my credit card over to the woman taking our order.

Rina went back to looking at the display counter, and I shook my head around a smile when she bent and almost pressed her face against it.

She was too damn cute for my smitten ass.

Our hot chocolate and cake soon came in, and as I grabbed the small box that had the rum balls in it, Rina picked up our hot chocolate cups before jerking her head towards the door.

"You don't wanna get a table?" I asked her.

She shook her head, so I let her lead me outside the store.

We'd only just gotten out, though, when I stopped, barely avoiding crashing into Rina, who'd halted quite abruptly. "Whoa, hey. Rina, what's wrong?"

She didn't move, didn't so much as shift.

I walked around her so that I could look at her. "Rina?"

She blinked and faced me, and when I saw a glimmer of pain in her expression, I cupped the side of her face and ran a thumb over her cheek. It's a good thing I had gloves on, otherwise she would've easily sensed my fear through my chilly, almost clammy skin.

"What is it?" I asked.

She pointed ahead, and when I followed her direction, I saw a group of people, dressed as elves and Santa, setting up a small platform across the street from us. There were wired microphones lying on top of large speakers, with Christmas props piled next to them, and even a fully decorated Xmas tree on the right side of the wooden platform. It didn't take a genius to realize what it is that these people were going to do.

"They're going to sing Christmas carols," I said to Rina.

61

Her chin wobbled a little as she nodded, and God, my heart *ached* for her, so much so that I felt blinded by it.

"Do you wanna leave?"

She shook her head and tapped her left ear.

She wanted to listen to them.

"Okay, then. Come on, let's grab a seat." I walked us to a small bench next to *Katherine Anne's*, and as soon as we settled down, Rina handed a cup of hot chocolate to me.

"Thanks." I opened the cake box, and we took off our gloves as we sat there in comfortable silence, eating our cake and drinking our hot choco while watching the group as they continued to set things up.

"I think I'm really starting to feel this cake right now," I told Rina. Maybe it was all the chocolate and truffle, or maybe it was the rum, but I felt pretty relaxed and elated.

She clicked her tongue, and then hiccupped loudly as she finished the last of the cake. She placed a hand over her mouth, and I chuckled.

"For the record: it was *you* who wanted these damned balls in your mouth, not me. Now we're both facing the consequence of your temptation," I said.

She gasped and slapped me on the arm, which made me laugh.

A screech of the microphone pierced the air. Rina and I looked ahead, just as everyone in the choir introduced themselves, announced that they were now accepting bookings for shows, and that this was a quick preview session for anyone who wanted to hire them, and then started singing *Deck the Halls*.

A small crowd had formed around them, their phones in front of them as they recorded the group.

I turned to look at Rina, and saw her watching the choir with longing on her face.

When she'd told me about her love for Christmas carols, she'd also told me how her and her dad would sing them every year from the beginning of November up until New Year's Eve, even though it wasn't exactly logical. She really enjoyed singing with him, and Christmas carols were just something that made her feel connected to him, even now.

I bumped my knee against hers, and she tilted her head upwards. Giving her a smile, I got to my feet and offered her a hand, which she took without hesitation. That little resolute decision of hers did something to me – something profoundly warm – and so, instead of trying to put a name to it, I embraced it fully.

"My, my; don't you look absolutely *lovely* in my arms," I said as I pulled her close.

She chuckled, but stopped as she hiccupped, and then perked up when the choir began singing *Silent Night*. Her eyes all but sparkled, and when I lifted a brow at her, she tapped the middle finger of her left hand against her chin twice.

I shook my head. "I don't get it." I really didn't like saying that to her. I wanted to genuinely invest my time in conversing with her like this, but my lack of knowledge in Sign was making it difficult for me to do anything in that department. I had to rectify that as soon as possible.

Rina must've seen the struggle on my face, because she ran her fingers over my jaw before giving me a quick peck on the cheek. She then pointed at the still-singing choir, tapped her left ear, and then gave me a thumbs up.

Ah, yes, now I understood what she meant. "This is your favorite Christmas carol," I said.

She beamed up at me, and then gave me another thumbs up. When I sighed, she touched her index and middle fingers to her mouth before moving them upwards.

"Sing?" I guessed.

She nodded, and then tapped my chest.

"You want *me* to sing?"

Another nod, followed by a hiccup.

"Rina, I can't, for the life of me, sing a carol, let alone *anything*," I told her honestly. "Even my bathroom walls start closing in on me when I occasionally hum in the shower. It's terrifying, trust me."

She laughed, and then once again signed for me to sing.

"No."

She tugged at the collar of my sweater with a look of plea on her face.

"No, Rina."

She pouted a little, to which I huffed.

"Fine," I relented, "but if people suddenly start throwing stones at us, don't be surprised."

She rolled her eyes and gestured for me to get on with it.

I cleared my throat, just as the choir started singing *O Come All Ye Faithful*. I decided to sing along, but softer so that only Rina could hear. I did warn her about the stones, but that didn't mean I was ready to experience them firsthand. No, thank you very much.

"*O come, all ye faithful, joyful and triumphant! O come ye, O come ye, to Bethlehem…*" I cleared my throat again, as if that would be of any reasonable help. "*Come and behold Him, born the King of Angels…*"

Rina brushed the tips of her slightly cold fingers over my mouth and smiled, just as a thin sheet of snow began falling on and around us. A few small flakes fell on her cheeks, and I followed them as they traveled from her chin to her coat.

"*God of God, Light of Light. Lo, He abhors not the Virgin's womb. Very God. Begotten, not created,*" I continued to sing.

She placed a palm on the center of my chest and smiled wider, so I took her hand in mine and pressed sound kisses on her fingers, her knuckles, and the inside of her wrist.

She blushed, and I leaned in before touching my nose to hers.

"Did you ever try doing it again?" I asked her.

Her forehead creased, and she lifted her head a little in question.

"Singing, I mean. Or talking," I said, and then swallowed. "You know, after your parents…"

She shook her head *no*, and then hiccupped again.

"Do you *want* to try it sometime?" I wasn't expecting her to, or even insinuating that she should. I just needed to know if she ever wanted to, and was perhaps hesitant to try.

Rina seemed contemplative, and then, a look of fatigue took over her features as she shrugged in response.

I wrapped my arms around her tighter. "I'm sorry if it was an invasive question. I didn't mean to put you in the spot or make you feel uncomfortable, I promise."

She patted her chest once, and then signed the letters 'O' and 'K' before running the back of her fingers over my jaw.

I sighed in relief. "I'm glad." I then canted my head a little. "You know, we could stay here, get some more of that Rum Cake and keep listening to carols, *or*," I said, "you and I can go to your shop, get my car, and spend the rest of the day eating Belgian fries, ceviche, empanadas, macaroons, and so much more at the *French Market*. What do you say?"

Rina grinned beautifully and gave me a thumbs up in return, and even bounced a little on her feet.

I chuckled, more relieved that I hadn't really hurt her with my earlier question, and, unable to resist the urge, I erased the small space between us before pressing my lips to hers.

16.

Carina

I parked my car in the driveway and quickly jogged up the stairs before making my way into the house. The living room was toasty, thank God, and as I closed the Dutch door, took off my boots, and began making my way up to my bedroom, I stopped when I saw *Avô* sitting on the leather couch, just inches shy from the left-side coffee table.

It was past 10, so it was unusual for him to be up this late.

I walked over to him with a smile, and then signed, *You're up late.*

He looked at me with an expression I couldn't put a label on, and then swallowed once. "Where were you the whole day, *pequena?*" he asked. "The only message you sent me was one during lunchtime, asking me if I'd eaten and taken my medications."

I grimaced at that. I felt deeply guilty for not having contacted him more throughout the day, and also ashamed to admit that I'd forgotten about it.

Myles and I had spent hours at the *French Market*, and he'd only driven us to *do Açaí* twenty minutes ago so that I could get my car and head home.

I knelt in front of *Avô*, fisted my left hand, and rubbed it in a circular motion across my chest. *I'm sorry.*

"I called the shop, but Remi said you were out with a friend," *Avô* stated. "Carina, where *were* you?"

I could see it on his face – the plea. He was silently begging me not to confirm his suspicion; quietly asking me to prove him wrong.

Well, I *couldn't.*

When I didn't answer him, his features pinched. "*Eu achei que você entendesse e soubesse melhor que isso, Carina,*" he said. I thought you knew and understood better than this, Carina.

I worked my jaw when it tingled. I then tapped my chest once, and crescented my hands before turning them upside down and moving them left and right to say, *I do.*

Avô's gaze hardened. "Do you really?" he challenged.

I clenched my hands to simmer my frustration at his insistent enmity towards this. I loved him so much, but that didn't mean I'd let him question my choices as if I were a thumb-sucking infant.

And so, instead of dragging a conversation that would most definitely turn into an argument, I got to my feet, signed *Good Night* to him, and ran up to my room. Once inside, I shut the door, pulled my phone out of my jeans pocket, and all but collapsed on my bed before sending Myles a text.

Me: *He knows I was with you today* :'(

Beauty: *Will I be shot in the head as soon as I get to your house tomorrow?*

I chuckled, and felt myself starting to relax.

Me: *Why would you say that?*

Beauty: *I've seen the rifle above your fireplace, Rina.*

I bit my lower lip to stop myself from laughing.

Me: *And how do you know it's real? It could very easily be a prop.*

Beauty: *Because Taron has one just like it. And also because I know what a real gun looks like.*

Me: *So what, you can't take a measly bullet for me? And here I thought we were star-crossed lovers.*

Beauty: *I'll negotiate and take a wedgie instead, how about that?*

I covered my mouth with a hand as I laughed.

Me: *Kinky. I like it* ;)

Beauty: *Pain isn't kinky* :/

Me: *It is for a lot of people.*

Beauty: *Seeing you blush as I touch you is my kink.*

I felt heat coursing through my body after reading that.

Me: *How did we move from you being afraid of getting your brain blown out, to you flirting with me?*

Beauty: *I'll always flirt with you, even if I'm bleeding out at your feet.*

I shook my head and smiled.

Me: *You're crazy.*

Beauty: *I'm blaming the Rum Cakes for my mental dysfunction.*

Me: *Or maybe the twelve cheese empanadas you had at the Market today.*

Beauty: *Those were pretty addicting, weren't they?*

Me: *And so were your kisses after that. Nothing tastes better than a pair of lips that are smeared with cheese and crispy dough.*

Beauty: *I love it when you talk dirty to me ;)*

I couldn't help but laugh again.

Me: *You think Avô will let you continue working at the house after that?*

He didn't reply instantly, so I sent him another message.

Me: *Did you get home alright?*

Beauty: *Yeah. Sorry for the late response. Mr. Ribeiro was texting me, so I had to get back to him.*

My heart pounded in my chest. Why would *Avô* text Myles?

Me: *What did he tell you?*

Beauty: *He told me where the keys were for when I come in tomorrow. He had to switch its place, because apparently, there's a cat in your neighborhood that steals things from the sneakiest of places.*

I swallowed my relief and quickly texted him back.

Me: *Yeah, that's Jack Sparrow. He's too stealthy for his own good.*

Beauty: *You gave him a name?*

Me: *Kinda. That's what everyone in the area calls him. He's been around for a while.*

Beauty: *But why call him Jack Sparrow?*

Me: *Because he doesn't have an eye. His left one was infected after a fight with another cat around four years ago, so everyone in the neighborhood came together to rise money and get him a surgery for it.*

Beauty: *And he still steals from you guys?*

Me: *I think it's his idea of fun. He doesn't steal anything, per se. He just hides it for a while and then puts it back in its place later.*

Beauty: *Aww :')*

Me: *Yeah. I love him. He's lovely.*

Me: *Can I ask you something?*

I flipped on my stomach and put a pillow under my chest as I waited for him to reply.

Beauty: *Of course.*

Me: *Why do you think my avô hasn't canceled your contract yet?*

Beauty: *Do you want him to?*

I clicked my tongue. He sure was slightly *louco*, that guy.

Me: *Of course not, you dummy. I'm just confused, given his reaction on me being out of the shop the entire day just to spend time with you.*

He didn't text back instantly. It made sense that he was just as confused about *Avô's* reason behind this as I was.

Beauty: *Maybe because he trusts me, knowing that you trust me, too.*

Me: *I think the trust factor is correct. He knows you're a good guy, but for some reason, he doesn't want us to be together.*

Beauty: *And what do you want, Rina?*

My heart raced again, but for an entirely different reason this time.

Me: *I don't wanna let go.*

It's one of the truest things I've said – ever. I wanted to try and not give up; I wanted to hope things would turn out great, but not hope too much at the same time.

Beauty: *Me too.*

I grinned.

Me: *I can't wait to see you in the morning.*

Beauty: *And I can't wait to kiss and hold you again.*

Instead of replying back with a text, I angled my phone against my face and sent him a selfie.

Beauty: *How dare you take the sleep off my eyes by sending me that photo!*

I snickered.

Me: *I'm so not sorry.*

Beauty: *I know. You're evil, plain and simple.*

He then sent me a photo of him pouting at the camera. His hair was mused, and he was wearing a grey t-shirt that hugged him snugly.

Me: *You really are a beauty, aren't you?*

Beauty: *If only you agree to be my Chip.*

Me: *I thought you'd call me your Gaston.*

Beauty: *Jeez, woman; I have a preference, and Gaston doesn't qualify for that.*

Me: *So you like underage people?*

Beauty: *That sounds so wrong and morally hurtful.*

Me: *I'm sorry!!! I was joking :(*

Beauty: *I know, and you're forgiven. What I meant was: my type is cute and curious, and you're both of those things.*

Me: *What am I, a rabbit?*

Beauty: *………*

Beauty: *We really need to work on your comedic timing. It's so off the rail that it's barf-inducing at this point.*

I started to laugh, but ended up yawning instead.

Me: *I'm tired. And full. And sleepy. Not in the exact order, but still.*

Beauty: *Ditto. I have a client meeting in the morning, so I have to be up early.*

Me: *Do people really come to your office at the crack of dawn and ask you to fix their broken shit?*

Beauty: *More like 8a.m., but yeah.*

Me: *The dedication, though.*

Beauty: *I know.*

My phone slipped from my hand, and I realized that I'd come close to dozing off and had lost my hold on it.

Me: *Okay, off to sleep I go. I almost dropped my phone on my face, and that's not a good sign.*

Beauty: *I wish I was there to see that.*

Me: *Why are you like this?*

Beauty: ◡◡◡

I laughed and shook my head.

Me: *Alright, I'm out. Byeeeee ♡_♡*

Beauty: *Look at you being all adorable and upping your emoji game for me.*

Me: *I have to keep up...*

Beauty: *I know :)*

Beauty: *Good night, Rina.*

I sighed and turned to my right.

Me: *Night-night.*

17.

Carina

"**O**kay, be honest with me: how big is his cock?" Ashleigh asked with a maniacal grin on her face.

A tattooed guy was passing by our table, but stopped and arched a brow at her, to which my dear, darling of a best friend, flipped him off. Not so subtly, too, might I add.

The poor man, God bless him, took that gesture good-naturedly, and chuckled before walking away.

I wanted to hide under the collar of my coat, but instead, I glared at Ash and signed, *What is wrong with you?*

When you Sign a string of words – a sentence, basically – the order of those very same words is different from if you were speaking them out loud. But because Ash has known Sign for just as long as I have, she understands what I'm saying without any issues.

"What?" She tried to act innocent. "That's the #1 question one asks when their best friend is dating a hottie, okay? It's so common at this point that it should be a rule. I'm only doing my due diligence here."

I rubbed both my hands over my face. That woman was a living, breathing migraine. One without a remedy.

I wasn't sure how to respond to her question anyway, because I didn't exactly know the answer to it. *Yet.*

We were at *The Publican* for our usual end-of-the-month brunch. The restaurant was a few blocks from Ash's workplace, and was also our go-to spot for whenever we needed those delicious, absolutely-necessary carbs.

72

We'd only just received our order of Frittata, cheese roll-ups, Blueberry Buckle, and Cherry Lime Rickey, when Ash had decided to ask me about the length of Myles's cock. I couldn't say I was surprised. I've known her for a little over two decades, and she's always been like this – inappropriately curious and alarmingly bizarre.

Given how maturely she'd behaved with a fellow patron just now – who'd merely been surprised by her interest in another person's anatomy, it was safe to say that Ash wasn't planning on changing in this lifetime. Not that I wanted her to, if I were being honest. It was good to have some level of madness in one's life, and Ash provided that in full, with a sprinkle of garnish on the side.

I wasn't talking about your question, I signed, and then pointed in the direction the tattooed guy had gone to.

Ash clicked her tongue. "He was trying to dip his toes in an undippable territory, so he got what he deserved." She then picked up a fork from the center of our table and stabbed it into a piece of Frittata. "Wait, is undippable even a word?"

I shook my head, both in slight annoyance and in answer to her question.

"Yeah, I thought so too." She began eating, so I did the same.

It was yummy, the Frittata, and was exactly what I needed.

"So, is Miguel still giving you shit for dating Myles?" Ash asked.

He was, up until the moment I left the house this morning, so I'd say yes.

Ash frowned and took a sip of her Rickey, and I shoved a tiny piece of Blueberry Buckle into my mouth before chewing it slowly.

Avô has been behaving rather curtly with me, which is very unusual, given our rapport. We haven't done our regular TV binges since that night, and he's even began ignoring Myles completely during his time at the house. I've seen Myles hurting when *Avô* walks past him without a glance, but he doesn't show any of it to me.

We've tried talking to him – separately and together – but he doesn't even stay long enough for either of us to get much out before dismissing himself without a word.

He does, however, leave notes on my nightstand during the days he goes to the shop, telling me he loves me, but doesn't respond to the texts I send him after that.

It was an overbearing behavior, if I were to judge it, but I didn't know if it'd be right for me to fault him for this, only because he's *always* been like this when it comes to the matter of me dating a guy.

I've only had two boyfriends in my life so far, both of whom decided to break up with me the moment my *avô* found out about them and decided to get himself acquainted with them. I've asked him multiple times why he does that, but he's never answered me.

Frustrating, I know.

"I really wanna tell *Avô* to get the stick out of his ass, but that'd be a burn on his cane situation, so I don't know…" Ash said, pulling me out of my train of thought.

Good Lord.

He's my grandfather, you idiot. I can't let you say that about him, I signed.

"But you can let him act like a domineering freak?"

I sighed.

He's not domineering; he just doesn't understand.

I had to spell out the word 'domineering', because there isn't exactly a sign for it.

Was it right for me to defend *Avô*, when he'd been nothing but uncooperative towards everything Myles-related?

"I'm sure he understands how attraction works, Rina," Ash stated. "He married Irene because they were in *love*. Surely that includes mutual liking – something you and Myles have also been feeling ever since the two of you saw each other for the first time."

She was right, wasn't she? I just wish I knew how to make *Avô* see things clearly.

He'll come around.

Ash huffed. "Yeah, when you're old and wrinkly, and Myles has put a ring on someone who isn't you."

You're fast-tracking too much. We've only just started dating.

"Doesn't mean you can't think of the future," Ash said, and placed a hand over mine. "I can see it in your eyes, babe, when you talk about him. I know you really like him, and I'm so proud of the two of you for going after what you want. Life's shitty as it is, and after everything that's happened in the world in the last couple of years, I'd say that being aware of your needs and being brave enough to admit the same, takes serious balls. Miguel needs to see that, and if he can't, then it's his fault. I don't appreciate you losing your ability to hope because he's stubborn and won't see reason."

I swallowed.

I just wanna be able to date Myles without feeling like I'm hurting Avô or doing something wrong. And, he's a great guy when he's not being awkward and silly.

The days when I was at home while *Avô* went to the shop, I mostly spent my time reading on my Kindle, or watching Netflix shows on TV while Myles and the others worked on the kitchen. But when *I* was at *do Açaí*, he'd come visit me during lunchtime, and we'd have burritos with Cruz and the others in the half hour I got to spend with them all without worrying about customers and sale numbers.

Myles and I have even managed to get a couple of dates in since the French Market. Even though said dates have been brief, they've still been wonderful and unforgettable. Especially our recent one at the *Oriole*, where he all but turned blue in the face after tasting the classic King Crab he'd ordered for himself. He'd told me – very confidently – that he wanted to try it out, so I'd gone along with it.

Little good that did him…

"Sooooo, you haven't seen his dick, then," Ash said flatly.

I blinked out of my reverie and scowled at her.

I'm going to kill you.

She laughed. "I was just trying to get your attention. You looked lost there for a second."

Was thinking about the restaurant thing.

Ash laughed harder. "He did look rather cute with that kinda-constipated expression on his face, though, not gonna lie. I'm pretty sure he gained at least a thousand new followers on his Instagram after posting that story."

I rolled my eyes.

I can't believe he put that on his social media.

"Well, I can believe it. I may not have met him yet, but with everything I've seen on his IG, and everything you've told me about him, he does seem like…a *unique* creature."

I chuckled. *He's pretty adorable*, I signed. *How's Dave?*

Ash all but swooned all over our table at the mention of her boyfriend. "He's hot, just like the last time you met him," she answered with a smirk.

I chuckled again and gave her a thumbs up.

Her and Dave have been dating for a year, and in the time I've known him, Dave has been nothing but amazing to Ash. I mean, he wouldn't still be breathing if he wasn't. I may look like I've stepped out of a Grimm's novel, but I was fully capable of conjuring up graphic, gruesome murders in my head, thank you very much.

I'm happy for you.

Ash grinned. "I know, and I'm so glad you've found someone like Myles." She then perked up a little. "We should go on a double-date soon. It'll be so much fun, I can already tell."

I nodded. It *did* sound fun, and I was sure Myles would be onboard with the idea.

As if summoned by Lucifer himself, my phone *pinged* with a text from him.

Ash let go of my hand and wiggled her brows at me, to which I smiled and shook my head at her.

Beauty: *Tell Daniel I said hi ;)*

I laughed.

Me: *I'm not at the shop right now, but I'll be sure to convey your message to him later.*

Beauty: *Ah, yes; you're out with Ash.*

Me: *Do you want me to say hi to her as well?*

Beauty: *If you want to… But my interests lie in a certain baker only.*

I giggled, and took a sip of my Rickey. Ash was busy on her phone while finishing up her Frittata.

Me: *You do realize that you're only fueling his fire, right? You're practically giving him more and more ammunition against you.*

Beauty: *It's not my fault he makes it so easy.*

Me: *He only flirted with you once, Myles. For TWO SECONDS. Come to think of it, it was more like an aspiration of his than actual flirting.*

Beauty: *So you're saying that all the free pastries he gives me when I visit the shop are for nothing? I'm hurt, Rina.*

I pursed my lips.

Me: *He gives you the extras from the day before, you sweet thing.*

Beauty: 0_0

I couldn't help but laugh again.

Me: *I'm sorry :')*

Beauty: *How could Daniel do that to me? I thought I was special!*

Me: *You are, just in a very different way.*

Beauty: *Yay?*

Me: ' ᵕ '

Beauty: *Mr. Ribeiro glared at me right before heading out for lunch. That's progress, right?*

My heart ached as I read that message once, and then a second time.

Me: *Oh, Myles; I'm so sorry :(*

I honestly couldn't understand why *Avô* had to behave this way at all, and I was so upset with the way he was treating Myles. Honestly, if it were anyone else, they'd have already quit the job and not even cared about the damn contract. That little fact itself should be enough for *Avô* to realize that Myles wasn't like the others. But I guess my grandfather really couldn't see past his mulishness to give my guy even a single chance.

Beauty: *It's okay, really. I'll prove to him that I deserve to be with you.*

I felt an array of emotions swirling inside me as I read those words.

Me: *But that's the thing, Myles: you don't have to prove yourself to anyone. I didn't want you to prove yourself to me, so Avô shouldn't want it, either. You're an amazing person, and that's all that matters to me. I just don't know why it's not enough for him.*

Beauty: *He is pretty strange that way, your grandfather. He won't talk to me; he doesn't want me to date you. But still, he wants me to continue working on the renovations, and even leaves us alone every alternate day to go to your shop. It's crazy.*

Me: *I couldn't have put it any better :/*

Beauty: *Anyways, I have to get back to finishing up the kitchen floor. I can't believe it's come together so fast. Did you ask Mr. Ribeiro about the appliances? I think he wanted a few new ones for you.*

I shoved a piece of cheese roll-up into my mouth before typing.

Me: *Yeah, we'd decided earlier this year to change them all after we got the kitchen renovated, so that's what we're going with. Amazon should deliver them tomorrow or the day after.*

Beauty: *Cool. Paul can help set them up once they're here.*

Me: *Yay :')*

Beauty: *Gotta go :(*

Me: *Nooooo.*

Beauty: *I can't have you running around a floorless kitchen, Rina. That's wrong on so many levels, that I can't even begin to count them on hand.*

I snickered.

Me: *Fine, go do your hammering and nailing. I'll see you when I get home.*

Beauty: *That sounded so wrong and inaccurate in terms of the flooring process, but I'll let it pass because you're uneducated in the field.*

Me: *Did you just insult me?*

Beauty: *Yes ◔_◔*

Me: *˙ ‿ ,˙*

Me: *I guess I deserved it.*

Beauty: *Again: yes.*

Me: *Fuck you :**

Beauty: *Aww, thanks.*

I chuckled.

Me: *I'll see you later, you weirdo.*

Beauty: *You're just showering me with compliments today, aren't you?*

Me: *There's more where that came from, if you're interested.*

Beauty: *I'm outta here. See ya later. Peace.*

I grinned and slid my phone into my purse.

I really did luck out with him, didn't I?

18.

Carina

I took the baking tray out of the oven, placed it on the brand-new counter, and plated my *Bolo de Fubá* before slicing a couple pieces of it. I then put the empty tray in the sink, and grabbed my Polaroid camera before taking a picture of my cake.

Bolo de Fubá. 12/01/2021

It was officially December, which meant it was time for my everyday baking tradition. I liked to make something new each day, up until Christmas, and I usually started with a Brazilian classic, *Bolo de Fubá*. It was simple and flavorful, and really helped in boosting my spirits.

I pulled out four serving plates, put two pieces of *Bolo de Fubá* in each of them, kept the rest of it in the refrigerator for *Avô*, sent him a text over the same, and grabbed a small notebook and pen from the coffee table before heading up to the storeroom. When I reached it, I knocked on the door, and smiled when Taron opened it a few seconds later. Him and the others were wearing caps, and they also had masks on to protect themselves from the dust. And let me tell you, that room was dusty as *fuck*.

Myles had told me that clearing up the storeroom would take at least two days, and once *that* was done, it would take a little less than a week to sand and prime the chipped walls for the tiling process. And that was just the beginning; turning the storeroom into a mini library would take longer than him and Taron had anticipated.

Not that I minded…

"Hey, Carina. What's up?" Taron asked around a smile.

The five of us had ordered takeout and had lunch together an hour ago, and then Myles had left, saying he had something he needed to do.

Him and the others had been on a weeklong vacation since Thanksgiving. *Avô* and I didn't celebrate it; it was one of *Mãe's* favorite times of the year. And so, the two of us had spent the day browsing Netflix and watching absolutely nothing.

And also, hardly speaking to each other unless necessary.

I knew *Avô* was giving me space – to get over my Myles-high and come to my senses, most probably – but it was starting to get on my nerves. I wanted to be able to talk to him like we always have, but he's blocked me out so adamantly that I don't know how to get through to him.

And, because I was just as stubborn as him, I'd decided to give him space so that *he* could come to *his* senses and realize that what I felt for Myles wasn't just a rush or infatuation, but something else entirely.

When I'd seen Myles in person earlier, after days of us interacting through text and video calls, I'd felt a sense of relief that I wasn't sure was even possible for me to experience. It was intense – what he did to me – like a roaring wave of something indescribable, yet inevitable.

I let go of a breath and began writing in my notebook, and once I was done, I flipped it around for Taron to see.

I baked something for everyone.

81

Paul and Greg shoved a couple of small boxes into a massive trash bag, and then moved onto a larger one to the right.

"You didn't have to, Carina," Taron said. Myles was right; he really did look like a lumberjack with the way he dressed: jeans, a flannel, and brown work boots.

I bake for almost the entire month of December. It's a tradition of mine.

He chuckled. "Well, lucky us, then. So, what've you got for us today?"

Bolo de Fubá. There's a plate in the kitchen for each of you.

Taron leaned against the doorframe. "Thanks, Carina, I'll get them in a bit. We have to trash these boxes, but we can take a break after that."

I grinned and gave him a thumbs up.

Don't forget to gargle and wash your hands before eating.

He gave me a two-finger salute. "You got it."

Where's Myles?

Taron straightened and jerked his head to the side. "In the van. He texted me a few minutes ago to tell me he's here. And," he lifted a brow, "if you're going to ask me what it is that he's doing in there, then don't, because I really don't know." He shrugged.

I frowned.

Alright, I'll go get him.

Taron nodded.

I pointed a thumb over my shoulder, and then waved at him before running down the stairs.

"Tell him that he really needs to get his ass inside so that we can finish cleaning this room, will you, Carina?" Taron hollered, just as I reached the living room.

I laughed as I looked at him, and gave him another thumbs up. He in turn gave me a quick wink before closing the storeroom door.

With a smile, I snatched my sweater, gloves, and beanie from the couch, put them on, covered the extra plate of *Bolo de Fubá* with foil, and grabbed it from the kitchen counter.

I half-assed my way into putting my boots on, and then shivered as I stepped outside the house and jogged down the stairs toward the glaringly out-of-place-looking brown van.

It was snowing like a bitch, so I wiped a hand over the driver's side window before knocking on it twice.

Myles was inside, with his headphones on and his eyes glued to his phone's screen. I couldn't make out what he was watching, but it must've been quite important, because he didn't even blink when I knocked on the window again. And *again*.

I scowled as I pulled the beanie further down my head, and then decided to bang the notebook against the glass. *Hard.*

God, I was *freezing*.

Myles jerked and finally looked at me, and when he saw the expression on my face, he quickly unlocked the passenger door from the inside and pushed it open.

I deepened my scowl as I walked around the van and settled inside, and then placed the plate I was holding, on the dashboard, before shutting the car's door and turning to Myles.

I raised my arms in question, just as he took his headphones off and shoved them in the front compartment. When I narrowed my eyes at him, he set his phone down in the coffee holder and shifted in his seat. I put my tongue to my cheek, and he wiggled his fingers at me.

"*Hey*," he all but sang.

What in the ever-infesting fuck?!

He motioned to the plate on the dash. "What's that?" he asked.

Cake.

He nodded. "Right…" He paused and glanced at it briefly. "Did you make it?"

Obviously.

"Obviously." He nodded again.

I glared at him. *What's wrong with you?* I wrote.

83

He cleared his throat. "I, uh…" He scratched his jaw. "So, I, umm, I'm kinda, sorta, a little bit, learning Sign?"

My eyes widened at his words. I was shocked, of course, but mostly, I felt…*important*, I guess.

Why?

He looked confused by my question. "What do you mean, why, Rina?" He gave me a soft smile. "I'm doing this because I wanna learn your way. I wanna be able to communicate with you better, understand you better instead of feeling helpless every time we interact face-to-face." He swallowed. "I signed up for these twice-a-week online classes, and I'm almost done with the course. I was just watching the newest session on my phone. I wasn't going to tell you anything until after I'd finished. I even had the whole reveal planned in my head, but now you know, and it isn't nearly as dramatic as I thought it'd be."

I ignored the snort that left me as I laughed while putting my notebook and pen away, and then fisted Myles's collar before pulling him to me so that I could kiss him.

He was wearing a teal-grey hoodie with the words '**I CAME. I SAW. I MADE IT AWKWARD**' written in bold letters on its center. I don't know where he got it from, or why he was wearing it, but it somehow went so well with him that I didn't wanna ask him about it. So, I instead cupped the side of his neck and grazed my teeth over his bottom lip, earning a slow grunt from him in return.

"C'mere," he whispered against my lips before kissing me again. He then tugged me towards him, and I went without hesitation. His hands splayed over the back of my thighs and squeezed as he leaned back in his seat, and I straddled him before brushing my tongue over his.

"You taste like unrelenting command, Rina," Myles said, and then touched his nose to mine. "One I can't help but feel grateful for obeying." He kissed me again, and I felt the back of his fingers brush against the inside of my right thigh.

I sucked in a breath, then let it go in a rush when he broke the kiss and lifted the hem of my sweater.

"Rina…" He gazed at me with question on his face.

I licked my lips and rose a little in a silent gesture for him to continue.

The smile he gave me was nothing short of roguish, and when he slid a hand behind the waistband of my sweats before finally touching my aching clit, I tipped my head back and moaned – loud and unabashed.

His fingers grazed me ever so slightly, but stopped a second later.

I frowned and looked down at him, only to find him staring back at me in shock.

What's wrong? I signed.

Myles opened his mouth, and then shut it, and then opened it again. "You…you moaned, Rina," he said incredulously. "You fucking *moaned*."

I blinked, and then realized that the reason why he was so surprised was because he hadn't exactly heard my voice until that moment.

I hardly did anything like this, to be honest, so I don't know why *I* wasn't shocked with myself. I guess it was because I didn't really care about my voice, or anything in context to it.

I did, I signed.

Myles huffed out a laugh and shook his head a little. "Do it again," he requested.

I arched a brow at him, and rocked my hips against his hand – the one that was still in my sweats.

He flashed his teeth at me, and then began running his fingers over the length of my pussy as he said, "Challenge accepted."

19.

Myles

I knew Rina was going to be a force that'd set an imprint on me for the rest of my life, but I wasn't even remotely aware of how much impact a little gesture from her could have on me. Of course, said gesture was one of complete rarity, and also one I wanted to earn at any given chance.

Every single element of that moan of hers was addicting, so fucking thrilling. Once was not enough; I needed *more*.

I watched her hair as it fell forward, her lashes as they subtly shadowed the peaks of her cheeks, her lips that looked slightly bruised from my kisses, and her throat as it moved when she swallowed.

When she smiled at me, I pointed a finger at her, and then rolled the fingers of my right hand across the front of my face in a clockwise fashion to say, *You're beautiful.*

Rina blushed, and damn if my entire being didn't light up at the sight of her – in front of me, straddling me, making me the luckiest fucking guy in the entire cosmos.

It was so elementary, and yet so radical, what Rina did to me. What she *meant* to me.

She shifted on my lap and gave me a curious look.

I chuckled. "Patience, woman." When she pouted a little, I grinned and slowly pushed a finger inside her pussy.

Goddamn, she was *hot*. And wet. And so, *so* fucking mine.

And I was so hard that it was starting to hurt.

"Lift your sweater," I told her when she gasped against my touch.

She'd all but challenged me to make her moan again, and because I was eager to hear that sound from her a second time, I'd taken her up on it.

She smirked at my words, and then not only lifted her sweater, but also pulled it over her head and threw it on the passenger seat.

"Fuck me," I mumbled when one of the straps of her ivory bra slipped down her shoulder.

Rina pressed her teeth over her lower lip and moved her hips back and forth, urging me to continue.

I pushed against my seat so that I could lean back a bit, and then began sliding my finger in and out of her.

She gasped again, and pressed her left palm against the van's ceiling as she rocked in time with my digit.

"Rina." I used my free hand to push down her bra, and groaned when her tits moved in time with her hips.

I sat up and started tracing my lips over the side of her neck, up to her jaw, then down to her collarbone, lower, and lower, and finally took one of her dark nipples into my mouth.

Rina fisted my hair as I sucked hard, pulled, and released her nipple before moving onto the other. And then, to my utter joy, she moaned out loud. This one, however, was hoarse. Desperate.

My cock hardened further, and I slipped a second finger inside her before running the pad of my thumb over her clit.

She moaned again – so fucking beautifully that I all but lost what little control I had over my impulses. Our eyes met, and she smiled before leaning in and kissing me again.

Mouths clashed, tongues touched.

A graze of teeth here, and a quick bite there.

A grunt from me, and a gasp from her.

It was a method, our passion – an increasingly volatile regime of give-and-take.

I pulled her closer and began finger-fucking her faster, which made her hiss.

"I wanna see you come undone, Rina," I told her. "Show me how you singe with desire."

She shuddered faintly, and then clenched herself around my fingers. Her lips parted, her lids hooded, and then, she gave me an urgent, almost bruising kiss as she came all over my hand.

I was mesmerized by her brief submission, completely intoxicated by her heat, smell, and satiating taste.

She let out a soft sigh as I pulled my fingers out of her and wiped them with the tissues near the dash. She then nuzzled her nose against the side of my neck and started dragging a hand down to my belt before tugging at it roughly.

I turned my face to hers. "I don't have a condom," I said with a frown. "Unless…well, unless you're on a pill…"

She moved back so abruptly that her forehead banged against my nostrils.

"*Jesus.*" I pinched my nose and grimaced at the dotting pain.

Rina huffed and fixed her bra, and then began signing something so quickly and furiously that I had to blink several times just to get a grip on my eyesight.

"Just because I've been learning Sign, doesn't mean I'm ready for hand-to-hand combat," I told her. "Can you slow down a bit, please?"

She rolled her eyes and grabbed her notebook and pen.

I said: HOW CAN YOU NOT HAVE A CONDOM?

I read, and then reread the words before looking at her. "Why did you write that in caps?"

She stared at me with no expression on her face.

"To answer your *politely* asked question: I *did* have condoms, but they expired. May they rest in peace." I shook my head in feigned sympathy. "I just didn't get around to buying new ones when I started working here. Tight schedule and all, y'know."

She put her tongue to her cheek and glared at me.

I cleared my throat. "Also, there's a sign for *condom*?" I asked. "I, umm, I didn't know that."

Rina's eyes narrowed. She made a fist and bobbed it back and forth, signing *Yes*.

I nodded. "Right, of course."

She scowled and pushed at my chest. *Asshole*, she signed, which made me laugh.

"You really love signing that, don't you?"

She tried to maintain her scowl, but it kept breaking as she fought a smile.

I wrapped my arms around her waist and pulled her to me again. "I promise I'll buy some today," I said. "Hell, with all the Christmas sales going on both online and at the stores, I can even get family packs."

She looked down at me like I was a rabid.

"Family pack condoms don't exist, do they?"

Fuck.

She shook her head very slowly, as if she was scared I'd grow another head if she moved hers too fast.

They are called VALUE packs, she wrote.

God, she was so stunned by me that she couldn't even Sign words. She had to *write* them instead.

I had officially broken Rina.

Time for a subject change. It was absolutely necessary, after all, both for me and my rapidly waning dignity.

"Sooooo…" I pursed my lips and jerked my head to the right. "Do I get to eat that cake now, or have I lost my privileges?"

Rina blinked at me for several agonizing seconds, and then flipped a middle finger *right* in front of my face.

It didn't take a genius to know what *that* sign meant…

20.

I touched the tip of my index finger to Rina's arm. "Are you...okay?"

Her eyes appeared all but glazed as she grinned up at me and gave me a *very* enthusiastic thumbs-up.

"Right." I slid my hands into the pockets of my jeans as I continued to walk next to her in the *Fiction* aisle.

We were at *Barnes & Noble* in Webster Ave, and in the thirty or so minutes we'd been there, Rina had made me circle the *Fiction* and *Romance* sections at least a dozen times. The struggle on her face as she looked around at all the books with undeniable longing, was almost comical, but also so fucking adorable.

I'd offered to take her out on a date to *B&N* as a thank you for all the baked goodies she's been feeding me, Taron, and the guys for the last few days. First, it was that yummy *Fubá* cake in the van, and then all sorts of Christmas cookies and pastries after that. I've been hogging them down with - 0% shame, so I thought it was about damn time I did something for her that I knew would make her happy.

I just...didn't know she'd get high as a fucking kite by the smell of inked pages and fancy book covers.

I guess it was a thing now in this world. I shouldn't be surprised; it's 20-fucking-21. If this world can have people who literally sell their farts in mason jars and become millionaires, then I guess we *could* have people like Rina, who got off on book-whiffs and hardcover jackets.

The world, after all, needs ample balance to function without a hitch.

Mr. Ribeiro was under the impression that Rina was at their shop, but with Taron and the guys working on the library without my assistance, I was pretty sure he must've suspected that both Rina and I weren't where we were supposed to be. I will admit, I had looked over my shoulder a few times since walking into the bookstore, half expecting Mr. Ribeiro to somehow show up and kick me in the balls, but that hadn't happened so far, so I'd decided to relax a bit.

Rina and I were about to enter the *Fiction* aisle for the eleventh time, most probably, when she stopped and grabbed a paperback from the last shelf in the *Romance* aisle before hugging it close to her chest.

I stood in front of her and gave her a smile. "Finally picked a book, I see."

It's the last copy, she signed, and then pulled her phone out of her coat before typing something on it.

When we started taking rounds, there were seven copies of this book here, but now there's only one.

She knows I can't understand Sign fully yet, especially if it's done in a long, consecutive sequence, so she alternates between signing and writing/typing certain things for me.

I pursed my lips at the now-empty shelf where the final copy of the book had been, pointed a finger at her, and then flattened my left hand with the palm facing up. With my right hand, I joined my thumb and index finger to form a circle, and then ran said circle along my left palm to say, *You counted?*

Rina smirked. *Obviously*, she signed.

I chuckled. "I shouldn't have asked." I plucked the book from her grasp and turned it around to read the title.

Bridgerton: The Duke & I

The book's cover was the Netflix series adaptation poster, one I'd seen so many damn times on billboards, social media, etc.

Rina snatched the book from me and hugged it even closer to her chest. *Have you seen the show?* she signed excitedly.

And there it was again – that almost-blinding gleam in her eyes.

91

She really did like the show, it seemed.

I shook my head in response to her question, and she jutted her lower lip out in return, making me chuckle. She then tapped on the dude on the book's cover, and then signed, *Beautiful*.

I crossed my arms and lifted a brow. "I beg your pardon?" I mused.

She snickered, and then typed something on her phone before showing it to me.

It's true; he's very beautiful. Regé is actually one of those actors who you fall in love with not just because of his looks, but also because of his insightful nature during interviews, and the message he sends with the way he carries himself.

I placed a hand over my heart and feigned being hurt. "And here I thought I was special," I quipped. "But now I gotta compete against a guy who is *insightful*." I huffed and raised my arms by my sides. "I was an idiot for thinking that my enviable IQ and calloused hands were enough to woo you unforeseeably."

Rina laughed, but stopped midway before gasping as she stared at something over my shoulder.

I turned, and saw a girl – a sixteen-year-old, at best – holding a boxset of some book series in her hands with so much glee on her face that it almost made me worried about her state of mind.

In the small amount of time I've spent here, I've come to realize that bookstores are a place where a completely different species of humans exists. And Rina was one of them. Or maybe it's the air in here that's turned her this way.

Or maybe she's always been like this…

I shifted so I could look at her, but before I could get a single word out, she grabbed me by the forearm and dragged me over to where the girl was.

We stopped in front of the aisle, and as I began searching the shelves for the boxset, I quickly realized that it was a waste, because the one the girl was holding was either from a different aisle, or worse – that it was the last of its kind available at the store.

I faced the girl with hope in my heart. Who knew things could get this stressful and cutthroat at *bookstores*?

"Uh…" I swallowed and motioned towards the colorful box in her hands. "Where'd you get that from?"

She barely gave me a glance. "Here." She pointed at the barren shelf dismissively.

No.

No, no, no.

I looked at Rina, and saw her expression change quickly from cheerful to crestfallen.

Fucking *hell*.

My shoulders slumped on their own accord when I realized that…it was time to get my hands dirty.

Jesus, take the damn wheel already.

21.

Carina

Myles cleared his throat and approached the girl. "Look, Samantha, I–"

"My name's not Samantha," she cut in with a scowl on her face.

"Right, of course." He scratched his stubble. "I don't exactly care about that, to be honest. I just wanted to put a name on you so that I didn't have to call you "girl" again and again."

She continued to scowl at him.

I pressed my lips together as I ping-ponged my gaze between her and Myles.

"Let me put forward a simple deal," Myles began. "I promise to pay you the full price of this boxset, *if* you decide to give it up by handing it over to me."

Supposed-Samantha turned to face him fully. "Are you out of your mind?!" she asked, and then held a hand up. "Wait, don't answer that. Of course you're crazy, because no sane person would propose such a stupid fucking deal."

"Language," Myles said.

"I'm eighteen."

"Are you?"

She hesitated for a second, and then shrugged. "None of your business. You're not getting the boxset from me anyway."

Myles raised a brow. "Oh, but I think I will."

SS (Supposed-Samantha) gave him a seething once-over. "Over my dead fucking body."

Jesus *Christ*.

She was dedicated, I'll give her that.

The thing is: the boxset she was holding was an exclusive *B&N* edition of Rainbow Rowell's *Carry On* series. I'm pretty sure I don't have to explain the rarity of this set to anyone, because if someone was willing to go all in for something like this, then it had to be important.

And it *was*, because try as I might, I hadn't been able to get my hands on this boxset. *Amazon, Book Depository*, the *B&N* online store, you name it, and I'd looked them up hundreds of times, only to be disheartened when I didn't find the set. Rainbow *herself* didn't have it up for sale on her official website, so yeah, there was *that*.

I loved her and her books, and I wanted that boxset in my possession.

No, I *needed* it in my damn life.

Myles narrowed his eyes at SS. "You shouldn't have said that, because now, Samantha, it's open *war*."

Oh God.

Oh dear.

Oh no.

Should I cover my eyes? My ears? I was so confused. And scared. And intrigued.

Myles grabbed the top corner of the boxset and pulled. "Give it to me…"

SS gasped and pulled the thing back towards her. "No. Way. In. Hell."

Myles scowled and pulled again. "Give it up, you *brat!*"

I placed a hand over my mouth to stifle my laughter.

A few people looked over at Myles and SS in complete shock, and then at me – giggling like an idiot next to the two of them – before walking away with either confused shakes of their heads, or while murmuring about how the three of us were probably limp in the brain.

Not that I cared.

Myles grunted and widened his stance. "Samantha–"

"STOP CALLING ME THAT, OHMYGOD!" SS yelled as she tried to break Myles's hold on the boxset.

I knew he wasn't using *all* of his strength on this, but just enough to make the girl give up on what should have been mine to begin with.

I would have taken his place, y'know, but to be honest, if I *had*, I wouldn't have gone this easy on Samantha-whoever. It would've gotten messy, loud, and probably bloody, so I'm glad it's Myles in front of her, and not me.

Anyone who says being an avid reader and book nerd is easy – yeah, they're fuckin' liars. They don't know what it's like being in our world. Shit ain't easy, especially when certain sources are limited or next to impossible to get our hands on.

Myles pulled again, and SS stumbled forward a bit. "Give. Itttttt!"

Okay, I was getting a bit worried, because if he managed to accidentally trip SS, and she broke her nose or chin or teeth, then he'd be in trouble. The last thing I wanted was for my boyfriend to get dragged out of my favorite bookstore by security. Or cops.

That's…certainly not how I'd envisioned this date would go.

I took a step towards Myles, ready to ask him to let go, because he was more important to me than this boxset, when…

"*Samantha!*" came an urgent voice from somewhere ahead of me.

I looked over *Samantha's* shoulder, and saw a middle-aged woman walking over to her with a concerned look on her face.

"Honey," the woman began, "where did you run off to? I've been searching for you everywhere in this God-forsaken hellhole."

Myles let go of the boxset and stumbled over to me. "*You think they'll get me arrested for this?*" he whispered.

I bit the inside of my cheek and shook my head, to which he sighed and relaxed. I then quickly signed the words *Name* and *How?* to him, because I was surprised at how accurate he'd been in guessing the girl's name.

He shrugged in a nonchalant manner. "*I don't know...*" he muttered. "*She just...looked like a Samantha to me, for some reason.*" He shifted on his feet. "*No offense to those with the same name, of course.*"

I pursed my lips to hide a smile, just as the woman looked up at Myles, and immediately, a stark blush creeped up her cheeks.

Her dark hair was tied in a low bun, and she was wearing a black pencil skirt, paired with a lavender silk blouse and black stilettos. With a Gucci bag on her wrist and a ridiculous pearl necklace around her slender neck, she was a mom stereotype which I thought only existed in TV shows and movies, but nope, the world has a way of surprising me.

All the damn time.

"Did she, uh…" The woman swallowed, still blushing. "Did she bother you?"

"Mom, *ewwwww*," Samantha said, to which both Myles and I coughed behind our fists.

The woman eyed us sharply, and then turned her attention to Myles again. "I'm sorry if Samantha said or did something harsh. Teenagers these days, you know…"

"Uh huh." Myles gave her a plastic smile. "It's all good; she's just a kid, after all."

Samantha glared at him.

"Oh." The woman grabbed the boxset from Samantha and examined it. "Is this yours?" she asked Myles, *totally* ignoring me, and then offered it to him. "Like I said: teenagers these days. So aggressive and irrational." She sent a saccharine smile his way.

Myles, with a too-smug look on his face, took the box before grinning at the woman. "Thank you. I appreciate it." He then handed it to me. "My girlfriend here saw it first and wanted it for herself, but Samantha got to it before we could, so we were simply sorting stuff out." He smirked at Samantha. "Right?" he addressed her.

She gritted her teeth and clenched her hands. "Right," she spat, and swiveled on her feet before walking away from us.

Myles's forehead creased in mock concern. "I'm sorry if I–"

"No, no," the woman cut him off with another too-sugary smile. "She'll get over it. They're just books, after all."

Right...

I wasn't surprised she'd said something so...shallow.

Books aren't *just* books; they are *life*. Adventures and romances and histories – they are a beautiful escape.

But I wouldn't expect Mommy here to understand any of that.

Myles waved a hand at the boxset I was holding, and then glanced at the woman. "If you want, we can give this to you so that you can–"

"Oh, no!" She shook her head elegantly. "Please don't. It's nothing she can't handle." She then finally gave me her undivided attention. "You have a keeper in your hands here," she said adoringly.

I do, I signed around a genuinely giddy smile, because Myles really was a keeper.

The woman's eyes widened as she stared at me. Her complexion paled, and she struggled with her words as she continued to look at me.

And there, on her ashen features, was the one thing I absolutely *hated* seeing from people who meet me for the first time.

Sympathy.

I must have stiffened against him, and he must've sensed it, because Myles wrapped an arm around my waist before pressing me so close to him that I immediately relaxed against his warmth.

"It was a pleasure to meet you," he said to the woman, who licked her red lips and swallowed as she finally took her gaze away from me and nodded at Myles.

"Yes, a pleasure." With a quick wave, she all but ran away from us.

Once alone again, I closed my eyes and sighed. *Breathe*, I told myself. *Breathe, Carina. It's okay, just breathe.*

These things usually didn't affect me much – people's reactions and their uncertainty in how to behave in front of me – but I guess sometimes they just...*hit* me, and hit me for *real*.

Why is it so hard to believe that there *are* people like me out there in the world? Wouldn't it be nice to simply accept and appreciate our nature? A little ease and understanding are more than enough. That's all I ask for.

We're unique in our own ways, and I'd really appreciate it if we weren't treated like disjoined parts of the society, but instead be seen as its cohesive variables.

That shouldn't be so hard to do, right?

"Hey." Myles ran a hand up and down my back. "I'm here."

I looked up at him, patted my chest once, and then tapped the tips of my fingers to the side of my forehead twice to say: *I know.*

He placed a knuckle under my chin and brought my face close to his. "You're perfect, Rina, just the way you are," he said against my lips, and then erased the space between us by pressing a chaste kiss on my lips.

And that – that was enough.

More than enough.

22.

Carina

Myles pushed open the door and motioned for me to step in. With a smile, I entered the condo, and sucked in a breath as I looked around the beautifully rustic interior of his home.

Everything felt so natural and pleasing to the eye – from the wooden walls and beamed ceiling, to the massive window in the center of the living room. From the classic leather couches to the plush ivory carpet on the floor.

As the two of us took off our boots next to the threshold, Myles shut the condo's door and placed the books and grocery bags he was holding, under the coatrack next to the entrance.

A faint smell of his cologne, along with the scent of burnt wood, hit my nose, and I sighed. I could almost imagine a silent lake beyond the house instead of the busy, traffic-laden street of Chicago as I watched the snow fall on the closed glass window.

Once we'd left the bookstore, Myles had suggested we go somewhere for lunch, but I didn't want that. I wanted to cook something for him, because other than desserts and cakes, I hadn't exactly made anything savory for him, especially a meal. And also because I wanted to reward him for his heroism at *B&N* earlier.

It was only necessary, of course.

Because going to my house and making him lunch was out of the question – due to *Avô*, obviously – I'd asked Myles if we could go over to his place. He'd said yes immediately. Although, he'd suggested we order takeout instead of me cooking, but I'd refused.

So, here we were, in his condo, after a quick visit to the grocery store.

I took off my beanie, gloves, and coat, and Myles did the same. He then hung everything on the rack before twining his fingers with mine.

"Come on," he said with a grin, and led me further inside the condo.

I hadn't seen his place before, so there was so much for me to take in as I continued to look around like a damn weirdo.

"That's my office," Myles pointed at the room to the left. "I usually do blueprints, designing, and financial stuff there. And here," he then pointed at the room next to his office, "Is where all the dazzling happens."

I lifted my brows at him.

"It's my bedroom," he clarified, and then clicked his tongue. "I don't know why I used the word 'dazzling'. Can you...just, can you pretend I didn't say that? Can you, I don't know, erase that bit from your memory?"

I laughed. *You're crazy*, I signed, to which he gave me a subtle wink.

"Oh, I know, babe."

I shook my head at him, and let him pull me towards the fireplace on the right.

There was a lovely wooden table in front of it, with some interior design magazines on it, followed by a few pencils, a couple sketchbooks, and an iPad. There was a sofa just opposite the table, and a small stand to its left, with a lovely lamp on it.

The kitchen was next to the fireplace, and despite the fact that there weren't a lot of appliances in there, the area still looked pretty well-used.

I walked over to the fireplace, just as Myles rekindled its fire and stood to look at me.

I love your house, I signed.

He smiled. "Thanks, Rina." He came behind me and wrapped his arms around my waist. "It's a contemporary rustic style. Roughhewn wood everywhere – my favorite."

I leaned against him. *Your house should be next to a lake*, I signed.

He pressed a long kiss below my ear. "Yeah?" he whispered.

I nodded, and gasped when his lips began traveling lower.

Myles softly dug his teeth into the side of my neck, making me moan. Goosebumps pricked every inch of my skin, and my heart began beating faster.

"Rina…" He kissed his way up to my ear again. "You're my bliss, my avalanche in the calm." He held me a bit tighter. "God, I'm so lucky to have you here with me." He pressed another kiss, but this time, to the back of my head, which made me smile.

I placed my hands over his, and when he bit my earlobe before nuzzling his nose against it, I chuckled.

That's when my eyes landed on something above the fireplace. And…and that's also when my body stiffened against Myles's.

23.

I felt the shift in Rina's body as soon as it happened. She straightened suddenly, and her hands over mine went slack.

I quickly let go of her and stepped to the side so that I could look at her. "Hey, what's wrong?"

She didn't even glance at me, and instead, walked closer to the fireplace before running her fingers over one of the framed photos that was on top of it.

It was a family photo, with a very young me, covered in mayonnaise and mud – don't ask – a laughing Taron, and our parents. Not my best moment as a kid, but Mom loves this picture, so I got it framed for anyone and everyone to see and get their fill of amusement.

I was nothing but a vessel of entertainment, after all.

Rina swallowed, her eyes still on the photo. She then pointed a finger at me, and tapped the tip of her left thumb on her chin, followed by the center of her forehead.

"Yes," I said. "Those are my parents."

She swallowed again, and then smiled faintly as she touched a corner of the photo.

"That's me," I told her.

I know, she signed, and then finally looked up at me.

"I was eight," I began. "I didn't wanna be in the photo, but Mom and Dad were pretty insistent about it. I was covered in mayo, so when they all but dragged me into the backyard for the shot, I rolled on the wet grass in…umm, protest."

Rina laughed, but the action appeared halfhearted. She then glanced at the rest of the photos, all taken during random, unexpected moments throughout the years, and signed, *You look happy in these.*

"Yeah," I said, but didn't elaborate.

She hugged herself and lowered her head a little.

"Rina, hey." I cupped her face between my hands. "I'm so sorry." I knew my words wouldn't fix anything, but I meant them, and I hoped she understood just how much.

She shook her head, and her expression turned to one of regret.

I'm sorry, she signed. *It's my fault. I shouldn't have ruined things by dampening my mood.*

"It's not your fault, and you didn't ruin anything," I told her, but she simply kept shaking her head.

"Rina."

No, she signed. *I'm sorry.* Tears started streaming down her cheeks. *I'm sorry.*

I brought her face close to mine. "*Listen* to me."

She stopped and looked at me, so vulnerable and wounded.

"You didn't deserve to lose them," I said. "But you did, and I'm genuinely sorry. I hate that there's nothing that can be done against what was taken from you, but Rina, you have people in your life who see you as a damn blessing." I pressed a kiss on her forehead. "Mr. Ribeiro, Ashleigh and your crew at the shop, their families." I swallowed. "Me."

She wrapped her fingers around my wrists, and her chin trembled a second before she started crying.

"Baby..." I pulled her to me and hugged her to my chest.

In the time I've known her, Rina and I have never discussed her parents. And to be honest, I'm okay with that, because the last thing I wanna do is upset her. I know this is a sensitive topic for her, so to bring it up on my terms really doesn't feel right. I, of course, would be okay to talk about it if *she* wants to. It is, after all, *her* choice.

She fisted the back of my sweater and pressed her face into the crook of my neck.

We remained that way for a while, and I was glad I could be there for her like this; that I could give her a moment of solace and comfort.

Trust was an imperative thing in a relationship, and for Rina to let me see this side of her – it meant more to me than words could explain.

She slowly, reluctantly pulled away from me, and gestured for me to give her something to write on as she all but slumped onto the sofa.

I nodded, and then grabbed a pencil and sketchbook from the coffee table before handing it to her and taking a seat next to her.

You know what hurts more than losing them? She wrote. *It's that I can hardly remember them. I miss them more than I can express, but I can't remember them. I have their photos and a few old videos in the name of memories, but I can't, for the life of me, put a recollection to any of them. When I think of them, all I can remember are the moments Pai and I would sing Christmas carols together, and the times Mãe would let me watch her bake in the kitchen. That's it, Myles; that's all I can remember. Nothing noticeable, nothing too specific. And it breaks my heart, because I love them, but I don't even know them too well. I miss them, and I can't even imagine their faces until I've seen their pictures. I don't know what that says about me, but I miss them and I love them and it hurts.*

My throat tightened, and my eyes burned after reading that. "You were very young, Rina," I said to her. "It's natural for you to not remember a lot. But at least you have those vague snippets of the past to know they were real, and that they most definitely loved you."

But it's not fair to them.

"What's not fair is you thinking it's your fault, when it clearly isn't."

Rina was shaking as she began writing again.

It is, though, isn't it? If I hadn't asked for that dress, we wouldn't have gone to the boutique, and they'd still be here.

"Rina…" I placed a hand over her knee. "You know 'What ifs' don't solve anything, right? They only make things complicated and painful. They are simply a way for you to drown yourself in doubt and unnecessary accusations. Please don't do this to yourself." I gave her knee a firm squeeze. "*Please.*"

If I'd gone back into the boutique with them instead of letting them go by themselves, then maybe–

I didn't let her finish writing; I grabbed the sketchbook and pencil from her before throwing them on the table.

"No." I shook my head. "Fucking *no*, Rina." I held her face again, and that's when I realized that my breathing was uneven.

"Don't *ever* let yourself go there, you got it? Grief and anger are valid emotions, but you can't let them define you." I leaned in and kissed her salty lips. "I won't let you do that to yourself."

She blinked at me, pain clear in her misty eyes.

"Tell me you understand me, Rina," I urged.

She sniffed as she scanned my face, and then let go of a sigh before placing a hand over my chest.

I do, she signed.

I kissed her again, and this time, she reciprocated it with equal vigor and urgency.

And that – that was hopeful enough for me.

More than enough, if I were being honest.

24.
Myles

I all but fell on the living-room couch in my haste of wanting to get off my feet, and wiggled my toes in relief as I pulled my phone out of the pocket of my grey suit jacket. It's funny how wearing formal shoes for merely 3 hours had left me wishing those damned things didn't ever come into existence. I was okay with sneakers and sports kicks, but those asshole-ish leather prisons my feet had to be confined in – yeah, those made me want to scream like a fucking banshee.

It was past 2a.m., and my family was arguing in my parents' kitchen about a late-night hot chocolate cap being beneficial or bad for health.

Just a regular day at the Reyes household, y'know.

Taron and I had decided to stay the night with Mom and Dad after attending Mass, which had made our folks super happy. Not that I minded their company. They were amazing, and Taron and I were so damn lucky to have them.

"But hot chocolate is LIFE!" my niece, Sienna, said. "It's basically comfort food."

"It's a beverage, hon, not an actual food item," added Tori, my sister-in-law.

"For the last time, guys: IT'S COLD AND I WANT HOT CHOCOLATE!" Taron all but yelled.

"Relax, sweetie," Mom requested, just as Dad muttered, "Oh, for the love of baby Jesus."

My back was to them, which meant I was saved from having to become an involuntary member of their…government-flipping discussion.

An absolute relief.

I shook my head and opened Rina's chat on my phone. I'd wished her a Merry Christmas just as the clock had struck 12, to which she'd responded almost an hour later. Can't say I minded, given how busy she must've been.

Every year, Mr. Ribeiro and Rina held a family dinner at Christmas Eve, and according to the latter, it ran pretty late into the night. Everyone from the shop, some of Mr. Ribeiro's and Rina's friends, including their families, were invited, so I could only imagine the amount of cooking and interacting that went down, let alone the cleaning and stabilizing.

I quickly typed a message to Rina, and drummed my fingers against my thigh as I waited for her to respond.

Me: *You free yet?*

To my surprise, she responded within a minute. I took that as a win.

Rina: *Yes, just done. Ashleigh and some of the other ladies stayed back to help, so I didn't have to do everything myself. They just left, so I'm about to head into the shower to freshen up. What about you?*

Me: *Just got back from Mass. Now I'm trying to zone out my family's voices in the background as they argue about the significance of late-night hot chocolate consumption.*

Rina: *Ughhh, don't even get me started. I could really use a cup. Or two. And you. And some cuddles :')*

A flush of warmth hit my chest at her words.

Me: *I could come over...*

God, how I *wanted* to go to her. Every second I'd been out, I'd thought about driving over to her place and crashing the damn dinner. But I couldn't, of course, given my flawless rapport with Mr. Ribeiro.

Rina: *Really?! Aren't you tired?*

I smiled.

Me: *Nope. Although, the glaring blisters on my toes would say otherwise. But hey, they won't mean shit if I get to kiss you and hold you tonight.*

Rina: *You can be extremely sweet sometimes, you know that?*

Me: *And that's a good or bad thing?*

Rina: *It's PERFECT.*

I grinned.

"Bro!"

Taron came up behind me and placed his chin on my right shoulder. If I moved my head towards him even in the slightest, I'd end up with at least an inch of his beard in my nose. Yeah, that's how close he'd pressed his face to mine.

"What?" I told him.

"Whatchu doin'?" he asked, like it wasn't obvious, given that he'd gotten way past invading my personal space.

I glanced at my phone in my hand, and then looked sideways at him. "Making love with my chest hair, of course," I deadpanned.

To my momentary relief, he moved back, but then came to stand right in front of me.

"You don't have chest hair," he said.

"It's creepy that you know that, you know?"

He rolled his eyes. "We work out together, you dumbass."

Ah, right.

"Well, you *did* initiate this conversation by asking a stupid question," I told him.

"It was rhetorical," he countered.

I raised a brow. "Was it, though?"

Taron clicked his tongue. "You're cray, bro."

Sweet baby Jesus, what the fuck?!

"Please stop spending so much time with your daughter," I said with a grimace. "You're turning into a massive...bearded..." I pursed my lips, "...and too-muscly version of her, and I am *not* here for it."

"She inspires me," Taron said casually. "She's my pride."

"Of course she is. I love her to pieces as well, but that doesn't mean you have to let her turn you into…this." I waved a hand at him. "'*Cray*', Taron, *seriously?*"

He chuckled. "She spent almost an hour trying to explain the meaning of that word to me yesterday. I *had* to use it somehow."

Good Lord.

"Well, go use it on your wife, man. Why am I your only target when you get a slang-itch?"

Taron folded his arms across his chest. "Because, Beauty, you wouldn't threaten to divorce me in return. You're a formidable option."

"*Ohmygod,*" I muttered, just as Sienna yelled, "Uncle Myles! Tell Grandma to gimme a mug of hot chocolate!"

I closed my eyes and let go of a long breath. "Mom, just give her the damn hot chocolate already."

"Language, Myles!" my mom countered.

"Sorry," I mumbled, just as my phone *pinged* back-to-back with new messages.

"Looks like *Chest Hair* wants your attention," Taron said.

I glared at him. "Ha-ha. *Very funny.*"

He laughed. "You get back to your texting, and I'll go handle my girl," he told me.

I chuckled, and bumped a fist against his as he walked past me and toward our family.

Alone again, I opened Rina's messages.

Rina: *Myles? Hello?*

Rina: *You still there?*

She was cute, wasn't she?

Me: *Yup, here. Taron just called you Chest Hair, by the way.*

Fuck. I don't know why I just texted her that.

Rina: *I'm sorry, WHAT?*

I put my tongue to my cheek.

Me: *Forget I said that, please.*

Rina: *I'm not even sure I fully understand what you meant by that anyway.*

Me: *Pretend I didn't say it, then.*

Rina: *Impossible. That text is literally there, staring me in the face.*

Me: *You're not a chest hair, Rina, I promise.*

Rina: *I'm so confused right now…*

Rina: *And scared.*

I couldn't help but laugh.

Me: *I'm sorry* • ‿ ,•

Rina: *Lol. Forgiven* (˘ ³˘)

Me: *You still want me to come over?*

Rina: *Why is that even a question?*

I laughed again.

Me: *Alright, I'll be there in twenty.*

Rina: *Yay! I made cookies for you earlier. Thought I'd give them to you when you stopped by the shop on Monday, but…*

Could she get any more perfect?

Mr. Ribeiro had asked me to halt renovation until January. So, because I couldn't meet Rina at the house, I'd decided to visit her briefly at *do Açaí*.

When Mr. Ribeiro wasn't there, *obviously*.

Me: *What flavor are the cookies?*

Rina: *Lofthouse* ✳ ‿ ✳

Me: *I could kiss you a thousand times right now.*

And then some, of course.

Rina: *Then come here and do it* ⌒ ‿ ●

I smiled.

Me: *I'm on it.*

I got to my feet. "Uh, hey, guys," I said to my family.

111

They looked up from where they were all sitting around the kitchen counter, sipping their hot chocolate.

No cup for me...

Nice.

"I'm heading over to Rina's," I told them. "I'll prolly go back to my place after and then come here in the morning for the gift-opening. That okay?"

Mom gave me a *look*. "Isn't it a bit too late to be visiting her?"

"She said I could come over, Mom."

My dad chuckled and placed a hand over hers. "He's not a child, honey."

She glanced at him, and then at me. "Well, as long as that horrid grandfather of hers doesn't come at you for visiting her at this hour of the night..."

"*Jesus Christ*, Michelle," Dad said, just as Taron grumbled, "The fuck, Mom," and Sienna and Tori muttered, "*Wow*," in unison.

I shook my head at her. "I'll be fine," I said to her, and then turned before hobbling over to the door.

Damn blisters.

"Wear your dad's sneakers, hon! They have that cushion thing underneath for comfort!" Mom called out after me.

I've never felt more like a kid than I did in that moment.

"Will do, Mom. Love you."

"Love you right back, sweetie!"

I put on my dad's shoes, grabbed my coat, and walked out of the house before closing the door behind me.

I'd only just made it to my car, though, when a new message came in.

Rina: *Don't knock.*

I sniffed against the chilly air and got into my car.

Me: *Of course I won't. I'll text.*

Rina: *Drive safe. And don't sing while you're driving. It distracts you from the road.*

112

I coughed out a laugh after reading that, and then started my car before turning on the heater.

Me: *Aye, ma'am. See you soon.*

Rina: *I'm counting on it* :)

25.

Carina

As I finished plating everything for Myles, I realized that I hadn't checked on the blue jays' food and water.

I pushed a strand of my damp hair behind my ear, and made sure to be quiet as I climbed up to my bedroom. *Avô* had headed to bed almost two hours ago, and I wasn't planning on putting a dent in his sleep, especially with Myles on the way.

I opened my bedroom door, grabbed the packet of wet wipes from my nightstand drawer, and made my way over to the window before sliding it open. I grunted as ice-cold air hit me right in the face, and then flipped open the food box so that I could clean it. A lone blue jay stirred as I put a hand inside the box, and chirped lazily when I began discarding the slightly snowy seeds into a small trash bag with the help of a couple wet wipes.

Once I'd replaced the food and water, I put the lid back on, threw the bag in the bin next to the window, and headed to the bathroom.

It was only when I pumped a dollop of hand wash into my palm that I realized my hands were shaking. Not from the cold, to be sure, but in time with the crazy beating of my heart, knowing that *he* was coming over to meet me. Knowing that I'd get to touch him in mere minutes.

God, the things Myles Reyes made me feel were extraordinarily irresistible. Dangerous, yes, but also madly addicting.

And damn if I didn't burn for him like the ember did for the still-roaring flames.

26.

I tapped my fingers against the steering wheel as I continued to drive through the illuminating streets of a very lively, late-night Chicago. I smiled when a couple of kids on the sidewalk waved at me, and bopped my head in time with the Christmas song playing on the radio.

As I took a left and entered Maplewood Ave, I started to hum, but quickly stopped myself when I thought of Rina's message from earlier.

She'd driven with me enough times to know how easily music could affect my attention. I could mostly never stop myself from singing or humming along to the songs on the radio, but that also meant I usually ended up either *almost* hitting an old lady on the street, or a random car driving ahead of me. It's definitely not something I'm proud of, but hey, at least I'm willing to work on getting rid of the habit for safety reasons.

It was only when I entered Rina's neighborhood that I realized that my stomach was in knots. Not because of an impending gastric episode, of course, but in time with the wild beating of my heart, knowing that I was about to meet *her*. Knowing that I'd get to touch her in just minutes.

God, the things Carina Ribeiro made me feel were massively compulsive. Risky, yes, but also madly inclining.

And damn if I didn't burn for her like a cinder did for an ongoing fire.

27.

Carina

I bent and shifted the cookie-laden plate that was on the coffee table, to the left, and then clicked my tongue before shifting it back to its original place. I pulled at my red sweater dress once, and then soothed it back down with a hand.

I moved the plate again. And again.

Wiggled my toes.

Stretched my legs.

Stared at the fireplace like it was Regé-Jean's ass from the 5th, and well, the 6th, episodes of Bridgerton.

Pushed my hair this way and that, as if that'd do anything remotely useful.

And then, just before I completely lost my sanity, my phone vibrated in my hand.

Thank *fuck*.

Beauty: *Knock-knock.*

I chuckled as I read his message.

Me: *Took you long enough.*

Beauty: *I have a...leg situation tonight, as you already know. Couldn't drive fast because of that.*

I got to my feet and made my way to the door.

Me: *I'm coming, hold on.*

Beauty: *That's what she said ;)*

I choked out a laugh.

Me: *I could keep you standing outside for that horrendous excuse of a joke, you know that, right?*

Beauty: *But baby, it's cold outside :'(*

I snickered.

Me: *You're lucky you're cute.*

I slowly, almost theatrically, opened the top latches, and then pushed the knob down before opening the door, only to blink repeatedly at Myles, who was standing on the *Welcome* mat with a grin on his face.

His hair was coiffed – something I'd *never* seen him do before. He was wearing a tailored-to-fit grey suit jacket, which complemented his complexion but clashed with his eyes, along with a black silk shirt and grey pants. He had his regular winter coat draped over his left arm, and when I looked down, I couldn't help but gawk at his shoes.

His *Dad Sneakers*, I mean.

They were neon green and white, and everything about them was wrong compared to the clothes he was wearing.

I quickly closed my mouth when I realized it'd hung open on its own accord, and took a couple steps back so that Myles could enter.

He limped his way inside, and I frowned.

What kind of shoes? I signed to him.

He grimaced. "Fucking Oxfords," he said softly.

I pressed my lips together, to which he rolled his eyes.

"Go ahead and laugh, Rina. I know you want to." He hung his coat on the rack, took off his…shoes, and then his socks, while I closed the door like the stealthy bitch that I was, before turning to face him.

I'm sorry, I signed.

He pulled me to him – so close that I could feel his belt press against my navel. "You're so not sorry," he whispered against my lips, and then kissed me.

I held onto the urge to moan, especially when I opened my mouth for him, and he took everything I wanted to give him without a care in the world.

My breaths labored when his lips travelled to my jaw and neck – unhurried – and the sharp sting of his stubble made goosebumps rise throughout my body.

His hands came to my waist, and he fisted my sweater before gazing down at me. "God, you're breathtaking, Rina." He dropped a soft kiss on my nose. "Who knew red wool could be such a turn-on."

I chuckled and ran a hand over the lapel of his suit jacket, and then flicked my eyes up to him before signing, *Wow*.

He smiled and took hold of my hand before placing soft, open-mouthed pecks on the inside of my wrist. "Thank you," he said, and a slight blush creeped up his cheeks.

I jerked my head to the side, and twined our fingers before walking us to the fireplace.

Myles shrugged off his jacket and placed it on the couch's armrest, and we then sat down with our backs to it. We stretched our legs out in front of us, and Myles's eyes widened a little as he looked at the things laid out on the coffee table. "You did all this for *me*?" he asked.

I'd set the tiny table with a couple cranberry candles, a tall glass of champagne, two small plates of Lofthouse cookies and *pavê*, and one full of cheese-flavored nachos, because I didn't have anything savory to offer him.

I nodded in response to his question.

Myles's expression softened, and he leaned in to press a kiss on my lips. "Have I told you how fucking awesome you are?"

I clicked my tongue and shook my head.

He grinned. "Liar," he whispered, and then kissed me again.

I cupped the side of his neck to deepen the kiss, and when we pulled back, I gently ran the pad of my thumb over his throat. I then let my gaze wander his frame, his jaw, the three undone buttons of his shirt, and the way the fire cast a shadow over his side profile.

"Hey," He placed a knuckle under my chin and lifted my face to his. "What's up?"

118

You are beautiful, I signed.

He chuckled. "Look who's talking."

I rolled my eyes and slapped his hand away. *Eat*, I signed.

With another grin, he straightened and grabbed a piece of *pavê* before examining it like it was an artifact or something.

"What's this?" he asked, and then, put the whole thing in his mouth before I could even answer him.

I stifled a laugh when he moaned while chewing it, and then grabbed the notebook and pen I'd set out on the couch.

It's called pavê. It's a Brazilian dessert made out of chocolate, walnut, pecans, bananas, etc. And, for the love of God, do NOT try to pronounce it.

When I showed him what I'd written, he read it quickly before shoving another piece into his mouth.

"I love it," he said with a mouth-full of *pavê*, but it sounded more like: "Ah wuv iff."

Once he was done, he sipped some champagne and nudged my shoulder. "How was dinner?"

I shrugged. *Okay*, I signed.

He raised a brow as he grabbed a pink cookie from its plate. "Just okay?"

I asked him to wait, and then began writing in my notebook while he finished his first cookie.

It was hectic. So much random gossip, boring this and that. Avô was happy to see everyone under one roof, but I felt a little suffocated, to be honest. I constantly felt like I needed air, but I couldn't possibly leave because I had friends who wanted to chat with me, and people I had to serve dinner to.

I'm glad it didn't last longer, or else I'd have lost it completely.

Myles frowned after reading that. "Is it like this every year?"

Not necessarily.

"You could've texted me, Rina. I'd have bailed you out."

I squeezed his free hand. *I appreciate it*, I wrote.

119

His frown deepened. "Are you sure you're okay?" he questioned, and then looked at the coffee table. "God, I'm so fucking inconsiderate. You've been running 'round cooking and cleaning and serving for hours, and I didn't even think about that *once* before stuffing my face like a damn asshole." He made to place the half-eaten cookie on the plate, but I grabbed his wrist in order to stop him.

He relented with a huff, and then shoved the cookie into his mouth.

I'm okay, I signed, but when he still appeared doubtful, I fisted my left hand, touched the index finger of my right hand to my chin, and slapped the palm of that very same hand over my fist to say: *Promise.*

He searched my face for a second or two, and then downed some more of the champagne before giving me a nod.

How was Mass? I wrote.

"Good," he said sincerely. "Mom cried for at least half of it, but that's nothing new; she does that every year. Dad and Taron tried to hush her, but she just doesn't get the memo."

I wasn't sure whether or not to laugh at that, so I just blinked at him.

He chuckled. "Wow, Rina; act at least a little bit amused. We don't want my mom to think she's lost her touch."

I laughed, and Myles moved closer to me before placing an arm on the couch.

Do you enjoy attending Mass? I wrote.

"Yeah," he said around a smile. "It's peaceful, and yet so powerful that it moves you in a way you don't mind being moved."

I returned his smile.

Must be nice.

"It is," he stated. "You ever attended?"

I shook my head.

But I want to.

"I'll take you next year," he told me with so much confidence that it made me swallow. "Screw the family dinner; come hang out with us Reyes for one

120

Christmas. And if you don't leave with your brain in your ass by the end of it, I swear to you that I'll change my name."

I placed a hand over my mouth to muffle the sound of my laughter, whereas Myles hid his face in my hair to do the same.

I sniffed as I regained my freaking sanity, and then punched Myles in the arm before signing, *Asshole*.

"You just love signing that, don't you?" he mused. "You find any and every excuse to show me your finger-hole."

I pursed my lips and gave him a look full of warning.

Stop.

"Why? Are you scared of making a noise and waking up your cranky ol' *avô*?" His eyes gleamed, and I saw the challenge in them – clear as fucking day.

He leaned in and bit the skin just below my ear, right before sucking it into his mouth.

My back arched against him, and he took that as an opportunity to cup my left breast from over my sweater.

I let go of a broken sigh, and Myles pulled my face to his before crashing our mouths together.

God, it was fire and pain; it was unashamed and wild. The way Myles kissed me was dizzying, all-encompassing.

He bit my lower lip, and I pushed my nails into his jaw.

He touched his tongue to the roof of my mouth, so I grabbed the collar of his shirt and brought him closer to me.

He pulled at my hair and fucked my mouth with abandon, and I cupped the back of his neck as I tried to remember where each of us began and ended.

"*Rina*," he all but pleaded, his voice a bit hoarse, and then tugged at the hem of my sweater. "Take it off."

I moved back a little and did just that, and watched as Myles's eyes roved over my white bra and underwear.

"Fuck me," he muttered. "Come here."

121

I moved toward him, and as he slipped my bra down to run his thumbs over my nipples, I pressed my lips to his so as to avoid moaning out loud, and began unbuttoning his shirt.

He helped me with it, and when he took it off and threw it behind him, I sucked in a breath before running my fingers over the defined planes of his body. I let my nails scrape his abs ever so slightly, and when I saw them contract against my touch, I went lower and unhooked his belt buckle.

"Rina…" His breath brushed my cheek, and when I unzipped his pants, he lifted up to take both it and his underwear off before kicking them to the side.

My heart was in my throat; my veins were on fire. Seeing Myles like this – for me – gave me a thrill I couldn't get enough of.

I wrapped my left hand around the base of his cock and began stroking him, and when he tipped his head back and groaned in response, I lifted on my knees and kissed my way from his chin to his throat, and then over to the taut muscles straining the side of his neck.

The smell of cranberry candles, paired with the burning logs in the fireplace, and Myles's orange-and-cedar cologne, was so addicting that I pressed my teeth into his skin, and then ran my tongue over it.

Myles groaned again, and then wrapped his right hand over mine – the one I had around his cock. With a smirk, he began stroking himself with me, and God, that was so damn hot I almost lost it.

He squeezed my hand, which in turn intensified the grip I had on him. "*Fuck*," he moaned, and then gazed at me before saying, "I want you."

I nodded without hesitation, because *fuck me*, I wanted him too – so much that I could hardly think past the rushing adrenaline in my head.

Myles let go of my hand, and I let go of him. He then snatched his pants from the floor before pulling his wallet out from inside it.

"Okay, so I have a regular one, a strawberry flavored one, a tingling one…" He turned to me with a bunch of condoms in his hands. "Hmm, yeah, there's also an ultra-thin one, a ribbed one, and, believe it or not, a glow-in-the-dark one as well." He shook his head when I stared at him in complete shock. "The freaky shit people like to get up to within the confines of their bedrooms, I tell you."

I... I was wordless. I mean *speechless*.

How many boxes did you get? I signed.

He scratched his jaw. "A bunch. These," he waved the packets at me, "are from a combo pack. One-of-everything kinda stuff."

Ohmygod.

I continued to stare at him.

"You wanna use the glow-in-the-dark one?" he asked me – so damn *casually* that it made me balk. "I'm not sure we'll even *see* the glow with the fireplace still so bright, but we could try and..." He trailed when he realized I'd frozen in place.

"Rina?"

I blinked and cleared my throat, and then grabbed the ultra-thin condom before slapping it on his chest.

Myles laughed as he put the others back in his wallet, and then placed said wallet on the coffee table before moving the latter out of the way.

He grabbed a pillow from the couch and threw it on the carpet, and jerked his head toward it as a silent command for me to lie down.

I got to my feet and turned my back to him, and as I looked at him from over my shoulder, he chuckled and joined me.

I gasped when his fingers grazed my spine, and as he unclasped my bra, I took off my underwear before discarding them both to the side.

Myles ran his knuckles over my arms, and then his hands found my breasts. I arched against him as he cupped them in an almost aching grip.

"You're *stunning*, Rina," he whispered in my ear, and dragged his hands down to my navel, and then to my pussy.

I let out a shaky moan, and pushed my ass against him when he touched my clit.

"So wet," he murmured, and then kissed my shoulder once. "Lie down."

123

I moved away from him and did as he'd asked, and as he turned to face me, he put the condom on and knelt in front of me.

"Spread your legs," he said to me, and when I did, his eyes darkened. "God, look at how bad you want me, baby."

I lifted my hips in response to that, which made him grin.

He hovered over me, and as our breaths merged, he widened my legs further before slowly pushing himself inside me.

My gasp was audible this time, and to stop myself from moaning out loud, I fisted the hair on the back of his head and touched his forehead to mine.

I couldn't believe we were doing this, when all it would take for *Avô* to see us would be to step outside his bedroom.

It was risky, what we were doing. It was uncontrolled and inevitable, yet also forbidden. But God if it wasn't the most satiating feeling in the world. I never wanted it to end; never wanted its taste to leave my mouth.

Myles panted a little as he began rocking his hips against mine, and every slide of his cock arose a fresh bout of thrill in me – one that was so damn overpowering and all-consuming.

I fisted his hair tighter, making him hiss. I couldn't possibly Sign anything even if I wanted to, because Lord knows I was too incoherent for that, so Myles would have to know that I wanted more through other methods.

"Rina…" His thrusts got faster, rougher.

I kissed him, and when he opened for me, I sucked on his tongue, and then bit down on it.

"Fuck," he rasped, and then pounded into me – so fast that it burned, but Christ, it was *still* not enough.

I placed both my hands on his chest, and then flung a leg over his waist before quickly changing our positions, in turn bringing us slightly closer to the fireplace.

He inhaled sharply, but laughed when I winked at him.

He pulled the pillow under him, and when he placed a hand behind his head, I got a front-row view of his body stretched out for me.

The fire crackled and brightened, and the sound reverberated through the room, mixing in with Myles and I's un-synced, dense breathing.

I rose, and then settled on him in a slow move, which made him moan low in his throat. "Faster, Rina," he said. There was a husk in his voice, and when I pinched my nipples before rocking forward just once, Myles grunted – in frustration, most likely – and grabbed my ass.

"*Faster*," he all but ordered. A sheen of sweat was visible on his temples, and so was the flush on his face and neck.

I pressed my teeth over my bottom lip and started riding him in earnest, and dug my nails onto his pecs when he filled me so deep that I could feel nothing but him. His crown hit the exact spot I wanted it to, and Myles's hips arched upward in the next thrust, making us both moan.

There was a sense of power that buzzed through me as our gazes met – him unkempt below me, and I, breathless above him.

I leaned over him, and my hair fell forward, shielding our side profiles from the fire.

He wrapped his arms around me, and I cupped the side of his face. "Are you close?" he asked in between thrusts.

I matched his pace and nodded in response.

"Come with me, then," he said. "Come all over my damn cock, baby."

I pressed my lips to his, and as he throbbed inside me, I clenched around him.

"*Jesus.*" He jerked unsteadily, and then groaned low as he came.

I hissed, and continued to kiss him as my shoulders shook in time with my blinding orgasm.

I could feel my pattering heartbeats in my ears as the two of us came down from our highs, and with one last kiss, I moved back to look down at Myles.

He tangled his fingers in my hair and smiled lazily at me. "How're you feelin'?"

I tapped a fist over the center of my chest twice as an indirect sign to say *Boom-boom*, and then signed the words *You* and *How?* separately so he'd know I wanted to know the same thing.

He nuzzled his nose against mine. "I feel…" He swallowed and smiled again. "I feel so *calm*, Rina, and not just because you gave me the best fucking orgasm of my life, but because it's *right* for us to be like this; to be this unrestrained and open." He pressed a chaste kiss to my lips. "I'm really happy."

As was I, and then some.

I extended the thumb and pinkie finger of my left hand before simultaneously pointing them in the opposite direction in a side-to-side motion to say, *Same*.

Myles exhaled. "Well, I'm glad. It would've gotten awfully embarrassing for me otherwise, given how I'm very much naked and at your mercy right now."

I laughed and shook my head, straightened, and then shifted to the side before standing up.

Myles stood as well, and then headed to the small bathroom next to the kitchen to dispose the condom.

It was a tiny area, one *Avô* had decided to add years ago for the times we have guests over.

When Myles came back out, I signed, *Shower*, and offered him a hand.

We both knew he'd have to leave soon, but taking a shower would give us a few more minutes together. I'd take that. Beggars can't be choosers and all that jazz, right?

With a smile, he nodded and took my hand. As we started climbing the stairs, I couldn't help but slap him in the ass. I mean, it was *right there* – all taut and asking for my attention.

I couldn't deny it the pleasure…

Myles stopped abruptly and narrowed his eyes at me. When I raised a brow at him, he smirked in a way that did unquestionable things to me.

126

"*Run*," he mouthed, that smirk of his still in place.

Goosebumps pricked my scalp, and as I stepped away from him, careful not to fall and crack my skull open, he whispered, "Run, Rina."

And so, I did; I fucking ran.

28.

I twisted in bed once, and when that didn't work, I moved to the other side and closed my eyes. And when that, too, failed to be effective, I huffed and sat up.

I took a deep inhale of the cranberry candle that was burning on my nightstand, and hoped and prayed that its lovely aroma would help me sleep.

But *nope*, it didn't.

It was so quiet outside, and if I looked through the window, I was sure I'd see nothing but snow and an empty, moonlit street.

I frowned and glanced at the digital clock on my bedside.

December 29th

3:23a.m.

I briefly thought about texting Myles, but he'd told me earlier that he was staying with his parents until the New Year, so I didn't wanna disturb him, in case he'd gone to bed late or something.

I ran my fingers through my hair, and then, with a sigh, I got to my feet before walking out of my room.

As I padded over to the one that was a few feet away from mine, I fixed my grey, silk pajamas and shirt.

I wasn't sure why I couldn't sleep. I'd had a nice, relaxing day, and had even texted Myles back-and-forth every hour, up until 12a.m., when I'd told him good night. Even the dinner was a yummy takeout feast with *Avô*, Ash, and Dave. The latter two had come to visit us, so we'd turned that into a mini get-together by ordering pizzas and cheese rolls and ice creams. It's a different story that Ash had tried to not-so-subtly coerce *Avô* into giving Myles an honest chance, and *Avô* had tried everything in his power to ignore her glaringly obvious suggestions. And *me* as well, of course, for still dating Myles, but other than that, it was a fun night.

Dave had managed to form a bond with *Avô*, and the two even planned a fishing expedition for next month.

Like, *wow*.

I swallowed and stopped outside the door, then knocked on it twice.

I bounced on the balls of my feet as I waited for him to open up, but straightened when I heard rustling on the other side.

"It's unlocked," came *Avô's* voice.

I slowly opened the door and stepped inside.

Avô was in bed, looking sleepy and concerned, and as I walked in further, his eyes searched my face.

"*Qual o problema, pequena?*" he asked. What's wrong, little one?

Can't sleep, I signed.

His shoulders relaxed at my response, and he threw aside his blanket before shifting a little to his left. "Hop on."

I went without hesitation, and all but curled up against him when he opened his arms for me.

My throat tightened as I placed the side of my face on his chest, and when he ran a hand up and down my back, I lost it and began crying on his shirt.

God, I felt so safe like this – cocooned against him. I didn't even care how I looked in that moment. All I knew was that I was okay and he was there for me.

"Carina..." *Avô* pressed a gentle kiss on my hairline. "What's wrong, hon?"

I sniffed, and as I moved back to look at him, I saw how starkly visible his wrinkles and worry lines appeared under the silver light that reflected against the window's glass and poured into his room.

I miss you, I signed, because it was the truth.

"I'm here," he said, but I knew that he knew exactly what I meant.

It's not fair to me, I signed, perhaps a bit more angrily than I'd like to.

Avô let go of a breath as he looked at me. "And how is it fair to *me*, Carina, when you won't respect my wish?"

He can't be serious.

Myles is amazing, Avô.

He raised a brow. "And you know that *how*, exactly? By sneaking out of the shop to go on dates with him? By going behind my back and spending time with him here, in this house, when I'm at the shop?"

If you already know I've been doing all of this, then why not fire him? Why is he still working on renovations if you aren't happy with our relationship? You're willingly letting us spend time together. Shouldn't you be doing the opposite of that?

He bunched his jaw as he stared at me. "Because I know what you're experiencing is simply a phase, one that *will* pass soon enough. I'm waiting for you to realize that by yourself and come to terms with it. Children need to learn certain lessons on their own."

I'm not a child.

"But you sure have been acting like one recently."

I fisted my hands. *Why are you doing this?* I signed. *Why won't you believe me when I tell you Myles is not like the others?*

Avô shook his head a little. "I trust him enough to know that he won't behave incorrectly with you, but that doesn't mean I think he's right for you."

Oh, he's *got* to be kidding me.

And you know what's right for me?

"Of course I do."

I roughly ran a hand under my nose. *You don't know anything*, I signed, just as a tear slid down my left cheek.

Avô's expression softened, and if I was right, I even saw a flash of regret on his features.

"Carina, come on–"

I put an index finger up to stop him.

You tell me you love me, and yet, you won't trust my decisions. You tell me you know what's right for me, but how can you? If only you'd spent a minute getting to know Myles instead of judging him so blindly, Avô, you'd know what I mean. You'd understand why I'm so drawn to him. But no, you're too proud to be sitting on your high horse to spare a second on people who deserve so much more than a bit of your time and attention.

I got to my feet and walked out of his room before he could say anything else.

He'd said enough already.

I didn't know what I was expecting from him, but it certainly wasn't *that*. I'd thought that maybe now that he knows that Myles and I are still going strong, he'd come to understand that I'm not backing down, but I guess I was wrong; I'd hoped for too much from him.

I marched into my bedroom, shut the door, and went straight to my phone.

Me: *I need you.*

I swiped a few angry tears from my cheeks as I waited for him to respond.

Beauty: *I'm here.*

An involuntary sigh left me after I read those two words.

Me: *Did I wake you?*

Beauty: *Doesn't matter. You okay?*

I swallowed as I wrote down everything that'd just happened, and hit send on the message. I then slumped on my bed and pulled my blanket over my legs.

Myles replied exactly 7 minutes later. I knew that because I was staring absentmindedly at my phone's time while waiting for him to text back.

Beauty: *Maybe he needs more time? Maybe I can talk to him.*

Me: *You won't talk to him.*

Beauty: *Rina, come on, babe. He's your grandfather, and you know I respect him.*

Me: *If you respect him so much, then why are you going against his will and dating me?*

131

I regretted saying that immediately after the message went through. *Shit*.

My heart pounded faster at each passing second as I kept staring at the screen.

Fuck, I shouldn't have said that.

Fuck, fuck, *FUCK*.

I all but jumped out of my bed when my phone vibrated with an incoming video call. My hands shook a little as I accepted it, and held my breath as Myles's face filled the screen.

I heard a click of a button, and then his bedside lamp turned on. His hair was an absolute mess, and one of the straps of his red tank top was sliding off his shoulder. But...but it's the expression on his face that was the center of my focus.

God, he looked *livid*. And rightfully so. I *had* sent him a very stupid, *stupid* message, after all.

I was about to tell him that I was sorry, but he beat me to it by saying, "Just because you're angry after the conversation you had with your grandfather, doesn't mean you get to throw shade at me, Rina," he said sharply.

Oops.

"You can't say shit like that to me and expect me to take it like a fucking punching bag," he continued, still *very* upset. "I understand that you need an outlet for your emotions, but I am *not* going to let you throw me under the damn bus just because I'm calm about Mr. Ribeiro's stubbornness and refuse to act against it. Just because you're angry, doesn't mean I have to follow in on it. I genuinely don't care about what he thinks of me as a person, or why he's convinced our relationship is a fluke, but by saying what you just did in that message, you're only proving his point." He clenched his jaw. "And I am not going to let you push me away, or let what he told you tonight affect your belief in us. I'm not going anywhere, and what I feel for you isn't weak enough to cower under the respect I have for your *avô*. I may see him as a reverent figure, but even *he* can't keep me from calling you mine." He lifted a

132

brow at me, and I all but melted all over my duvet. "Are my words clear enough for you, Rina?"

I nodded, because really, what else could I do? I was entranced by him, and so grateful for him for saying everything he had.

I'm sorry, I signed. I *didn't mean to upset you.*

Myles shook his head and gave me a faint smile. "It's okay. I just wanted you to know that I'm in this for a long haul, and *nothing* can keep me from you. Not even your emotionally charged texts."

You acted quite dramatically.

He narrowed his grey eyes at me. "I so did *not*," he countered.

Wanna bet?

"I'm not giving you money for calling me out like that."

I chuckled, both in amusement, and in relief that we were okay.

Thank God.

You look crazy right now, I signed, and then pointed at my head to show him exactly what I meant.

Myles put his tongue to his cheek. "Wow, babe, *thanks*. It's not like I've just woken up from a deep sleep or anything," he said, but didn't make a move to fix his hair.

I laughed, and then yawned behind a hand.

"Hey, we should do that cheesy movie thing where the couple keeps the call going while they go to sleep so that it appears as if they're next to each other instead of miles away," Myles suggested with a grin.

Cute – that's what he was.

I nodded. *Okay*, I signed, and then smiled.

"Perfect. I've always wanted to do that."

I shook my head at him. *I'm not surprised*, I signed.

He chuckled. "*I'd* be surprised if you were."

We shared a laugh, and then quickly lied down in our beds. I pulled open my phone's holder and set it next to me so that I could watch Myles, while he did the same on his end.

"Night, Rina," he said, and then switched off his bedside lamp.

Good night, I signed, and then closed my eyes.

When I woke up around 4 hours later, the day had opened, and I could hear the blue jays chirping outside my window.

I glanced at my phone, and saw that the call was still going, and on the other side, Myles was asleep. He looked silly with his mused hair and slightly parted lips, but also perfect – in every way that mattered to me.

I was about to end the call, but stopped when he stirred, and then started mumbling something in his sleep.

I leaned in so that I could hear him better, but I couldn't understand anything he was saying. He clearly hadn't woken up, and every few seconds, he'd stir, mumble something incoherent, and then nuzzle his nose against his pillow.

I couldn't stop watching him, and after a while, I realized I was laughing. It seemed that even in his slumber, Myles was capable of making me happy; of putting a too-wide smile on my face.

And if *that* little factoid wasn't enough to let anyone know that he was a keeper, then I don't know what was.

29.

I wrapped my shawl around me tighter, and leaned a shoulder against the doorframe as I watched Myles pull a thick screw out from between his teeth. He grabbed two short pieces of polished wood, placed one horizontally and the other vertically, and then drilled them together by their respective edges.

I had absolutely no idea what he was doing, but the way he moved and the way he did things, was so fluent and thorough that I couldn't help but admire him as he worked.

He was wearing clunky boots, dark jeans, a pink cable-knit pullover with its sleeves pushed up, and a black beanie. A few strands of his caramel hair were sticking out here and there from under said beanie, and every other second, he'd try helplessly to swipe them back with a gloved hand, but then huff when it did nothing.

It was the first day of 2022, and *hardly* 9a.m., and Myles and the crew were already back at the house for the renovation. It was clear dedication on his part, and not an uncontrollable urge to sneak in as many breathless kisses as him and I could before *Avô* woke up.

Nope, that was *so* not the reason.

Vila do Açaí was set to open on the 3rd, so until then, I could shamelessly ogle my *very* hot boyfriend without restrictions as he worked on creating my dream room.

Complete bliss to my eyes.

The storeroom looked like…*a work in progress*. The old floor tiling had turned slightly jagged and messy; the walls were chipped and sanded, but void of any tiles or paint. The corners of the ceiling were clustered with support beams, and in its center was a massive, circular glass for sunlight to pour in, in abundance.

I couldn't wait to see the end result. Myles really was onto something with the way things were going, and I trusted him to do a wonderful job with this, not only because it was going to be a place of solace for me, but also because I knew he's never done anything like this before and was excited to bring his ideas to life.

I shifted on my feet, and the doorframe creaked a little against my weight.

Myles immediately looked up from where he was working, and grinned when I waved at him.

He got to his feet, dusted his hands on his thighs, took off his gloves, threw them on the ground, and walked over to me.

"Hey, gorgeous," he said around a smile.

I looked over my shoulder briefly, then grabbed him by his sweater before pulling him down for a kiss.

He tasted like coffee and bubblegum, and even though it was an unusual combination, it was perfect because it was *his*.

Someone wolf-whistled, and Taron muttered, "Spare my astonished eyes, man," which made Myles and I chuckle.

He pushed some of my hair behind my ear before moving back a little. "I was actually hoping to talk to you."

About what? I signed.

"Furniture arrangement." He back-walked into the room and pulled a marker out of his jeans pocket. "I'm currently thinking of installing 3 bookshelves," he began, and then tapped the tip of his marker on the wall behind him. "The broadest one could be placed here." He moved to the right. "And the other two could go...here." He waved an arm towards the empty area next to him, and then placed both his hands on his hips. "You like that placement?" he asked me. "Or do you want the shelves to go on the opposite side?"

136

I like what you suggested, I told him honestly.

He grinned. "Perfect." He opened the marker and began writing measurements and other…interesting, numerical things on the walls where the shelves would be, and then turned to me again. "Where do you want the sofa and armchair?"

I stepped into the room, careful not to trip over the uneven floor.

Myles came next to me and kicked a few broken pieces of wood away from my feet.

Sofa, I signed, and pointed at the space exactly opposite the square window on the left. *Armchair,* I then signed, and pointed towards the far-left center of the room.

Myles looked at his brother. "Make a Word doc with all the detailed positions and measurement notes, will you?" he said to him, then walked over to the places I'd picked and wrote down a bunch of things on the respective walls. "Done." He sighed in relief and returned to me.

Paul and Greg got back to doing what they previously were, and Taron began moving around the room while also typing info into his phone.

As Myles got close to me, I pressed a kiss on his chin before signing, *Thank you.*

He looked surprised. "What for?" he asked.

I gestured around the room and signed, *For this.*

He smiled. "It's my job, Rina," he said. "But even if it wasn't, I'd still do it, because I know it'd mean a lot to you, and that thought itself would mean the world to me."

My breath hitched at his words. God, if only there were enough Signs in existence for me to show him how happy he made me, and how special I felt with him in my life.

I cupped his face in my hands and rose on my tiptoes before kissing him once, and then a second time.

You are amazing, I signed after giving him a third kiss, to which he chuckled.

"Just too smitten with you, that's all," he told me matter-of-factly.

I shook my head and asked if he wanted something to eat or drink.

"Coffee," he said immediately, which made me laugh.

Okay.

"For all of us, if possible," he added sheepishly.

Of course, I signed. *Some biscuits, too?*

Myles nodded. "That'd be great." He took my left hand in his and pressed his lips to the back of my fingers. "You rock, you know that?"

I smiled and slapped him playfully on the chest, and as I turned to leave, he grabbed my wrist and turned me to face him.

Our eyes met, right before he bent and kissed me – so hard that it left me utterly breathless and aching.

Now, if 2022 was going to be a year full of moments like these with the man in front of me, then I was more than ready to embrace it with open arms.

And a hopeful yet completely helpless heart, too.

30.

"**D**id you get that, Uncle Myles? Did you???" Sienna all but screeched.

I sighed as I lowered her phone. "Yes, you insufferable migraine of a human," I grumbled.

She clicked her tongue and sashayed over to me. "You shouldn't frown like that. You look like Grandpa when you do."

I placed a hand on my hip. "I do *not*."

"Do too," she countered. "Let's go there," she pointed at the fountain on the far left. "I think the lighting there is just *perfect*." Her floral dress went crazy with the wind as she began running, and, because I had no other choice, I stomped-followed her.

We were at the *Millennium Park*. It was Sunday, so me and the crew were off work, which meant that I was free, and also a very open prey for my niece to snatch onto for her weekly Instagram photoshoot session.

I've been a victim of it several times, which is why I try my best to avoid her calls on Sundays, but because Tori had fallen ill and Taron was busy looking after her, I was the only one remaining on Sienna's hit-list.

I had, of course, asked her why she'd picked *me* instead of her friends for something like this, to which she'd simply turned to me and said, "*Because you take the best damn photos of me. You've got a talent, Uncle Myles, and you should be thankful I discovered it before you lost all the hair on your head and teeth in your gums. You could be a legend, all because of me!*"

I wasn't sure how I could respond to that, so I'd kept my mouth shut and agreed to do her bidding.

The weather was pretty nice for a Chicago winter morning, and as I looked around me, I saw several people enjoying it as well, by either taking pictures, or simply walking around with relaxed smiles on their faces.

"Uncle Myles!" Sienna called.

I turned my attention to her. "Yes, demon?"

She rolled her eyes, flipped her long black hair over her shoulders, and then struck a pose in front of the fountain – something very similar to the ones I'd seen those fashion models doing on luxe clothing store banners.

"Snap," she all but ordered.

I scowled as I clicked a few shots of her from different angles, then handed her the phone so she could check them.

"OMG, Uncle Myles! These came out so good!" she said. And yes, she literally *voiced* 'OMG' instead of saying 'oh my God'.

"I'm glad you like them," I told her.

She shoved her phone in my hands again. "Okay, now I need you to take a few more…" She glanced around for an *aesthetically pleasing backdrop*, then gasped and pointed at the lush-with-flowers section of the park. "Here!"

I followed her, of course, and raised my brows while taking her pictures because…the poses she was doing here seemed more, I don't know, delicate and candid.

I never had a doubt that my niece was beautiful, but with each click, I realized that these photos were not like the others, but something of a more…special nature.

I immediately stopped snapping and gave her a stern look. "What's up with these poses?" I asked. "Why are they not as flashy as the others?"

Sienna straightened and crossed her arms over her chest. "Because these aren't for Instagram; these are for my boyfriend."

I'm sorry, WHAT?

Boy…boyfriend?

Oh God, Taron was going to skin me alive and wear me as a winter garment if he learnt what I was helping Sienna do.

I swallowed and cleared my throat. "Your...who? What?"

She rolled her eyes again. "My *boyfriend*, Uncle Myles. His name's Jeremiah and we have the same classes. You do realize that I'm almost sixteen, and it's only natural for me to have a boyfriend, right?"

Natural? I didn't know about that. But this sure would lead to my brutal execution if I didn't tell Taron about it, *stat*.

But wait, what if he knew about it already?

"Are your parents aware of this... Jeremiah person?"

"I mean, they know who he is, but they don't know we're dating," Sienna said.

Queue crying baby sound effect.

I was *so* dead.

"And you haven't told them because...?"

Sienna sighed. "You've met my parents, Uncle Myles; you know how they are, especially my dad."

I couldn't help but chuckle. "Oh yeah, I *know*. Your mom's manageable, but your dad?" I made an abort gesture.

She laughed. "You won't tell them, though, right?" she asked, then looked at me with plea in her grey eyes.

"Do you think skinned and bleeding-all-over-the-place will be a good look on me?"

She grimaced. "*Ewwwww*, why would you say that?"

It was *my* turn to roll my eyes. "Because if Taron finds out that I know about your dating situation and didn't tell him about it, he'll turn me into a ready-to-eat chicken."

"But he won't know anything if you don't tell him."

I shook my head. "He could find out on accident, or from one of your friends, Si."

Sienna grabbed my hands. "He won't. My friends know not to say anything, and Jeremiah and I are always careful about things." She let go of a breath, and in that moment, I realized how her situation was so in sync with mine and Rina's.

"If anyone can understand what I'm going through, Uncle Myles," she told me, "it's *you*. You know what it's like having to live under restraint, when all you wanna do is scream your lungs out and tell the world how badly you wanna be with this person. I promise I'll tell Mom and Dad about Jer and I, but just not now. Can you please not say anything to them for the time being?"

I worked my jaw as I looked at her, and because everything she'd just told me felt so honest, especially with the way her eyes lit up every time she said the guy's name out loud, I sighed and relented. "Fine, but only because I know exactly how you feel."

She squealed and began jumping up and down. "Thank you, Uncle Myles!" She hugged me. "Thank you, thank you, THANK YOU!"

I laughed and hugged her back. "Alright, alright." I pulled away and placed my hands on her shoulders. "But be careful, Si. And, if this guy ever breaks your heart or hurts you, you come to me, okay? I'm here for you."

She nodded, then showed me a selfie she'd taken of the two of them.

I had to admit: they looked adorable together. And, if Sienna really had found happiness with someone she knew well enough, then who was I to get in their way?

"Hey." She tapped my arm. "Let's go to the café and get some Frappuccino. I'm tired and hungry."

It took us fifteen minutes to get to the café. On a weekday, it'd take us twice as long, but because the traffic was minimum and the streets were clear, I could protect myself from getting an ear bleed against Sienna's K-pop marathon.

I parked my van outside the café and faced her. "You stay here," I told her. "And if you need anything else other than a Frap, just gimme a call."

"Okay," she said, and then began playing some BTS song on her phone.

I groaned and got out of the van.

As I pushed open the café's door and stepped inside, the welcoming smell of coffee and bread hit my nose, making me sigh.

I realized there was a line in front of the order counter, so I slid my hands into my coat pockets before standing behind a guy ahead of me.

"I don't understand, ma'am," I heard Suman, the order lady, say to someone.

There was some commotion up front that I couldn't hear clearly, so I rose on my toes to see if I could make out what was going on, but it was a pretty crowded line, so I couldn't see anything.

"Ma'am, please; I cannot understand," Suman said, this time in clear frustration.

More unclear commotion.

Some customers started fidgeting and began murmuring to each other.

Fuck this.

I got out of the line and made my way to the front, but around halfway through, a guy grabbed my arm in order to stop me.

"Whoa, hey. Where do you think you're going, dude?"

He was still in his PJs, and his breath smelt all but rotten as he gave me a once over.

I jerked my arm out of his hold. "To see what the fuss is about," I told him. "Because clearly, you or the others don't give two shits about it." I took a step forward, but stopped and faced him again. "Also, the next time you plan on getting out of the house, make sure to at least brush your teeth, *dude*. It'll save lives, trust me." I didn't wait for him to reply; I marched straight up to the order counter.

"What's wrong, Suman?" I asked the barista.

She relaxed when she saw me. "Myles, hey." She then gestured in front of her. "I've been telling this lady that I have no idea what she's saying, but she won't budge, so it's put a hold on the rest of the line. And, it seems like she's alone, so that's made things harder."

I looked to my right, and saw an old lady glancing between me and Suman. When she saw me looking at her, she walked up to me and began signing furiously.

"See?" Suman said. "That's all she's been doing for the last few minutes."

I ignored her and gave my complete attention to the lady.

Hi, I signed. *I'm Myles. Are you here by yourself?*

She beamed up at me, and the relief on her face made me smile.

I'm Annabeth, she signed. *The woman behind the counter has been driving me crazy. My son is out running an errand, but he should join me soon.*

I chuckled. "That's okay. You can tell me what you'd like to order."

Annabeth tapped both of her ears, and then shook her head with a frown on her face.

Ah, so she couldn't hear me.

I'm sorry, I signed. *Can you tell me what you would like to order? I can convey your message.*

She nodded, then told me exactly what she wanted: two cream coffees, no sugar.

Anything else? I asked her.

She pursed her lips and looked at the long display case in front of us. Then, with a gleam in her eyes, she flattened a hand, palm up, and shaped her other one as an upside-down C before touching it to the open palm in a sign to say, *Cupcake.*

I grinned. *You got it,* I told her, and then turned to Suman. "Two coffees, no sugar, and two chocolate cupcakes."

She nodded, her eyes wide.

"Do you have sugar free cupcakes?"

She nodded again.

"Perfect." I faced Annabeth. *Your order will be ready soon,* I signed.

She smiled. *Thank you.*

"What's your order, Reyes?" Suman asked me.

"Uh…" I glanced at the growing line. "I–"

144

"Listen up, everyone!" Suman hollered at the customers. "This man just helped someone in this line, so he gets his order first as compensation. If any of you have a problem with that, then you can go find yourself another café."

A couple of baristas working the coffee stations laughed, and the customers mumbled briefly before going back to waiting patiently.

I looked at Suman. "Thanks," I told her. "I'll take a chocolate Frap with extra drizzle, and a hazelnut coffee, one sugar. Both to-go, please."

"You got it." She passed on both Annabeth and I's orders to the baristas. "Wait period: six minutes."

"Gotcha." I looked at Annabeth. *Can I get you a table?*

She nodded, and let me walk her to an empty table-for-two near a closed window on the left.

As she settled down, she gestured for me to take a seat opposite her.

I obeyed.

You are very handsome, she signed. *Are you married?*

I chuckled. *Thank you. No, not married yet.*

She briefly placed an elegant hand under her chin, then moved her right thumb down her cheek once, followed by clasping the index fingers of both her hands together in one direction, and repeated the motion again, but in the opposite direction to say, *Girlfriend.*

I grinned. *Yes*, I signed, then slowly spelled out Rina's name. I was still learning to shape the alphabets properly, so it usually took me a while to even think of their forms before I could actually Sign them.

That is a lovely name, Annabeth signed.

I smiled effortlessly. *Yes.*

Photo? she asked.

I nodded, and unlocked my phone before showing her my homescreen. It was a selfie of Rina and I. The sides of our heads were touching, and we were smiling at the camera like complete idiots because we were just so damn happy.

It wasn't specifically a unique photo or anything; just one of the many we'd clicked together. But I simply loved this one because it was unfiltered and warm, and it made my heart thud a little faster when I looked at it.

Annabeth placed a hand on the center of her chest, and her eyes crinkled at the sides as she glanced at my phone first, and then at me.

You two are beautiful together, she signed.

Thank you, I told her.

She handed my phone back to me. *Bless you both.*

You are very kind, I said to her.

"Excuse me?"

I turned, and found a man standing behind me. He was maybe in his mid-forties, with grey hair and stubble, and bright blue eyes.

When I stood up, he looked at Annabeth, then smiled at me.

"You must be Myles," he said. "I'm Stephen. The counter person told me you're the one who helped my mom with her order."

"Hey, yeah." I offered him a hand, which he shook. "It was no problem, really. Your mother is absolutely lovely."

He chuckled. "That she is."

"One order for Annabeth. One order for M. Reyes. Collection counter is No. 3."

"Umm, I should go," I told Stephen. "My order's here, and I'm pretty sure if I leave my niece alone any longer, she's going to trash my van as a punishment for keeping her waiting."

He laughed good-naturedly. "I get it. And hey, thanks again for the assist with my mom. I appreciate it."

"You got it." I turned to Annabeth. *I have to go, but it was nice to meet you*, I signed to her.

She got to her feet, and Stephen and I helped her walk around the table. She smiled at her son, then at me, and took my face in her hands before placing a gentle kiss on my forehead.

Thank you again, she signed.

146

I squeezed her hand once, and then waved at her and Stephen before making my way over to counter 3.

As I grabbed my order and left the café, I couldn't help but notice a bounce in my steps.

Man, I couldn't *wait* to tell Rina about this.

31.

Myles

I shut the van's engine and got out before locking it. I jogged up the small flight of stairs, and once I was near her front door, I pulled my phone out of my pocket and sent her a text.

Me: *Knock-knock.*

I hadn't spoken to Rina much during the day, what with me being busy photographing my annoying niece *for the gram*. And, because Rina was going to be at the shop tomorrow morning, and I would hardly get to see her with all the work that I had to do in the storeroom, I'd decided to spend some time with her tonight.

It was after 11. Rina had texted me twenty minutes ago asking me to come over. Only after being perfectly sure Mr. Ribeiro had gone to bed, of course.

Rina: *Who's there?*

I chuckled.

Me: *Honeydew.*

Rina: *Honeydew who?*

Me: *Honeydew wanna build a snowman? Or ride my cock until it's dawn?*

Rina: *OHMYGOD.*

Her next message was a string of cry-laughing emojis.

Rina: *Why are you like this?!*

I blew air into a fist and laughed after reading that.

Me: *Baby, I was born this way* B-)

Rina: *I do not doubt it* :')

I shivered at the cold and stepped closer to the door.

May God damn the damn snow.

Me: *I'm freezing; come get me* • ‿ ‚•

Rina: *Coming, hold on!*

Me: *Yay! My savior* ♡‿♡

I slid my phone back into my pocket, just as the front door opened and I was pulled inside by a grinning Rina.

She didn't even let me get a breath out before she pressed our bodies together and began kissing me.

I moaned into her mouth.

Christ, her warmth felt *so* good against the chill I was experiencing. Her tongue felt so good; her touch felt so fucking *nice*. And she smelled *amazing*, too – like marshmallows and chocolate and desire.

Rina pulled back, much to my dismay, and quickly locked the door.

I took off my shoes and hid them under the carpet behind the coatrack.

We'd come up with the idea after realizing that there was a chance Mr. Ribeiro could walk into the kitchen one of these nights and discover my shoes by the threshold. Because the coatrack was in a corner and provided ample shadow behind it, Rina and I'd decided to hide my shoes there.

I didn't like that we had to do all of this – the sneaking and hiding – but there was nothing else we could do until her grandfather came to his senses. It wasn't like I could go on a run with her. We were educated people, and all we wanted was for someone important in Rina's life to acknowledge her happiness and support her in it. So, until that miracle occurred, we'd have to pretend we were characters from one of Shakespeare's romantic plays or something.

Rina took my hand in hers and dragged me to her bedroom, and I tried my hardest not to trip and fall in the process of following her as my socked feet kept slipping against the hardwood floor.

Once we were safe inside her room, I took off my coat and beanie and threw them on the plush chair to the right.

Rina slowly clicked the lock shut, and just as she turned, I wrapped her in my arms and all but crashed our lips together.

Who says making out is off-fashion for adults? I find the act to be just as hot and necessary as sex, if not more. *Especially* when your partner tastes and feels like Rina does.

I began pulling her silk shirt over her head, but stopped when I remembered…

"Wait." I was panting, and so was she. "I wanna tell you something."

What'd happened at the café had been the highlight of my day, and the only reason I hadn't texted her about it was because I wanted to tell her everything in person.

What? Rina signed.

"Let's sit." I walked her over to her bed, and after the two of us settled in – cross-legged, face-to-face – I told Rina about Annabeth.

"I'm…I'm so damn happy, Rina," I said without restraint, and then laughed. "I've been bubbling with emotions the entire day, waiting to talk to you about this, and now that I have, I feel…*good.*" I grinned at her, and found her looking at me with so much joy on her face that I couldn't help but lean in and kiss her.

She fisted her right hand with the thumb sticking out. She then used the thumb to trace a path up the middle of her chest, and went on to point at herself first, then me, to say, *I'm proud of you.* And that right there – that meant *so* fucking much to me.

"None of this would've been possible without you," I told her, and when she shook her head, I took her hands in mine. "*Listen* to me, Rina."

She blinked and inhaled softly.

"If I hadn't met you, I never would've known what it's like to feel this accomplished at something I never even knew I could be good at," I began. "I know it isn't exactly a huge deal, but for *me* it is a monumental one. Every moment I spent with Annabeth today made me realize how important bringing her momentary relief and comfort was to me. When I first saw her, she looked

150

lost and frustrated, but when I said goodbye to her, the smile she gave me – it made me wanna *burst*." I sniffed and squeezed Rina's hands. "Thank you for inspiring me; thank you for being so damn special. I don't wanna say I'll owe you one for the rest of my life, but I will, and there's no changing that."

She started crying, so I leaned in and touched our foreheads together.

"You mean more to me than words can explain," I said to her, "and I'm so fucking grateful that you chose to forgive my initial screw-up and decided to give me a chance."

She ran her knuckles over my jaw and smiled at me. *You are worth more than everything in my world*, she signed. *I have never doubted that, and I never will.*

"That high on your list, huh?" I quipped.

She chuckled softly and slapped me playfully. *Yes, you idiot*, she signed.

"Jeez, no pressure or anything, right?"

She rolled her eyes, and then sat back before asking, *Can I show you something?*

"Of course," I answered.

Rina shifted and turned on her bedside lamp, then grabbed an album from her nightstand.

What you said to me at your house that day made me want to face this part of my past, she signed, and then opened the album.

I moved closer to her and looked down at it.

The album was full of pictures of her as a kid – some with her friends, while others with her family.

"Wow, those are some *serious* cheeks," I mused as I pointed at a photo of a very tiny yet chubby Rina sitting next to a pile of plushies and looking blissfully at them.

She elbowed me, to which I chuckled.

"I'm serious," I told her. "It's kinda sad you lost all that baby fat. You'd look even hotter if you had at least a little bit of it now." I turned the page, and immediately felt a weight on my chest as I looked at the picture on the bottom right.

It was Rina with her parents – in a bedroom, I think. She looked to be four in the picture, and was sitting between them, laughing, while they shared a carefree smile with each other.

Rina ran her fingers over the photo.

I swallowed. "You look so much like your mom," I managed to say. Her dark hair and complexion were most definitely courtesies of her dad, but her facial structure and eyes...

I looked away from the album and glanced at her. Rina's cheeks were wet with tears, so I swiped a thumb over them, which made her meet my gaze.

This photo – it's one of those standstill memories I can't even remember making, she signed, and then licked her lips. *Why can't I remember them, Myles? It's like a different kind of incapability – one I can't even find validation in.* More tears slid down her mournful eyes.

"Trauma infests deeper than we can comprehend, Rina," I said. "It takes away the good and leaves you with nothing. Those who refuse to let it win are usually the ones who come out of it empty-handed." I wiped away her tears. "You're one of them, but just because you've lost the fragments of your past, doesn't mean you can't fill the space you now have with fresher, happier memories. Life's brutal, that's for sure, and you can either let your fallen memories haunt your thoughts, or let the possibility of a positive future excite your days. The choice, if you ask me, is very simple. You just have to make up your mind and go with it. Don't let yourself feel regret or guilt. What happened wasn't your fault, but what you choose to do next will definitely define the kind of path you want to take." I placed a kiss between her brows. "Whatever you decide, though, know that I'm here with you – here *for* you. I'll walk whatever road you pick, and I'll walk it with so much confidence that it'll shake the whole damn cosmos. I've got you, baby. All the way to the end."

Her breath hitched, and a second later, she began sobbing.

I immediately took her in my arms and hugged her close to my chest, and as she cried into my hoodie, I kept pressing soft kisses on her temple.

We stayed that way for a few silent moments, and then Rina slowly moved back before looking up at me.

Thank you, she signed. *You are a blessing to me, Myles.*

I gave her a smile. "And you, Rina, are my devotion."

She lowered her gaze and pushed some of her hair behind her ear. *Stop it*, she signed, her cheeks flushed.

I smiled further. "But it's true." I pulled at a stray thread on her checkered sweater. "Can I ask you something?"

She gave me a nod.

"Do you…" I started, but stopped to think. I then touched the tips of my index and middle fingers to my throat before lifting them up twice to say, *Voice.*

I still have it, Rina signed.

I shook my head. "I know that." I swallowed. "I don't mean to pry, Rina. I just…I guess I just wanted to know if you ever miss…" I swallowed a second time.

Talking? she signed.

"Well, yeah," I said.

She grabbed a notebook and pen from her nightstand drawer, and then started writing. *I've lived almost all my life without words, Myles. My silence is my comfort, my advantage against the occasional screams in my head. It's strong, and it makes me feel powerful. I like myself with my silence, and I don't know if I'd feel the same if I knew how to physically use my words.*

I stared at her after reading that, and my heart all but warmed with pride for her. The positivity she exuded was nothing short of inciting, and yes, her decision to stay the way she was, was selective, but it was still her *own* decision – one she'd learnt to use as an advantage rather than an outlet of pain and despair to hurt herself for what happened all those years ago.

153

We don't always do things the right way when we're hurting, but when we do, it definitely comes from a place of ease for ourselves, and honestly, there's nothing wrong in being slightly selfish and thinking about yourself when you're down and need a way out.

Everyone has a different way of dealing with things, as they say. Rina's was unconventionally amazing, and I appreciated her unconditionally for telling me about it.

When I told her just that, she closed the album, put it aside, and surged forward before wrapping her arms around my neck.

I chuckled, and she rose on her knees so she could straddle me. The moonlight pouring into the room illuminated her features as she grinned, while the lamplight acted as a dim halo behind her.

I scanned her face for a beat or three before touching our foreheads together. I then reciprocated her grin as I slowly ran my thumbs over her wet cheeks.

"Tell me how you feel," I urged her.

She shifted closer to me, and our noses brushed. *Happy*, she signed.

"Why?"

She lifted a shoulder, then signed, *You make me happy*.

I let go of an unsteady breath. "I do?"

She nodded and kissed me softly.

Everything inside me tightened, and then expanded at the sincerity in her gaze.

"You make me happy, too," I told her honestly. "*So* much that I can't believe you've picked *me*, of all people, to be yours."

She sucked in a breath at my words. *Say it again*, she signed.

I furrowed my brows. "Say what?" I asked.

Her sable eyes gleamed against the nightlight as she touched the tips of her fingers to my mouth. *That you are mine*, she signed.

I inhaled, and then exhaled against her skin. "I'm yours, Rina," I said. "I sometimes can't believe it, but it's true. I'm yours, and I think I always have been." I kissed her once. "I always want to be."

She placed a hand over her heart, and then brought it over to mine in a way to say, *I'm yours*.

God, this woman was *everything*. I didn't know what to say, what to *do*.

She bent and kissed me, full of honest need, so I gripped her waist and pulled her closer to my body.

"Rina…" I breathed against her, and pressed my lips to hers again.

She was perfect – the kind that fit so well with my crazy. I was at her mercy as she rocked against me; I was all but swimming in her gentle moans and delicate gasps.

And, when my words began to waver under the weight of our growing desires, I couldn't hold back, and so, I caved.

Until I couldn't hear past the roaring in my head; until we couldn't feel our legs or much less care about what was happening around us.

Because nothing else mattered when we were together, especially not the world or its limitations and boundaries.

32.

Rina's nails dug into my bicep, right before she made a little sound of discomfort from next to me. She had her right cheek pressed on my shoulder, and just as I turned my head to look at her, she made that sound again.

"Hey, you okay?" I asked with a frown.

She let go of my arm and excused herself, and I set her iPad next to me on the bed as I watched her head into the bathroom and shut the door behind her.

We were watching *Pokémon: Mewtwo Strikes Back – Evolution*. She'd suggested it, of course, but I'd sensed her distraction from the moment we'd sat down to watch the movie.

She was supposed to go to the shop, but didn't because she'd gotten her period. I only knew about it because I'd seen Mr. Ribeiro asking her to stay at home and get some rest while he opened shop instead. I'd just walked into the house after a coffee run when I'd seen them. Rina was hunched over the kitchen counter eating waffles and breakfast cream with a look of pain on her face, and Mr. Ribeiro was standing next to her. Only when she nodded in agreement to what he'd said, did he leave her and head upstairs to his room.

I'd managed to make my escape before he could see me, though, because the last thing I wanted was for him to incinerate my ass with his signature glare.

I sighed and glanced at the bathroom, then wiggled my toes in frustration.

I knew Rina was in pain, and I wanted to help her. I didn't know how, but I wanted to help nonetheless.

With another peek at the bathroom, I huffed and grabbed my phone.

Me: *You know any home remedies for period pain?*

She responded after a couple of minutes.

Mama Llama: *Dark chocolate, lemon tea with sugar, eucalyptus oil over the navel and pelvic areas.*

Me: *You rock, Mom.*

Mama Llama: *Oh, I know, hon :) Tell Rina I said hi.*

I chuckled.

Me: *Will do.*

Mama Llama: *Love you, sweetie. I'm in the middle of a session right now, but shoot me a text if you need anything.*

Me: *Thanks, Mom.*

My mom was a retired professor, and now an online student counselor. Given how she's an amazing mother, her choice of profession was actually pretty spot-on.

The bathroom door opened, and Rina all but stumbled outside with wide eyes and…fear on her face?

"What happened?" I stood and ran over to her. "Are you all right? Are you in pain? Tell me!"

She hastily grabbed her notebook and pen before scribbling something on a blank page.

I DON'T HAVE PADS! MYLES, I DON'T HAVE PADS!

I stared at the words, and then at her. "Why did you write that in all caps?"

She groaned and began writing again.

I NEED PADS! PLEASE CAN YOU GET ME PADS? OHMYGOD, I DON'T HAVE PADS, MYLES!!!

"Rina, babe; relax." I fixed her hair, because it looked like a family of seaweed had taken residence on her head. *"Relax* for me."

She shook her head.

"Please? You can do this. I have faith in you."

She glared at me.

157

I cleared my throat. "My mom said hi?" I told/asked her, and then waited a few seconds to see if she did anything in response to that.

She *didn't*.

"My mom's 'hi' didn't calm you?"

Her glare intensified.

"Umm." I scratched the back of my head. "Pads – you need pads, right?"

She tilted her head to the side, and *my God*, she looked *so* fucking scary when she did that.

Period temper was a real thing, apparently.

"I…I'll go get you your pads," I said, like I even had a choice that suggested otherwise. "And…chocolates? One of every kind?" I quickly put a hand up when she narrowed her eyes at me. "*Two* of each, then."

Yes, she signed.

I sighed in relief and grinned at her. "Great." I took a step back, and then another. "I'll…I'll be off now." I pointed a thumb over my shoulder. "But please don't turn into Drogon by the time I come back. You may be fierce, babe, but dragon-skin is *so* not a good lewk."

Go, Rina signed with a scowl on her face.

I turned, and, as my luck would have it, my ankles clashed and I went toppling on the ground. My hands were splayed on the floor; my ass was in the air. My freaking *dignity* had slit its own throat and was convulsing in front of me as it took its last breath.

It was a whole thing, I'm telling ya.

But, because I was a damn phoenix and had the determination to rise from the ashes, I gracefully got to my feet, marched out of Rina's room, and headed for my van. I didn't look back at her as I left, even though I could feel her laughter trailing me like Casper the fucking ghost.

But hey, if you didn't see it, then it didn't happen, right?

…Right.

33.

If the Earth is a massive ball-sack, then the women's sanitary essentials aisle is the under-skin of a cock right after an orgasm…

I have no idea why I said that, or what it even means, but my brain decided to stop functioning when I entered the women's section in *Walmart*, so my thought-vomit had taken a dark and twisted turn.

My deepest, most sincerest apologies.

I was standing in front of pads. Packets, upon packets, upon packets of pads.

So many pads.

So.

Fucking.

Many.

My eyes were being assaulted by wrappers that were black and pink and purple and blue and green and… What the hell kind of color even *was* that?!

Peach?

Orange?

Sherbet?

RETINAL DEATH?

I dragged both my hands over my face and considered ringing for backup. My mom wasn't an option, because there was *no way* I was asking her if I should get Rina an S, M, or XL pad. Sienna would think I'm crazy if I consulted her about this, and Rina would probably reach out of my phone and breathe fire into my eyeballs if I texted her about her…size preference.

Which meant I had only one option left.

159

"Myles! Oh, dearie, if only you'd warned me beforehand about the video call, I'd have found a secluded place for us to chat," Daniel said after picking up my call.

FYI: I was regretting this already.

"Where are you?" I asked him. "It's so dark that I can barely see you."

"Where do you think?" The camera angle moved, and I saw a familiar hearth behind Daniel's smug face.

"Ah, you're at *Vila do Açaí*."

"But of course, buttercup. Who else is going to bake all the cupcakes and breads, if not yours truly?" He took a seat in front of the hearth and lifted a brow. "But any*who*, what's up with you? You look like you've seen Cruz without his pants on."

Cruz, who was also in the baking room, spat a curse at Daniel, resulting in us both to laugh.

"I need your help in picking pads for Rina," I told Daniel.

I heard him gasp, and in the distance, Cruz muttered, "Lord, please take me now."

"*Scandalous*, aren't you?" Daniel mused.

"Try *desperate*," I countered, and then sighed. "Look, I have no idea how this works. You have a wife, Daniel; I'm sure you know about–" I stopped when I realized his phone was on speaker. "Wait, can Mr. Ribeiro hear me right now?!"

Oh God, oh God, oh fuck-me-sideways God.

Daniel clicked his tongue. "No. He's out having lunch with Remi's grandfather. You're safe, don't worry."

I ran a hand through my hair. "Okay, but can you tell me which pad to get Rina so that I can leave this fucking aisle already?"

A woman and a little girl were passing me by, but stopped briefly to give me the stink eye before continuing on their way.

Great. Just what I needed: looks full of murderous intent.

"Get an all-night pack," came Daniel's voice. "That's the safest option."

I looked around the groups and subgroups of packets, and my eyes finally landed on a black box with the moon and the stars printed on it. There was a fluffy bunny sleeping on top of the moon, and the packaging claimed the following:

All Night Protection. 100% absorbent. 0% leaks guaranteed. Gel lock.

Bingo! Jackpot! Hallelujah!

I was about to grab the massive box, but stopped when I saw...

Size: S

I groaned in defeat. "You have *got* to be shitting me."

"What's wrong?" Daniel asked.

"There's a size selection for these as well," I muttered as I glared at the boxes. I needed a breathing bag. Or a stress ball. Or a hammer so that I could destroy this entire fucking aisle.

"Uh..." Daniel scratched his jaw. "Look, you're going to have to figure that out on your own. Or, maybe you could simply ask Rina. But please do *not* expect me to tell you an estimated size of her vagina. I'm too young to die from a coronary."

I scowled at him, to which he pressed his lips together and gave me a shrug.

I sighed and glanced at the bunny-pads once more. Uttering a silent prayer to the guy high above, I grabbed the box that said *M* under the size column, and threw it into my cart.

"Yay! You did it!" Daniel cheered, and I realized that the video call was still going.

"I don't know how your wife deals with you," I told him as I walked out of the women's section. "You're like a heartburn with a face. It's annoying."

I heard Cruz's laughter in the background as Daniel stared at me with his mouth hung open.

"What? Cat got your tongue?" I mused as I entered the chocolate aisle.

"Are you forgetting that it was *you* who called *me*?" he said.

I put a *Snickers* and *Mars* double-pack in my cart, and then grabbed a box of *Reese's* before adding that in, too.

"Yes," I answered Daniel, "I remember. And I also recall regretting my decision the second you picked up the call."

"Rude, Myles. *Very* rude."

"You deserve it, though," Cruz chimed in. "This, and a lot more."

I chuckled as I went around adding more and more chocolates to my cart.

"You know what, Reyes?" Daniel began. "No free cupcakes or pastries for you anymore. You've shown absolutely zero respect to my kindness towards you and your sweet tooth. You are officially cancelled from my list of favorites, however gorgeous you might be. You're evil incarnate, a devil in Adonis skin. A complete monster!"

I rolled my eyes. "Whoa, Daniel; stop with the compliments already. I'm about to drop dead swooning on this germ-encrusted floor."

He pursed his lips. "Are you sure you don't want those free cupcakes?"

"Nope, I'm good," I said with a smile. "They were leftovers from the day before anyway. I'm better off without them, to be honest."

Daniel inhaled sharply. "Who told you that?" he questioned. He looked *so* baffled, it was funny.

I smirked. "Who do you think?"

His expression became comically perplexed. "Right, okay." He nodded. "Yes, I see that now."

"You finally broke Daniel, Myles," Cruz said, and then finally appeared next to him.

"Hey, man." I waved at him, then pushed my cart further ahead.

"Hey yourself." Cruz placed an elbow on Daniel's shoulder. "I was actually hoping to steal my partner here," he smacked Daniel in the chest, "for a quality-test on the new batch of cookies that I just pulled out of the oven."

"Of course," I said. "Talk to you guys soon, yeah?"

"For sure," Cruz promised. "Bye, Myles."

"Bye, Heartbreaker," Daniel added, which made Cruz roll his eyes.

I, on the other hand, couldn't help but laugh.

"Later, guys." I disconnected the call and put my phone away so that I could explore the rest of the chocolate aisle without any interruptions.

34.
Carina

"Is it a Prince Albert?" Daniel guessed. "Just to spite your overly religious family and maybe shorten their lifespans?"

I choked on my *CW Jr.*

Yes, I am well aware that it's a kids blend smoothie, but it's one of the best *Smoothie King* has to offer, and I simply can't resist the banana-and-strawberry combo.

"What, *no!*" Remi exclaimed in response to Daniel's suggestion, and then huffed. "Come on, man; you can do better than that."

"A nipple piercing? Navel piercing? Toenail piercing?" Daniel said, looking a little disinterested at this point.

"Why do you think it's a piercing?" Remi asked. "It could literally be *anything.*"

Daniel waved a hand in front of his face. "I don't know, Remi; I've just got an intuition, *okay?*"

Sitting behind the main counter at *Vila do Açaí*, I sipped some more of my *CW Jr.* as I glanced between the two of them.

Remi had walked into the shop fifteen minutes ago with a blinding smile on his face, and had asked us to guess 'what he'd gotten'. The question was very vague, and he wasn't even willing to hand out clues so that we could make more concrete assumptions.

Simran was sitting behind her counter, busy tapping away on her laptop as she blew chewing gum bubbles every so often. She was a universal mood, in my opinion, and I respected her so much for that.

"Fuck your intuition, man," Remi said to Daniel.

"Okay, okay," Daniel straightened from where he was standing at the bakery's entrance. "I've got it."

"What?" Remi asked skeptically, but there was still a flash of hope on his face.

"Pussy," Daniel announced triumphantly. "You finally got some pussy. After years of lusting over eligible women in Chicago, you finally found the one who let you cash it in."

I coughed behind a fist. That was *savage*.

Remi shot daggers at Daniel. "I give up." He crossed his arms over his chest. "You're helplessly ridiculous, you blue-eyed parasite." He then turned to me. "Rina? Can *you* take a guess?" he asked hopefully.

Uh...

A flamingo tattoo on your ass cheek? I signed. I had to spell the word flamingo as it had no specific Sign.

Daniel began cackling. "And you called *me* a parasite," he told Remi, and then continued to laugh.

I bit the inside of my top lip to stop myself from joining him, and blinked innocently at Remi when he sent a glare in my direction.

"Seriously, Rina?" he said, which made Daniel laugh harder.

Simran just rolled her eyes at him and muttered, "Degenerate," before pulling out a set of order receipts from her printer and giving them her full attention.

Sorry, I signed to Remi.

He clicked his tongue. "It's fine; you're forgiven."

"What about *me*?" Daniel inquired.

"*You*," Remi pointed a finger at him, "need to go fuck yourself, asshole. You didn't even *say* you were sorry."

"That's because I'm not," Daniel said easily.

I chuckled, and even *Simran* deemed that funny, because she smirked briefly.

"Fine, whatever." Daniel shook his head. "But at least tell us what you got."

Remi puffed out his chest a little. "This." He pointed at the full-sleeved t-shirt he was wearing. "It's been unavailable for *months*, but last week, I got an email from the brand saying they have a limited stock up on their online store for sale. I was lucky enough to get my order in before the damn thing got sold out again." He grinned as he looked between the three of us.

Ohmygod.

I stared at the tie-dye t-shirt, at the *Flintstones* guy printed on it, and the words '*Yabba Dabba Doo*' that were written above his head in a curved manner.

Nice, I signed, and forced out a smile.

"Christ Almighty," Daniel said, and placed a hand over his heart. "I rattled off so many valuable, *meaningful* guesses, just to be beaten by…*this*?

"Not everyone finds happiness through acts of sexual nature, Daniel," Remi countered.

"Clearly not." It was almost comical how horrified Daniel looked. He reminded me so much of Tom Ellis's character, Lucifer Morningstar, from Netflix's *Lucifer*.

I cleared my throat and clapped my hands.

My crew looked at me, and I raised my brows at them before signing, *Get to work, everyone.*

"Yes, boss," Daniel said with a smirk, and then disappeared inside the bakery.

Simran gave me a thumbs up, whereas Remi sighed and began rearranging the takeaway boxes on his counter.

The electronic bird on the shop's door chirped. A second later, a bunch of high school kids walked in, and my phone *dinged* with a new message.

I took a sip of my smoothie as I read it.

Beauty: *Requesting status report.*

I smiled.

Me: *I'm fine :')*

He'd texted me at least twenty times asking if I was okay since I'd left the house two hours ago.

Beauty: *Are you having cramps? A headache? Knee pains?*

I chuckled.

Me: *Yes to all, but they're bearable.*

Beauty: *Do you need more chocolates? I could bring them over if you'd like.*

Me: *Shouldn't you be working?*

Beauty: *Fuck work, babe.*

I finished my smoothie and slid the empty cup to the side.

Me: *Hey, now. I want my personal library* ◔‿◔

Beauty: *I know, and you'll get it. Me worrying about you doesn't affect the renovation process.*

Me: *Yay!*

Beauty: *So, chocolates? Or maybe lemon tea?*

I chuckled again.

Me: *I'm good, Myles.*

"Special delivery!" Daniel placed a mini tray on the counter with a flourish. "Cruz sent these cookies for ya."

I smiled. *Thank you*, I signed.

Daniel gave me a wink before walking away.

Beauty: *Okay, if you say so.*

I shoved a warm piece of cookie into my mouth.

Fuck, that was *good.*

I could taste *Açaí* and cinnamon and something nutty in it, and with how soft it was, it melted almost immediately into my mouth.

Me: *Can I ask you something?*

I finished an entire cookie as I waited for Myles to reply.

I had payroll sheets to finalize and stock receipts to sign, but here I was, shamelessly eating baked goods and distracting my boyfriend when he, too, was supposed to be working.

Beauty: *Of course.*

I bit my lower lip as I typed out my question.

Me: *Have you ever considered getting your dick pierced?*

I fully blamed Daniel for putting that thought in my head.

Beauty: *Daniel, is that you? Have you hijacked Rina's phone? Is this your way of getting back to me about yesterday?*

I laughed, then put my phone aside so that I could ring up the high-schoolers. I collected their cash, handed them their slips, and then grabbed my phone again when they stepped out of the shop.

Me: *What happened yesterday?*

Myles told me about him having video-called Daniel to ask for his assistance on getting sanitary pads for me, and how the whole thing had basically turned into him and Cruz roasting Daniel.

The pads Myles had picked out for me were…insufficiently inaccurate. They were a little too small for my liking, and I had to use two of them at a time to double their length. But hey, I genuinely appreciated his help, and I knew he'd done the best he could, given his lack of knowledge in the department.

Also, the incident had taught me to be better prepared for the next month, and to triple-check my sanitary stock beforehand to avoid such unexpected emergencies.

Me: *You people are really hard on Daniel. He's just trying to exist in this world by being his inappropriate self. Give him a break.*

Beauty: *He deserves it, especially for all the leftovers he's tricked me into eating.*

I smiled as I shook my head.

Me: *You didn't answer my previous question.*

I don't know why I was pushing it. Maybe because I wanted to get a laugh on, on Myles's behest, or…

Maybe because I was hoping our conversation would actually make him consider getting a piercing. It's not like I wanted him to, but if he *did* get one, I wouldn't complain about it.

Beauty: *I'm willing to do anything for you, Rina. ANYTHING. But just not this. I'm too fragile, and my cock has already hidden all the way into its shell in complete horror just by me having read that question.*

I placed a hand over my mouth and snort-laughed, earning curious looks from both Remi and Simran.

Me: *Its SHELL? Seriously, Myles?*

Beauty: *Scabbard? Sheath? Capsule? Canopy?*

I just couldn't stop laughing like a damn moron.

Me: *Stop it.*

Beauty: *Well, YOU'RE the one who had an objection to my initial choice of word, didn't you?*

I sniffed and shook my head.

Me: *Go back to work.*

Beauty: *Abrupt change of subject ʘ_ʘ I see you, babe.*

Me: *Do you really want Avô to find you texting me instead of working on the library?*

Beauty: *That's low, Rina ˙ ‿ ,˙*

Me: *I didn't have a choice. I had to pull out all the stops.*

Beauty: *Are you trying to get rid of me?* ಥ_ಥ

I smiled and rolled my eyes.

Me: *Never (˘ ³˘)*

He didn't respond immediately, so I passed the time by opening up all four payroll pdfs on the shop's laptop and updating Cruz's sheet first.

I had only just started working on Daniel's, though, when my phone lit up with a new text from Myles.

169

Beauty: *You were right; Mr. Ribeiro caught me. In the guest bathroom, no less.*

I chuckled.

Me: *I warned you, didn't I?*

Me: *Also, what the hell were you doing with your phone out in the guest bathroom?*

Beauty: *I know this looks scandalous…*

I laughed.

Me: *It so does.*

Beauty: *You're making it sound like it is.*

Me: *Well, then tell me what IS it?*

Beauty: *My phone was already in my hand when I went into the bathroom. I needed to pee, and I also had to text you. I was only keeping my priorities in check, but now I'm pretty sure your grandfather thinks I was sending you nudes. Or worse, that I was sending nudes to someone else* •⌣•

I was tearing up with how much I was laughing.

Me: *As if your reputation with him isn't strained enough already.*

Beauty: *I don't know what to do. I saw my life flash before my eyes when he found me.*

Me: *You brought this on yourself.*

Beauty: *You're supposed to be on MY side.*

Me: *But I like my head on my shoulders :')*

Beauty: *Traitor.*

"Yo, boss."

I looked up from my phone, and saw Simran standing on the other side of the counter.

"The inventory guy just texted me," she said. "He's on the way here. I've printed the invoice already, so I just need your signature."

I grabbed a pen from the second drawer and signed the invoice, and after I handed it back to her, I signed, *Take Cruz with you.*

She nodded, then walked over to the bakery before yelling, "Cruz, get your meaty ass out here! I need your help with inventory."

A second later, a sprinkled-with-flour Cruz stepped out of the kitchen and scowled at Simran.

She ignored his expression, of course, and turned her back to him before marching out the shop's back door.

Cruz huffed, dusted himself a little, and followed her out to the alley.

We had a room just above the shop for storing our monthly inventory. Usually, it was Simran who kept track of everything, but occasionally, Cruz liked to help her just so he could stay up-to-date with the quantity of stuff we ordered, and its manufacture + expiration dates.

The landline on Simran's counter went off, startling me a little.

Remi stepped away from his counter to receive the call, just as the shop's door opened and a group of our regular customers walked in.

I immediately got to my feet and took Remi's place behind his counter.

He was busy writing down a bulk order from the customer on-call, so I'd have to be the one to handle the incoming crowd.

I realized that I hadn't responded to Myles's last message, so as I waited for one of my customers to pick something for me to box for them, I quickly sent out a text.

Me: *The usual morning rush has started. If I don't text you for a while, know that I'm busy schmoozing and making money.*

Beauty: *You got it. But try to get off your feet a little, okay? It's still your second day, and I read online that it's a painful one :/*

Ugh, he was too sweet.

Me: *I promise :')*

Beauty: *Good. I gotta go piece together one of your bookshelves. Text me when you're free.*

Me: *Will do.*

I slid my phone into my back pocket, and grinned broadly as Mrs. Hudson, one of my regulars, stepped in front of the counter and rattled off her order to me, while a group of others waited behind her for their turn.

Hoo, boy.

It was going to be a *long* day, that was for sure.

35.

I placed a gentle hand around Rina's mouth and moved my hips forward as I thrust into her from behind. "I can't believe I'm saying this," I whispered in her ear, "but don't you dare moan. *Unless* you want him to hear us, that is."

She lifted her ass and rocked against me, making me groan.

God, her pussy felt so good wrapped around my aching cock.

I pushed into her harder, and she let out a broken moan – one that made me grin. "I thought I asked you to stay quiet," I told her.

I heard murmuring from outside her bedroom door, which made me pick up my pace.

Rina widened her legs further for me, and when I all but pumped into her heat, our skin slapped together.

When Mr. Ribeiro had come to check in on me and the crew a few minutes ago, I'd silently asked Taron to keep him busy so that I could slip out of the storeroom and into Rina's room. She'd just walked out of the bathroom after freshening up when I'd entered. Our eyes had met, and she'd all but ran over to me. I'd only just managed to lock her door before our lips had met, and then, I'd turned her around, shoved my jeans down, lifted her t-shirt dress up, and hastily put a condom on before sliding into her.

Not being able to have her for five days had left me mad with want, so my haste in wanting to be inside her again was natural enough.

She whimpered softly, pulling me out of my thoughts.

"Rina…" I rasped against the back of her neck as I fucked her. I pulled my hand away from her mouth and brought it down to her pussy. "Shh." I began circling a finger over and around her hardened clit, and earned a gasp from her in return.

I could hear Taron talking to Mr. Ribeiro – most probably stalling on my behalf – but I couldn't make out the words they were exchanging.

Not that I cared, given how occupied I was.

Rina palmed my ass and pushed me further against her, and I wrapped the fingers of my free hand around her throat before turning her face to mine.

Her eyes were glazed over; her hair was a mess above her head. I could smell the sweat on her flushed skin, mixed with something sweet – her moisturizer, maybe. She tasted like mint and insanity as I kissed her, slid my tongue into her mouth, and swallowed another one of her silky moans.

Taron's voice filtered into the room, so Rina began rocking back against me harder.

I felt my balls tighten at the increased pressure. "Are you close?" I asked her as I continued to rub my fingers over her clit.

She nodded.

I kissed her again, hard enough to make her groan. She clenched around me, arched her back against my chest, and fisted my hair in a vise grip as she came.

Charged by the pain in my scalp, paired with her lips on mine and the thrill of knowing that we could run out of time at any given second, I placed both my hands on Rina's waist and pushed into her as I orgasmed.

I shook a little at the intensity, then sighed when Rina let go of my hair and smiled lazily at me.

"I always think you're as hot as the Indian summers," I panted against her mouth, "but *Christ*, woman, you're even hotter after you've been thoroughly fucked. Satiation is a good look on you." I slowly pulled out of her and turned her around so that I could see her better.

Her t-shirt dress slid down her thighs in the process, and she chuckled as she wrapped her arms around my neck.

The outside murmuring came to a stop.

Rina and I stared at each other as we waited to see what happened next. Then, a few heartbeats later, the sound of three consecutive staccato knocks filled the silence, and I let go of a relieved breath.

"It's Taron," I told Rina.

She relaxed and stepped back, then pressed a chaste kiss on my lips before signing, *That was so good.*

I grinned. "Try *mind-blowing*," I said, then pointed at the bathroom. "Be back in a few."

She nodded.

I quickly trashed the condom, cleaned up, and fixed my clothes. When I walked over to Rina again, she smiled and let me kiss her until we were both out of breath.

"Let's watch a movie together later," I told her. "Preferably not a *Pokémon* one, though."

She laughed and signed, *Okay.*

With another kiss, I opened her bedroom door and walked out as quickly as I'd entered.

I'd only just stepped into the storeroom, when Taron turned from where he was tiling a section of the wall, and faced me before saying, "You owe me, asshole."

I raised my hands in front of me. "I know, I know." I then gave him a brief once-over. "Though, I can't believe you managed to deal with Mr. Ribeiro for longer than two minutes. He would never willingly spend that much time with *me*."

Taron rolled his eyes and threw the trowel he was holding, on the floor, before walking over to me. "First of all: he likes me. I *think*. Second of all: even *I* wouldn't willingly spend that much time with you, and I'm your brother. And third of all: you smell of sex, so you better stay the hell away from me."

Greg and Paul laughed at that, but one glare from me shut them up.

175

"So, the next time you try to use another one of the slang words you learn from Sienna, on me, I'll just remind you of everything you just said to me," I told my brother.

"I'll use my slang on Miguel instead."

I scoffed. "He already thinks you don't have a brain. You acting like a bearded version of Sienna is only going to solidify his claim."

Taron narrowed his eyes at me. "Did I, or did I not, just buy you time to have a quickie with your girl?"

I put my tongue to my cheek as I looked at him. "What we did in there is *our* business, and our business *only*."

Taron rolled his eyes. "Don't worry, I'm not going to ask you to give me a play-by-play. I'd rather get my balls waxed than hear you tell me about your sexcapade."

"I wasn't even offering…" When he sneered at me, I chuckled and said, "Look, I'm really grateful for your help, man. Mr. Ribeiro isn't an easy man to fool, so what you did just now means a lot."

Taron shrugged. "I mean, I'd argue and say that you could've easily waited until he left to go to the shop to do whatever it is that you wanted to do instead of throwing me to the wolf, especially when I've only had a single cup of coffee since waking up, but I guess it's rather too late to complain about any of that now."

I lifted a brow. "Is this your way of asking me to buy you coffee as a favor for what you did?" I asked him.

He shoved his hands into his jeans pocket and lifted a shoulder. "So what if it is?"

Technically, I *did* owe him for the assist, so I couldn't exactly deny him.

"Fine, I'll go get you a macchiato." I pointed a finger at him. "And I'll also get you a chocolate chip muffin and an extra greasy croissant, because I'm feeling quite generous today."

Taron wiped a non-existent tear from his cheek and touched the center of his chest. "Always the thoughtful one."

I shook my head around a smile, then flipped him off when he laughed, before pulling my van's keys out of my hoodie's pocket and jogging down the stairs.

36.

"**W**ell, that's absolute *shit*, isn't it?" I heard Myles say. He sounded angry, and the tone of his voice made goosebumps rise throughout my body.

"Look, I dunno how this happened, man, but at least it's a good thing we caught the issue before it became fatal," came Paul's response.

"*Are you fucking kidding me right now?*" Myles all but hissed. "You messed up, Paul. Admit it instead of trying to get out of it by fucking with me."

Yikes.

"I'm not the only one who was working on piecing together this damn bookshelf, okay, Myles?" Now even *Paul* sounded angry. "This is just as much your fault as it is mine."

"Guys, come on; calm down," Greg said. "It's not like it's an unfixable problem. We can easily work on it today and leave the pending stuff for tomorrow."

"Exactly," added Taron. "Me and Greg can pitch in with ideas, even if we aren't that great with wood-work."

I'd only just stepped out of my room to go say good morning to Myles and the crew, when I'd stopped in my tracks after hearing them argue.

It was almost 10a.m., and I knew *Avô* would be heading out to open shop soon.

"*But it still doesn't change the fact that we screwed shit up, Taron!*" Myles yelled. My God, he was *enraged*.

"I've never let anything like this happen before, and you know that," he continued, now sounding defeated. "It's almost February, and we're still working on putting together the same fucking bookshelf that we started the year with. We're already getting close to crossing the budget Mr. Ribeiro set for us, and the last thing I need is to discuss financials with him. In case you guys aren't aware, him and I don't exactly have a camaraderie going on here."

"But the budget only went up because we made the mistake of ordering a bookshelf from a company whose installation was garbage," Taron provided. "It's not our fault they refused to give us a refund when their policy clearly suggested otherwise."

"This isn't right, Taron," Myles said, and my chest tightened because his voice seemed so small and tired. "I should have been able to fix this; it shouldn't have taken me this long to work on a single thing."

I finally decided to stop eavesdropping and walked into the storeroom.

The guys immediately turned to look at me, and Myles's entire demeanor shifted when I reached him.

"Morning, gorgeous," he said with a grin, then gave me a quick kiss.

I scanned his face. *You don't have to pretend with me*, I signed.

He gave me a rueful smile. "You heard us, didn't you?"

I nodded, and then placed a hand over his chest before running it up and down in order to let him know I was here to listen.

Myles sighed. "Remember the broad bookshelf I told you about? The one that's supposed to be placed opposite the door?"

I nodded again.

"Yeah, so that's not exactly coming along. We're almost done with tiling the walls and finalizing the ceiling, but because the shelves aren't ready, we can't exactly do the floors, because we work in this room itself, and the new flooring could take serious damage due to the wood-work we still have to do. And..." He scratched the top of his head with a look of distress on his face. "The reason why we still haven't finished the bookshelves is because we keep piecing the bigger one incorrectly, for some reason." He took my hand in his

179

and led me further into the room. He then waved an arm at the incomplete shelf that was standing against the front wall. It was as tall as Myles, made of bare wood and thick nails.

"See this?" he pointed at the shelf's foot. "It's always crooked, no matter what I do. This is the second time I've trusted a new company to send in a shelf, and because we're already low on budget, I don't wanna ask your grandfather for extra money for another shelf." He looked at me. "I dunno what to do, Rina."

Is it bad that it's crooked? I asked him. *I mean, it's still standing.*

"If I leave it as it is, there's a strong chance it'll fall off, especially if you put your books in it," Myles told me. "And, there's no point in keeping it crooked and continuing to build it when it can't do the one thing it's supposed to: hold books. It's a liability, at best."

"It almost fell on Myles the other day," Taron said as he came to stand next to his brother. "Good thing Paul caught it before it hit him in the head."

My heart started doing that *boom-boom-boom* thing it does when I'm scared, because Christ, I was *terrified* after having heard that.

I stared up at Myles. *What the fuck?* I signed.

He gave Taron a glare before looking down at me. "I'm fine," he assured. "It was nothing, babe."

Nothing? I signed, then shoved him. *Why did you not tell me?*

"Rina." He grabbed my wrists and pressed my hands to his chest. "It was nothing, I *promise*. I was simply sitting too close to it while working, and it just happened to fall while I was there. I'm *fine*, I swear to you."

I realized I was breathing too hard, so I swallowed and began working on my self-control, because all it was telling me to do was to strangle Myles.

Stop working on this shelf, I signed to him, and then jerked my head toward the two dismantled shelves on the floor behind him. *Work on those. And if they are just like this one, then I can simply get premade shelves from the store.*

I had to spell the word 'premade' slowly so that Myles could understand.

180

He shook his head. "We're low on budg–"

I shoved him again. *No*, I told him. *It's my room, and I get to decide what I want in it. I'll not have you getting injured for a few shelves.*

"Rina–"

I put a hand up to stop him. *No*, I signed.

"Uh-oh," Taron quipped at Myles. "Looks like you're in trouble, baby brother."

Myles glanced his way with ice in his gaze.

Taron chuckled and stepped back, then motioned for Paul and Greg to follow him outside the room.

Once alone, I shoved Myles a third time. It was, after all, the next best thing to strangling him.

He sighed audibly. "I'm sorry, okay? I should've told you, and I didn't. I apologize."

It isn't that, I told him.

"Then what is it?"

I stared at him briefly, then at the shelf, and then back at him.

Scared, I managed to sign, and swallowed.

Myles's expression softened. "I know." He stepped closer to me and wrapped his arms around my waist. "But I'm tougher than this, Rina; I've worked with far dangerous shit. Trust me, I'm *okay*."

Be careful, I signed.

He smiled. "I will."

I will discuss the budget with Avô, I then told him. *For premade shelves.*

"No, Rina," he said, and then frowned. "If I wanted to add store-made shelves in this room, I'd have done so days ago and saved us all the time and hassle. I've been making things by hand from the very beginning because I want this room, and everything that it's built with, to be special to you. I want you to sit in here weeks from now, and know that every inch of this space was made for you, and only you."

Oh, Myles…

As if he hadn't already stolen my heart by being himself, now he had to go and steal my breath away, too.

I rose a little and gave him a long kiss. *Everything you do for me means the world to me*, I signed. *I appreciate what you said, Myles, but you come first for me. Not this room, not the shelves, not the budget, but…* I tapped his chest twice to say, *You.*

His eyes gleamed a little against the mellow sunlight as he searched my face. "How did I end up having such luck?" he asked, more to himself than me, I realized.

I fixed the collar of his sweater as I smiled at him. *I will speak with Avô, and we will think of something together*, I signed, then flung my arms around his neck before cupping the back of his head.

"What if he says no?"

I simply shook my head.

Myles sighed and gave me a nod, then brought his face to the crook of my neck before exhaling against it. His shoulders slumped, and his hold on my waist tightened.

I hugged him close to me, and as I began massaging his scalp, I felt him relax further and further in my arms.

"You're amazing, Rina," he mumbled against my skin.

I closed my eyes, nuzzled my nose against his cheek as I breathed in the smell of his aftershave, and placed a kiss on his jaw in response to his words.

37.

I burped out loud, then coughed at its intensity.

"*Sweet baby Jesus*, Myles," Taron muttered as he hid his nose behind his shirt.

Paul simply grimaced as he continued to play *Angry Birds* on his phone.

I burped again, and then pointed an accusatory finger at Greg as I sat on the floor in the storeroom. "This is all your fault."

Greg clicked his tongue. "Seriously? I only took you hooligans out for lunch as a *treat*. I didn't ask you to store six months' worth of food in your body like a damn camel or something. So no, Myles, your reeking acidity is not *my* fault, but yours, and yours *alone*."

Greg had offered to take us all out for lunch, and because Rina was at the shop and we had no plans of meeting during our respective break times, I'd said yes to his offer. Little had I known, I'd turn into an unashamed hog after entering *Eduardo's Enoteca*.

Italian food was brilliant, and I simply couldn't resist a good *Diavola* pizza.

I took a big gulp from the soda bottle – one of the many we'd gotten from the grocery store after leaving the restaurant – before rolling my eyes at Greg. "It's still your fault," I told him, and when I burped again, Taron scowled and glared at me.

"You're disgusting, Myles," he said.

"Am I, though?" I finished my soda and placed the empty bottle on the floor. "If I'd called *you* that when you farted right in my face not twenty minutes ago, you'd have thrown a fit and prolly scratched your own beard out in rage." I stretched my legs out in front of me. "So, *deal with it*, brother."

But Taron was right; my burps smelled...*toxic*, to say the least. I was so glad Rina wasn't here, because if she was and we'd kissed, she'd most definitely have passed out on me. God, my bathroom was going to *hate* me in the morning.

Taron walked over to me with his hands fisted at his sides. "You little–" He stopped when three consecutive taps sounded on the door.

I looked towards it, and immediately got to my feet when I saw Mr. Ribeiro standing at the threshold.

It's weird, but it's the first time I *actually* noticed his cane. The head of it was a typical J, the shaft was mostly void of polish, and the ferrule was chipped – so much so that its ends were curved towards the sides.

"Myles?" Mr. Ribeiro's voice made me stop my inspection and look at him.

"Yeah?"

He jerked his head to the side. "Take a walk with me." He didn't wait to see if I'd follow.

Of course I *would*. I may be an idiot, but I sure as shit wasn't a halfwit.

I signaled for the crew to continue working, and all but ran after Mr. Ribeiro. On the way out of the house, I quickly grabbed my coat and beanie from the coatrack, and then hastily put them on whilst also shutting the front door.

He stopped halfway down the street to button up his winter coat, and as I caught up to him, he glanced at me from over his shoulder before continuing down the road.

The weather was actually quite lovely, with soft, icy wind blowing in every other direction, and snow falling gently as it drifted sideways against the chilly breezes.

I took a couple of long strides, and then Mr. Ribeiro and I were walking side-by-side.

"Carina told me about the budget problem yesterday," he began. "I'd have thought that you'd manage the money I gave you, with care. Using it carelessly on failed installations is not very wise, Myles."

I guess I deserved that, but still, *ouch.*

I cleared my throat and slid my hands into my jeans pockets. "I do realize that, and I'd like to apologize profusely. I thought I could do everything within the budget *and* on time. I was wrong, clearly. I put in the extra hours and cash because I wanted everything to be authentic and custom-made for Ri–" I stopped myself and bit my tongue. "For *Carina*, I mean." I swallowed and avoided Mr. Ribeiro's gaze when he turned to look at me.

We were silent for a while as we turned down the next street, and I watched as he smiled and waved at a few passersby.

"I take it you're still dating my granddaughter, Myles?" he said after a while.

I looked at him. "Yes."

"Hmm." He nodded, his gaze on the bustling street instead of me. "So, how much will it take for you to break up with her, then?" he questioned so casually that it took me a second to realize he'd even asked something like that to me.

I stopped walking as I stared at him. "Excuse me?" I didn't know what he was insinuating through that question, but I had a bit of an idea as to where this conversation was going, and why he wanted to talk to me alone.

Realizing that I wasn't following him, Mr. Ribeiro stopped, too, and turned to face me. I was so glad there was an ample amount of space between us, otherwise he'd have very easily heard the pounding of my heart as I waited for him to answer me.

"*Money*, Myles," he finally said what I already knew he was going to say. "How much of it will it take for you to break up with my granddaughter?" He faintly tilted his head to the side, and something like sorrow marred his features. "She's all I've got left; all that's left of my family. I simply *cannot* lose her. So, if sacrificing an ounce of her happiness, along with some cash, is what it'll take for me to keep her close to me – to keep her *safe* – then I'm willing to play the hand." He swallowed. "I'm going to give you some money for the library anyway, so why not add to it and shoot two birds with a single bullet?" He tapped his cane on the snow-covered ground once. "Carina will obviously not know how much I'm giving you, so I was thinking of taking advantage of that by seeing if you and I could have ourselves a deal."

A *deal*…

I knew he was a man of strange morals, but this – *this* was absolutely repulsive. It was a slap against my feelings for Rina; against everything we have and share.

And yes, I understood the reason behind his cruel selfishness, but that didn't mean I was going to stand there like a damn moron and let him insult my ideals.

"Is this how you got rid of her previous boyfriends?" I asked. It is then that I realized that my hands were clenched inside my pockets. "Did you pay those two to break up with her? Is that why you met them once you learned about them from Rina?"

He had the audacity to look surprised. "Of course not." He relaxed his stance. "Those idiots bailed on her right after I had regular, civil conversations with them. I asked them a few questions, and they failed to answer them. I told them just who I thought they were, and they came to their senses. But *you*, Myles…" He gave me a once over. "You are way past those questions. Given how Carina behaves when you're around, and how you look at her, I'd like to think that asking you those questions would just be a trivial formality at this point. Words won't work in swaying you, I can tell, but perhaps money will." He raised his brows at me.

I could *not* believe him. Even if he was offering me money as a bait to see if I'd take it, he was wrong. I didn't give seven shits about his cash. What Rina and I had was so much more than a cheap bargain. It was sickening that Mr. Ribeiro didn't see or understand that.

186

"I can't even begin to comprehend the fact that you're honestly willing to *buy* a breakup for your own granddaughter because you think she's not safe with anyone but you," I stated incredulously. "Are you really going to stoop this low and steal Rina's happiness from her? Because I seriously thought you loved her and cared for her. But what you just said to me goes against everything Rina and I stand for, so I don't know if I even judged you the right way to begin with." All the respect I had for him was dwindling by the second. I was shocked and hurt, but most of all, I felt revolted by his offer.

"Oh, do get off your high horse, Myles," he said. "We both know you're simply toying with my Carina, and once you're done, you'll leave her heartbroken and move on like nothing ever happened between the two of you."

Oh, he did *not* just say that.

Christ, I wanted to punch him in his too-old face, but my manners and basic humanity stopped me from doing so.

I ran a hand over my jaw and scoffed, and when Mr. Ribeiro looked coolly at me, I took a step towards him. "I can't believe I'm saying this, but with everything *you've* just said to me, I think you deserve it." I leaned in a little. "*Fuck you*, Miguel. Fuck you so fucking much. Fuck you for your dissent towards Rina and I's relationship; fuck you for not seeing how happy she is when she's with me. Fuck you for treating me like I don't deserve an inkling of your time or energy, and fuck you even more for trying to bribe me into breaking Rina's heart." I straightened and twisted around, but then turned and looked at him again. "Also, I don't need your money – for the renovation or for the absurd offer. I'm not going to quit this project, because this library is Rina's dream room, and me and the crew will bring it to life for her no matter what. I know you won't fire me, because I know you're scared you'll push Rina away if you do so. So, listen up, *asshole*: I will invest my own money into making my girlfriend's library, and when I'm done, I'll continue to date her and make her happy because it's something that brings me joy and makes me feel alive. So, take your cash, shove it up your rigid ass, and never, *ever* undermine or underestimate my feelings for your granddaughter." And with that, I finally pivoted on my feet and walked away from him.

38.

Carina

I felt like a pendulum, bouncing between emotions of absolute shock and shame. Shock because I'd never have even *dreamed* of assuming that my avô would say something like that, and shame because I didn't know how to look Myles in the eye and pretend like I didn't feel utterly humiliated on my grandfather's behalf. But then again, feeling *anything* on his behalf didn't seem right, especially when I was so hurt by the offer he'd made to Myles.

It was past eleven, and when I'd let Myles into the house and my bedroom around thirty minutes ago, the very first thing he'd told me was, "Your grandfather took me on a walk this afternoon and proffered to pay me money to break up with you."

I'd gone completely numb after hearing that, so much so that he had to shake me multiple times in order to snap me out of it and tell him I was okay.

"Rina?"

I stared at my turquoise blanket, at the totem designs printed on it, at every single fiber of it that was visible to me – *anything* to avoid meeting Myles's gaze.

"*Rina.*" His voice sounded insistent this time, but I still didn't look at him. "*Rina!*"

I sucked in a breath and finally brought my eyes to his.

Myles's brows were pinched together, and his lips were turned down. When I blinked at him, he gave me a barely-there smile and swallowed.

"Hey," he said, then ran the knuckle of his forefinger over my left cheek once. "Why are you avoiding my gaze?"

189

You know why, I signed.

He shook his head. "Miguel's words or actions don't define you or the kind of values you like to follow, Rina. What happened shouldn't alter your behavior towards *us*. I don't blame you for any of it, and I don't want you to think I'll see you any differently after today."

Still, I am sorry, I signed.

Myles clicked his tongue. "Don't do that; I'd never want you to apologize for someone else's fuck-up."

Does not mean I don't feel mortified.

He tugged me towards him, and when I leaned in, he grabbed me by the waist so that I could straddle him.

"Listen," he began, then tucked a few short strands of my hair behind my ears, "just like you, even *I* couldn't believe when your *avô* made that absurd offer to me. And why? Because he wanted to say 'I told you so' to you and get the satisfaction of being falsely correct?" He scoffed. "That's ridiculous, and you and I both know that. But hey, it happened, and we can't change it, as much as we'd like to." He wrapped his arms around my middle, and this time, gave me an all but magnetic smile. "If anything, Miguel's offer made one thing *very* clear to me. It's crazy I didn't realize it sooner, but I guess I wasn't sure I could feel something like this so early on in our relationship. I was definitely *wrong*."

My heart was in my throat as I waited for him to continue.

"Rina…" Myles searched my face before smiling again. "I love you," he said, and my world all but turned on its axis. "I love you *so* fucking much, babe, that it's almost insane. At first, I thought my restlessness during the hours we spent apart was because of the newness of what we had, but now I fully realize what it is that I was really feeling." His bubblegum breath brushed against me. "Now I realize that it was love all along – growing every second of every day to become what it is in this moment."

I looked at him – *really* looked. There was a welcoming chaos of emotions right in the center of my chest that was begging to be released, so I took an essence of it, cupped Myles's face, and poured every inch of myself into the kiss I gave him.

When you know someone is right for you, you mold into them with everything you have. It's a raw, trustworthy back-and-forth of reliance and desire; of hope and happiness. And with Myles, it's been like this from the very beginning; it's been a journey of absolute certitude from the moment our eyes met three months ago.

I touched my forehead to his after breaking the kiss. Then, when he gazed openly at me, I stretched up my right thumb, index and pinkie fingers, held the hand out with the palm facing away from me, and moved it back and forth slightly to say what I've known for a short while now.

I love you.

Because I did, so much so that I felt a buzz go up all the way from my toes to my scalp after finally having signed that.

Myles grinned as he pulled me closer to him. "Do that again," he said.

I chuckled and did as he'd asked.

"Again."

I love you, I signed, and he kissed me.

I moaned and cupped the nape of his neck with both of my hands before opening my mouth for him.

Myles groaned, fisted the sides of my t-shirt, and pushed our bodies impossibly close together. "Fuck, how I yearn for you, Rina," he rasped, then gently bit my bottom lip. "How my very soul *aches* for yours because I can't get you close enough. I can breathe you in right now, but it's still not enough. I can feel your heat against me, but I still want more. I can hear your heartbeats in sync with mine, but I still want them to be louder, faster. The more you give me, the more I'll want, and the more you take from me, the more I'll want to give you. Baby…" He kissed me slowly, almost delicately. "You're my everything; you're my fucking sanctum. You lift me up and make me whole, and when my words waver against my feelings for you, you know just how to bring me back to myself. I'm so grateful for you, and my God, I love you *so much*."

We kissed again, not only because we loved each other, but also because everything he'd said, he'd said it for the both of us. He'd mirrored my conviction and feelings perfectly, and I knew for sure that if I ever ran out of signs, Myles would know just what to say to make things meaningful for us both.

I grazed my tongue over his lower lip and pulled away, and when he smiled lazily at me, I let go of a breath and signed, *I may not have words, but everything that I do have is yours. You complete me in ways no one ever has, or ever will. You have changed my outlook on life and hope ever since you walked into my life, Myles, and I can only hope that I'll continue to be enough for you – enough for you to want to stay forever.*

"Rina…" He swallowed and took my hands in his before pressing sound kisses on the inside of my wrists. "You'll always be enough – so much *more* than just enough. You're a damn blessing to me, and I promise to never take you or your humanity for granted." He tapped my chest first, then his, stretched up the index and middle fingers of both of his hands, and orbited them around each other once before bringing them together in an X to say, *You are my universe.*

And you are mine, I signed. *Slightly crazy and highly awkward sometimes, but still mine.*

Myles chuckled. "Good, because I wouldn't belong anywhere else anyway. I like myself here, with you in my arms, and me ogling you with absolutely no shame whatsoever," he said.

I laughed because he was right, and then, I kissed him yet again because I just couldn't help it.

And also because I loved him so much that the instinct was pretty much natural.

39.

Carina

I was standing by the door and bouncing on my feet as I waited for him. I was tingling with anticipation, and all but squealed when my phone vibrated in my hand.

Beauty: *Knock-knock.*

Myles knew *Avô* had already left for some golf session with his friends, but because the *knock-knock* text had become our thing, I looked forward to getting it from him rather than having him ring the doorbell.

I flung the door open, pulled Myles inside by the collar of his black leather jacket, and rose on my tiptoes to give him a kiss.

He shut the door and moaned against me, but I quickly pulled back and let him take off his boots so that I could drag him into the kitchen.

Once inside, I turned and looked at him, and all but came in my jeans when he grinned at me.

I'd never seen him in a leather jacket, so excuse me for going nuts about the fact. And those faded jeans he was wearing? Yeah, they were doing *everything* for his thighs and my shameless eyes.

"Happy Valentine's Day, babe," Myles said as he walked over to me.

I melted into his arms when he kissed me, but managed to grab the plate that was on the counter behind me.

I slowly pushed him back, and when he raised his brows at me, I presented him the massive Lofthouse cookie I'd made for him.

It was round, doughy, perfectly sweet, with an ample amount of pink buttercream frosting, and loads of sprinkles – just like Myles liked it.

His eyes widened when he saw the cookie. "Rina, you didn't have to." He looked at me. "You told me not to bring you a gift, so–"

I placed a finger on his mouth to shush him, then jerked my head at the cookie.

With a smile and a slight shake of his head, he grabbed it and took a massive bite of it. "*Fuck*," he all but groaned. "It's *so* good, Rina."

I chuckled as I set the plate aside, and, because I was feeling a little something-something after seeing him in a leather jacket *and* moaning after eating the cookie I'd made him, I placed my hands on his arms and turned him around so that his back was to the inner counter.

"What're you–" He stopped abruptly when I went on my knees before him.

"Rina…" His chest rose and fell at an unsteady rhythm. "You don't–"

I shushed him, then signed, *Eat*, before unbuckling his belt.

He looked like he was in a daze as he swallowed, nodded, and then took another bite of the cookie.

I unzipped his jeans and pushed its flaps aside, put a hand behind the waistband of his underwear and wrapped my fingers around the base of his cock, then pulled him out before rising a little on my knees.

"*Rina…*" Myles sighed when I stroked him slowly – just once. He then grabbed the hem of his white t-shirt and lifted it up.

I smirked and leaned in to place open-mouthed kisses on his hipbone as I began stroking him proper, and he hardened more and more in my grasp with each press of my lips on his skin.

Myles inhaled sharply, and I felt his abs contract at my touch.

It was a different kind of pleasure knowing that he trusted me enough to let me take him on a high that was uncontrollable and wild. It was a sensation so untamed that it drove me mad, made me hungry for more.

I moved back, and when our eyes met, I ran the tip of my tongue over his crown, making him grunt.

194

"Rina, please," he said. The grey of his eyes looked all but obsidian as he stared at me.

I grinned, and parted my lips before finally taking him into my mouth.

"*Fuck.*" Myles's hips thrust forward, and I gagged a bit.

Pushing his underwear down further, I pulled him out of my mouth and began sucking on his balls.

I moaned, and my nipples hardened at the taste of him.

God, he felt *so* good.

"Fuck!" I felt him spread his legs a little, and when I tightened my grip around his cock before stroking him faster, his breaths turned audible, uneven.

I looked up at him, and when I saw a small piece of cookie in his hand, I arched a brow at him.

He quickly shoved it into his mouth and began chewing on it, making me chuckle.

The vibration from that action made him grunt again, and when I pulled his balls out of my mouth before gently tugging them downwards with my free hand, Myles clenched his jaw and groaned.

"I'm close," he rasped, and pulled his t-shirt higher.

I took his cock into my mouth again, but this time, I let him slide deep. I pushed my head forward and took him in to the back of my throat, and gagged out loud. Pulling him out, I spat on his crown, applied more pressure on the hold I had on his base, and started sucking him again.

He rocked his hips in time with my head, and when I felt his balls tighten in my hand, I looked up at him again.

Myles arched and roared as he came into my mouth, and the way his entire body stiffened under the pleasure *I* gave him, made me feel so fucking powerful as I swallowed almost every drop of his come.

"*Jesus-Mary-Joseph,*" he whispered when I got to my feet and wiped my lips with a thumb. "You broke my brain, woman."

I laughed, just as the doorbell rang. Daniel and the others were here, it seemed.

I glanced at Myles, all flushed and relaxed, and gave him a wink. *Clean up*, I signed, then turned around before sashaying out of the kitchen and into the living room.

40.

"**C**hits, please," Daniel said as he went around swinging the glass bowl up and down.

I watched as he collected chits from the others, and when he came to stand in front of me, he gave me an '*Eh*' look before raising a brow.

"Chits," he all but spat the word.

I tried not to laugh as I put mine in. "You can't possibly still be salty with me," I told him, then flashed my teeth at him. "You know you don't want to."

He gave me a once-over. "Are you flirting with me?"

I lifted a shoulder. "Depends."

"On?"

"On whether or not it's doing something to your Hulk-like ego," I quipped.

Rina snickered from next to me, and Daniel scowled before giving her a glare.

"*Chits*, boss," he said to her.

When she excitedly placed both her chits into the bowl, Daniel walked away from us with an air of defiance in his steps.

Rina grinned as she looked up at me with glimmering eyes, to which I chuckled and nudged her hip with mine.

My mind was still in a buzz from that epic fucking head she'd given me. It was so unexpected, yet so damn hot that it'd left me speechless for minutes after.

197

Daniel had suggested that instead of doing the usual date and gifts shebang on Valentine's Day, the whole squad should gather with their respective partners at Rina's house to play a game of *Dare*. No truths, only dares. And not just any dares, either, but ones that *had* to be at least slightly inappropriate, and also '*up to the par of humorous*', according to Daniel.

He'd made each of us write two separate dares, and as I fully came to terms with what was about to happen, I realized that I hadn't been thinking straight when I'd agreed to this shit.

Me and the crew were off work for the day, obviously. Just like I'd promised Miguel, I'd invested in installing a couple small bookshelves in the storeroom myself, and me and the crew were in the process of merging the faulty bookshelf with the spare ones we'd ordered in January from that shitty company. We had loads of materials from those shelves anyway, so we'd decided to put it all together and see if it worked.

But we'd hardly started on that bit, though, so there was still stuff to be done before the library was complete.

I sighed and looked around at everyone who was gathered. Cruz and Daniel were here with their wives; Taron and Tori were also present. Ash and Dave had come together, and because both Remi and Simran were single, they'd decided to come as a pair. Paul and Greg – those bastards – had declined coming to the mad-fest, and had instead taken their dates on a damn picnic.

A sweet, *regular*, Valentine's Day picnic.

I was starting to think they'd done the right thing.

I didn't know what level of dares I was supposed to expect from the others. Even from Rina, because when I'd asked her to let me read hers, she'd turned her back to me like those kids do in school in order to hide their test sheets.

Oh well.

The one's that *I'd* picked, though, were simple – because, you know, I'm a *good person* and all.

1) Eat 12 hot peppers and recite your filthiest sexual fantasy in complete detail, without taking a water or milk break.

2) Try to capture a burp or a fart in a mason jar and make your partner smell it.

See? Simple and completely doable.

Told ya I'm a nice person…

Even though business at *Vila do Açaí* was crazy on V-day, Rina had somehow convinced Miguel to keep the shop closed, and Daniel, our Saint and savior, had booked a VIP golf session for Miguel and his friends at *The Beverly Country Club* to keep him out of the house so that he could murder us all in this cult gathering that he'd organized.

I didn't trust those sparkling blue eyes of his, but Rina was excited, so I had no other choice but to do Daniel's bidding.

"People!" he called out to us. "Let's all sit down in a circle, because the dares are in. It is game time!" He opened a kitchen cabinet and grabbed a bottle of *Ardbeg* from inside it. When he turned and our eyes met, he shrugged and said, "Just in case, y'know? If the dares get intense and someone needs liquid courage."

"It's 10a.m., Daniel."

He shrugged again, but slowly this time. "Your point?"

I rolled my eyes and followed Rina into the living room.

As I sat next to her on the floor, with Taron on my left, Daniel strutted over to the cult circle and sat opposite me. Brianna, his wife, was on his left, and Cruz was to his right, with *his* wife, Valeria next to him.

It'd been a genuine pleasure getting acquainted with them, as they were really good people to talk to and share a laugh with. So were Ash and Dave, honestly, but I guess the former was a bit more eagle-eyed towards me at first, clearly because it was her job as Rina's best friend to judge my very existence until she was happy with everything she saw and heard.

I didn't blame her.

Daniel cleared his throat, placed the chit-filled bowl in the center, and set the bottle of scotch in front of him before saying, "Are you guys ready?"

We all murmured our yeses.

"Great." He slapped his thigh once. "Oh, and if you end up getting your own dare by accident, you get to pick another one. No one is supposed to perform their own dare. We're not here to watch you fulfill your fetishes, so please, for the love of baby Jesus, *spare us*."

I laughed and looked at Rina. When she smiled at me, I bent and gave her a quick kiss.

"Okay, everyone, so who wants to pick the first chit?" Daniel asked.

Simran crawled forward and grabbed one before anyone could say anything, and then after having read it, she simply turned to Remi and said, "Lift your armpits."

The poor guy paled. "*What?!*"

"Wait, wait," Daniel cut in. "That's not how it works! You have to read the dare out loud before performing it."

Simran rolled her eyes. "*Smell someone's armpits for 10 seconds,*" she read casually.

"Oh God." Daniel ran a hand over his face, then looked at Cruz. "It was you, wasn't it? You're the one who wrote that?" When Cruz didn't respond, and instead chose to keep his eyes on the floor, Daniel lifted his arms in defeat. "I said *R-rated* or *humorous* dares, you pile of meat! Armpits are neither of those things! They're gross and Satan's curse to humanity!" He waved a hand at Simran. "But whatever, do the dare so that we can move on."

He just *had* to mention Satan to solidify my suspicions about this being a cult gathering, didn't he?

May the Almighty save my soul.

Remi reluctantly raised his arms, and Simran spent 10 seconds smelling each of his pits.

Rina shifted, and our knees bumped. When I glanced at her, I saw her looking at Remi and Simran with a horrified expression on her face.

200

"Changed your mind yet?" I asked.

She scrunched up her nose, but shook her head, making me chuckle.

"Your loss," I quipped.

"Shh!" Daniel chastised. "Okay, good job, Sim. Who's next?"

Remi picked up a chit. "*Make out with someone of the same sex as you.*" He looked around, then pointed ahead. "Dave, you in?"

Dave nodded, and Ash smirked. She sat back and watched gleefully as Remi and Dave put Massimo Torricelli to shame with the way they kissed each other.

"Whoa..." Daniel opened the bottle of scotch and took a huge gulp from it. "Okay, so *that* just happened." He drank some more.

Brianna punched him in the side, to which he chuckled and kissed her.

Rina got on all fours and took the bottle from Daniel, then downed a small amount of it before giving it back to him.

Oh*kay*...

Dave was next in line for the dare, and when he got one where he had to make his partner come in under 30 seconds, Ash didn't waste time in stripping down to her underwear.

The two of them headed into the guest bathroom, and within 20 seconds, we heard Ash's moans filtering out and reverberating through the otherwise silent room.

I swear this was getting crazier by the second.

The pair walked out soon after, and Ash, *thankfully*, put her clothes back on.

Rina looked so flabbergasted that I wanted to laugh, but had to control the urge by clearing my throat instead.

The game went on, with each dare more questionable than the other, until Taron reached forward and grabbed a chit. "*Leave an R-rated voicemail for an ex.*"

I couldn't hold it in, then; I laughed. Full body-shaking, teary-eyed laughter that went on for quite some time, until Rina finally placed a hand on my shoulder to stop me.

Everyone was looking at me like I'd popped a brain cell, and maybe I had, but I didn't care about that.

Taron glared at me. "What's so funny?"

Tori pressed her lips together as she looked up at him. "Babe, I'm the only girlfriend you've ever had," she said with a frown.

I laughed again, and this time, everyone else joined in.

Taron appeared flustered as he faced Daniel. "What do I do?"

"Put this one back and pick another, silly," he said matter-of-factly.

Taron did just that, then balked at the new chit in his hands. "*Pinch your partner's nipples while reciting the nursery rhyme,* A Sailor Went to Sea." He glanced around. "What the fuck?!"

Cruz's wife, Valeria, shifted as she tried to hide a smirk behind a fist.

Taron threw the chit in with the other used ones, looked at his wife, and said, "You wanna do this?"

She nodded excitedly. "Yup!"

Oh, *Christ.*

Is this seriously what my life has become? I have to watch my elder brother pinch my sister-in-law's nips while reciting a kiddie rhyme? For real?!

I averted my gaze as Taron completed the dare, and when Tori pulled a chit out, it was even worse than her husband's.

"*Dry-hump your partner until they come,*" she read.

I wasn't even surprised at the intensity of the dare, so when Tori got into position and began going at it with Taron *right there and then,* I only sighed and ran my hands over my face.

This was the most *ridiculous* V-day of my life so far, and yet somehow, I was starting to find humor in it.

I'm crazy, I know.

After listening to 27.6 seconds of Taron panting and huffing, and then *finally* coming, the group cheered the pair on for pulling off a dare so risqué with a crowd in attendance.

Yay to the Valentine's spirit, I guess.

Taron went off to clean up, and when he came back, Rina jumped forward and grabbed a chit.

Sweet mother of bountiful heaven.

She read the chit, then handed it to me with a grin so maniacal, that it made a chill run down my slightly perspired spine.

I shakily – *yes*, I was shaking in complete dread – took the chit from her and read it out loud. "*Bite your partner's ass.*"

I whipped my head at Rina. "No."

She grinned wider. *Yes*, she signed.

"Baby, *no*." I swallowed. "Pretty please?"

She shifted a little and clapped her hands. *Yes*, she signed again.

I started wracking my brain for a way out of the…situation, but then, to my utter, unfortunate dismay, my darling of a girlfriend started unbuckling my belt.

"Yasssss, gurl! GET!" Daniel chanted.

I sent a brief glare his way, then looked at Rina again. "Babe?"

Her eyes met mine.

"You don't want everyone to see what's yours, do you?" I said/tried to convince her out of going all cannibal on my ass. "I mean, I didn't take you for someone who'd want to share my…stuff." Yeah, I wasn't being very convincing about this.

Rina gave me a '*Really?*' look, then tugged hard on my belt.

"Fine, fine." I got to my feet and unzipped my jeans. "Christ, woman; patience." I stood and faced the group so that they couldn't see my trembling cheeks, then pushed my jeans down to my knees and bent my upper body forward.

Daniel smirked at me, and I knew this was his dare without even having to ask him about it.

Rina stood and came behind me, and this time when she went on her knees, I knew she'd serve me pain instead of pleasure.

I looked at her from over a shoulder. "If you make me bleed, there'll be consequences," I told her.

She laughed, pushed aside my underwear, and leaned in.

And then...

Then there was only pain.

Agony.

Torment.

Affliction.

PAIN.

So. Much. Fucking. Pain.

I yelped and practically jumped off the ground when Rina's teeth pressed onto my right ass cheek. That creature bit down on me with sheer force – one that all but blinded me as a sharp sting coursed through my damn ass, all the way down to my toes.

"Fucking HELL!" I screamed as I stumbled away from Rina and put my jeans back on. "You...you Goddamn piranha!"

She was laughing so hard she was tearing up. Even her face was flushed from the amusement she'd gotten from seeing me so out of it.

I heard more laughter, so I turned around, and found all ten idiots who were sitting in the circle, cackling at my behest. Simran was among them, and that says a lot, because she *never* laughs.

Great. Fucking fantastic.

I took what was left of my dignity, and sat back down. But as soon as my ass hit the floor, a new wave of pain shot through me, making me hiss.

Taron cleared his throat. "It's called karma, brother," he whispered to me, his expression smug.

"Fuck you *so* very much, *brother*," I whispered back, resulting in him to chuckle.

Rina slid over to me and sat down to my right, and when I glanced at her, she sent an air kiss my way.

My lips twitched. It was hard to stay mad at her, however occasionally undomesticated she might be.

"Pick a chit, Myles," came Ash's voice.

I nodded at her, then sent a prayer before reluctantly grabbing a chit from the bowl.

As soon as I read it, though, I realized that my plea to the Lord above had gone in vain, because the dare…it was…

"*Have someone wax your armpits*," I read out loud, and all but died on the inside because…

WHAT. THE. FUCK.

41.

Myles

"**W**hat the fuck is it with you and *armpits*, Cruz?!" Daniel all but exploded, but I couldn't stop staring at the chit that held my execution sentencing.

Rina tapped my thigh, and when I looked at her, she signed, *Are you okay?*

I blinked at her. "Am I a cult sacrifice?" I asked. "Was today just a ploy to get me here and offer me up to some demon you guys worship? How did you rope Taron and Tori into helping you? Was that blowjob you gave me earlier your way of saying sorry to me because you're going to gut me and eat my intestines in order to achieve immortality?"

Rina searched my face for a beat too long, and I knew she was fighting back a smile with the way she kept pursing her lips every other second. But, after a while, she regained herself, then signed, *I'll get the wax*, before getting to her feet and running up to her bedroom.

The universe was playing with me. Or maybe it was the Illuminati...

Satan? Yeah, maybe he was behind all of this.

I honestly couldn't tell.

"Applying some talcum powder on the area that's to be waxed makes the process more bearable," Cruz said.

I took my eyes off the chit so that I could glare at him proper. "I thought you were a *saint*," I all but hissed at him. "But even geniuses can be wrong, so I only have myself to blame for falling for your saccharine act of companionship."

Cruz frowned. "Sorry, man. I really wasn't expecting you to get the dare. I was hoping that this idiot," he pointed at Daniel, "would be the one to pick up my chits."

Daniel acted offended. "Ex-*squeeze* me?! My armpits are hairless and innocent, thank you very much." He clicked his tongue. "Serves you right for trying to get unnecessary revenge on me when all I've wanted us to do today is have fun."

Before Cruz could fire back a response, Rina came bounding down the stairs with actual, *literal* glee on her face, and a small, pink box clutched in her right hand.

God, I'd accidentally fallen irreversibly in love with a real-life Harley Quinn.

Fuck me twelve ways to Easter.

She came to a stop in front of me, a little out of breath, then signed, *Take off your jacket and shirt.*

"*Absolutely not,*" I told her. I was still sitting cross-legged on the floor, so I had to crane my neck a little in order to look at her.

She placed her hands on her hips and huffed, then turned to Cruz with a silent command on her face. She then gave another kind of scary look to my brother, and I watched, dumbfounded, as both the giants in the room rose to their feet.

No.

Não.

Non.

Níl.

Óxi.

"Stay. The *fuck*. Away. From me." I dragged myself away from the two towering heaps of muscles, but they continued to advance toward me. "Fucking *stop*!"

"Don't make this hard, bro," Taron said. "It'll be over in seconds; just co-operate."

"EASY FOR YOU TO SAY!" I yelled, and slid back more. My bitten ass was burning, but that's the least I had to bear in order to save my *life*.

"Calm down, man," added Cruz. "It's just wax."

"You…" I pointed a finger at him. "*Fuck you.*"

"I deserve it," he agreed. "But you're being a damn baby about this. You're a constructor, for Christ's sake. Surely you've had injuries in the past that hurt far more than wax ever will."

"That's beside the point," I told him. "Those were *necessary* injuries; this – this is *TORTURE.*"

"Look…" Cruz started, but stopped abruptly and grabbed my legs. Before I even knew what was happening, two large arms hooked themselves under mine and lifted me, and then, Cruz and Taron were carrying me over to the center of the gathered circle.

"STOP!" I screamed helplessly. "SOMEONE HELP ME! PLEASE, HELP ME!"

The giants placed me back on the ground, and when I tried to get up, Rina came next to me, pushed me down, and straddled me.

"Babe…" I swallowed. "Come on, we don't have to do this. I love you, and you love me. *Is that not enough?!*"

She clicked her tongue and again signed for me to take off my jacket and t-shirt.

I gave her my best *Puss-in-Boots* eyes, but when she didn't budge, I sighed and did what she wanted me to, then lied on the floor like the sacrificial lamb I knew I was.

"Dear *God*, look at those abs," I heard Daniel say. "I could mold cookies shaped as them."

"Ugh, you're so *weird*," Simran told him, and *everyone* muttered their agreement to her statement.

Taron and Cruz headed back to their places, and Rina opened the pink box she was holding before pulling a flat strip from inside it.

Nooooo.

Ohgod, ohgod, OHGOD.

She briefly rubbed the strip between her palms, then gestured for me to raise an arm.

"Baby, I–"

She glared at me, so I quickly obeyed her order.

She slowly pulled the strip apart, handed a piece of it to Ash, then leaned in before slapping the other one right over the smattering of hair on my right pit.

My heart was in my damn throat as I watched her press the strip onto my skin. She rubbed it continuously for a few seconds, and once she was satisfied, she looked at me and signed, *Ready?*

I nodded, because really, there was nothing else I could do. It was too late; the damage had already been done.

Rina grabbed an edge of the strip, pulled down my skin, and then – then she ripped.

R I P P E D.

And oh, *man*, did it hurt.

It hurt *so* bad that my eyes began to sting, my jaw started to tingle, and my mouth all but dried out because I was sucking in air in anticipation of the incoming pain.

And the burning sensation I was feeling? Yeah, that was 250 times more intense than that ass-bite.

"*FUCK!*" I all but howled, and my hips arched on their own accord, making Rina jump a little.

She chuckled, and I knew why.

I'd felt her heat on my crotch, and she'd most definitely felt my cock between her thighs.

At least there was that little thing going on below my belt to keep me sane, shameless as I am to admit it.

Rina shifted, and I met her gaze. *Raise*, she signed, then pointed at my left arm.

209

I swallowed and did just that, and as she repeated the process of placing the strip on my skin and then rubbing it, I puffed out air through my lips and waited for darkness to take over.

And Lord, it *did*.

My hands clenched into fists; my vision turned spotty and hazy. My breath left me in a *whoosh*, and my chest tightened as I shrieked, "FUCK YOU ALL, YOU DEMON-WORSHIPPING CULTISTS!"

Another fresh hell of pain zapped through my body post that pull, so I closed my eyes and thought to myself: *This is how you're gonna die, dipshit – with a chunk of your ass bitten out, and two swollen, blood-red, freshly-waxed armpits.*

What a way to go…

"Alright, it's game-over, everyone!" Daniel hollered, then cleared his throat. "Uh, Pizza! Who wants pizza?! Everyone wants some pizza, right? *Right???*"

Everyone said 'Yes' in unison, and when I opened my eyes, he looked at me with a wobbly, almost grimace-like smile on his face. "Do you have a topping preference?" he asked softly.

I sniffed and sat up, then groaned as I brought my arms down.

Rina, who was still straddling me, pursed her lips as she fixed my hair, then signed, *I'm sorry.*

"No, you're not," I told her immediately.

She fought back a smile, to which I rolled my eyes.

"You're evil, woman," I said. *"Pure evil."*

She grinned, gave me a long kiss on the lips, and grabbed something from inside the wax box before waving it in front of my face.

I took it from her and read the packaging:

Aftercare oil with aloe and almond. Massage over waxed skin to ease any irritation or swelling. Do not wash after application.

I handed the packet back to her and arched a brow. "You have better be using that all over my armpits in the next minute or so, or else I'm banning sex for at *least* an entire month." The burning sensation in my pits had turned into a constant throb, which made me clench my jaw against it.

Rina's mouth formed an 'O' as she stared at me over my threat to her, so I just gave her a grin and looked at Daniel.

"Extra cheese, olives, slightly burnt pineapples, and fresh basil," I told him, and when he blinked at me, I added, "My pizza topping preference."

"Right." He nodded. "Of course."

I turned to Rina again and smirked at her. "Now, then; how about that armpit massage, huh, babe?"

42.

Carina

"**I** am yours, Daphne! I have always been yours!"

I almost dropped my paperback copy of *Cinderella Is Dead* when I heard Myles's resounding voice cut through the otherwise peaceful environment at *Vila do Açaí*.

I whipped my head up, just as a few customers laughed before making way for him to walk up to the main counter.

What. The. Ever. Infesting. Fuck.

My eyes all but popped out of my sockets when I looked him up and down.

He was wearing a grey tank top, ivory joggers, his usual Blackhawks beanie, and…and a 19th century crimson suit coat/jacket that looked *exactly* like the one Regé-Jean wore in *Bridgerton*.

Daniel and Cruz stepped out of the bakery, and the former sucked in a breath when he saw Myles. Cruz, on the other hand, just ran a hand over his face, then began finger-combing his beard in frustration. I could only *imagine* the looks on Simran and Remi's faces.

"Daphne! I mean, *Rina*." Myles drummed his fingers on the counter and gave me a grin. "I have the best news."

I blinked, still trying to get a handle on his outfit, because *Lord*, he looked like a fucking *hybrid* in those clothes.

He hadn't come to the house in the morning, so it's the first I was seeing him since yesterday. And *man*, what an eccentric view he provided.

I set the paperback I was holding, next to my work laptop. *What?* I signed.

"Remember that choir from last year?" Myles asked. "The one we'd seen outside the café in November?"

I nodded.

His grin widened. "Yeah, so I follow them on Instagram, and they shared a post an hour ago saying that they're doing a little *Bridgerton* inspired musical down the street for those who can't afford to, or couldn't get tickets for, *The Queen's Ball: A Bridgerton Experience.* We can even donate some cash to the choir so that they can keep doing these shows, but bigger." He leaned in. "Would you care to indulge me, Miss Ribeiro? A little bit of *this*, and a little bit of *that* – with yours truly."

I looked down at my pink sweater dress, beige yoga pants, and brown winter boots, then gave Myles another once over.

Where did you get the jacket from? I asked him.

He fixed the lapels of said jacket and gave me a wink. "I borrowed it from one of the performers. Told him I wanted to impress my girl and shit."

I chuckled, just as Daniel said, "Rina, kindly remove this *mutant* from the premises. It is scaring away our customers and putting a major damper on our business."

Everyone, including Cruz, laughed.

Myles only flipped Daniel off in response, earning a few giggles from the female shoppers in the store.

"Mature as always, I see," Daniel stated with a belligerent roll of his eyes.

Myles blew him a kiss. "Had to make sure it matched your level of intellect, bestie," he quipped.

I snorted, but quickly placed a hand over my mouth when Daniel glowered at me.

The electronic bird chirped, and as another group of customers entered the shop, almost all of them gave Myles either confused or incredulous looks before going about their business and browsing the display cases and framed menu boards.

He didn't care about any of that, of course, and brought his attention back to me. "So, you coming?" he asked around a smile. "I know you love the show, and I've also sorta, kinda, a little bit, found sense in it. It'll be fun – just you and me, and some ear-splitting crescendos."

There will be other people present, I signed. *It is a street, after all.*

Myles shrugged. "So? Big deal, Rina. When has that ever stopped you from being *you*?"

I shook my head as I chuckled, because he was right.

Of *course* he was.

Okay, I told him, then looked at Remi from over his shoulder. *Take over for me*, I signed to him.

He nodded and gave me a thumbs up.

I then looked at Laurel and Hardy – I mean, Daniel and Cruz.

Assist Remi, please, I signed.

Daniel crossed his arms over his chest. "If you come back wearing a corset and an empire-waist dress, I swear to God I'm going to refuse to identify you and most definitely disown you as a friend," he said.

Cruz kicked him in the shin, making Daniel yelp in surprise and glare at him.

"What he *means* is," Cruz began, then gave Daniel a bored look, "we'll look after the shop and help Remi if there's a customer rush. You go enjoy the choir."

I love you, I said to Cruz. *You rock.*

"He *doesn't*," Daniel objected.

"You'd wish that, wouldn't you?" Cruz told him, then signed, *Have fun; love you*, to me, before grabbing the back of Daniel's collar and dragging him back inside the bakery.

"Wow…" Myles scratched his jaw with a contemplative look on his face. "I always wonder if those two are real, or just crazy side characters from a quirky romcom novel. But then I also think about how I don't really give any number of shits in regards to that little idea, and then go about my business."

Huh?

God, I was so confused.

"*Anyways.*" Myles grinned at me again. "Should we get going, or what?" He offered me a hand.

I nodded, slid my phone into my dress pocket, placed my hand in Myles's, and let him lead me out of *Vila do Açaí*.

Once we'd stepped outside, Myles began running down the left side of the street, and I laughed as I tried to keep up with him.

I noticed that every single streetlight on the stretched-out pavement was turned on, because even though it was early morning, the day was rather muted due to the chilly weather and steadily falling snow.

Myles and I sidestepped a few cars in our haste, and because I'd forgotten my coat at the shop, I pulled his beanie from his head and put it on as decently as I could, while also trying not to get hit by oncoming vehicles.

We took a sharp right, and when Myles began slowing down, I matched his speed, then came to a halt when I looked at the meager setup just a few steps ahead of me.

The group had hung fairy lights over the streetlights, which made no practical sense, but aesthetically, it looked adorable. A lavender carpet was draped over the platform they were standing on, and they'd even erected a floral-wallpapered photography wall on top of it to give the whole thing a thematic appearance.

Come to think of it, 'meager' may not be the perfect term to describe the setup the group had come up with; maybe *quaintly duplicate* was.

A small crowd was scattered around the platform, either talking amongst each other, or tapping away on their phones.

"Here you go, man; thanks for letting me borrow it," Myles said to the performer who was on the stage, then handed the velvet coat to him.

"No worries," the guy said around a smile. "I hope it helped."

Myles grinned and jerked his head in my direction, and when the guy looked at me, I gave him a smile and a wave.

"Hey." He waved back, and I may be crazy for saying this, but he looked kinda like Regé-Jean Page, and that slight resemblance was enough to make me blush a little.

Sorry not sorry.

"I'm Jayden," he told me. "It's nice to meet you. Myles here says you're one in a million, and also a hardcore *Bridgerton* fan. Thanks for stopping by today; it means a lot."

The other performers were bustling around the setup. Some were rehearsing, some were fixing their hair and makeup, while the others were either taking selfies or working on tweaking their musical instruments.

I'm Carina, I signed to Jayden, hoping he'd understand. *It's nice to meet you as well.*

He flashed his teeth in a megawatt smile, and I wanted to sob because he really *did* look like Regé.

I hope you enjoy the show, he signed, and in that moment, I came to the conclusion that he could *not* get any more perfect than that.

I loved Myles to pieces, but that didn't mean I couldn't fangirl every once in a while, *okay*?

"You know Sign?" Myles asked Jayden. "That's great, man."

Jayden nodded. "I do, yeah. My younger sister has sensorineural hearing loss, so we communicate through Sign, among other things. It's as natural to me as speaking is."

"It's kinda the same for me, even though I've only known Sign for around three months," Myles said to him. "Learnt it for Rina, and I'm so damn glad to have done it."

Jayden smiled at him, then at me. "It sure is a completely different feeling to interact via Sign, isn't it?"

"It is," Myles agreed, just as one of the performers hollered, "We're ready for show time!"

Jayden put on the Simon-coat and pointed a thumb over his shoulder. "I gotta go double-check my mic. You two have fun, okay?" he told Myles and I.

"We sure will," Myles stated.

Donation box? I signed.

Jayden pointed at a red box on the far left of the stage, then, with another wave, he joined the other members of the group behind the stage.

I walked over to the donation box and slid a $20 bill inside it.

Myles did the same, then took my hand in his before leading me back to the area close to the platform.

"I made Taron binge the show with me last week," he told me, and then wrapped his arms around my waist. "Four episodes in, and he started losing his shit. He began looking for 19th century gowns for himself, and even drew a digital sketch of a carriage he wanted to make for himself. But…" He paused for emphasis, "…before he could actually make true on *any* of that, I stopped him. A couple of chokeholds here, a few arm twists there. I think I even used his beard as a leash at one point, but it's kind of a blur right now." He faintly lifted a shoulder. "It worked, though, so who am I to complain, right?"

I stared at him in absolute shock.

At this point, I know that I shouldn't be surprised by anything Myles says, or does, or *both*, but it's impossible for me to not lose a slice of my commonsense every time I hear him say something as aberrant as what he'd told me.

You and Taron belong in a museum, I signed. *You two are crazy.*

Myles chuckled. *I know*, he signed back, then said, "You should be ready for shit like this by now, Rina. I can't drop these bombs and have you standing here gawking at me like you have no idea what to do with yourself. It's very unbecoming, babe; live up to your damn reputation."

You said you used Taron's beard as a leash. How was I supposed to expect that? I asked. *My bravery can only stretch so far.*

"We've done worse to each other than that, though," he stated casually.

I rubbed my hands over my face in utter frustration, which resulted in Myles to chuckle again.

217

"You'll get used to it, I promise," he assured, like it even *was* something I needed assurance on.

Asshole, I signed, just as a loud screech of the mic, followed by the mellow sound of a piano, filled the air. One of the musicians began playing the familiar tune of *We Could Form an Attachment*, an original *Bridgerton* background music, on the piano, and the crowd around us started cheering and taking pictures. A few moments later, Jayden and a female performer walked on stage, just like Simon and Daphne had walked into the Vauxhall gardens at the end of episode one. The two bowed ceremoniously, then fell into a beautiful waltz, and surprisingly, so did a lot of the couples in the crowd.

Myles grinned down at me, and I couldn't help but laugh at him.

"Stare into my eyes, Rina," he commanded.

I would have rolled *my* eyes at him for quoting Simon, but I just couldn't, because the way he was looking at me – it defied every single level of intensity any fictional character has whilst looking at their love interest.

Because *this* was real. *We* were real.

And nothing – not even my love for a period drama and its lead guy – meant *anything* compared to what Myles meant to me.

I stepped closer to him and gazed up at him. Even under the dim daylight and shadowing streetlights, I could clearly see the bright flecks of grey in his eyes. I ran a hand up and down his chest, then draped my arms over his shoulders before gently cupping the back of his head.

"Would it be right for me to presume that you don't know how to waltz?" he asked.

I nodded.

"Great." He playfully fixed the beanie on my head and gave me a subtle wink. "Let's wing it, then."

And boy, wing we did. We started taking short steps from left to right, then from front to back. The loop was far from perfect, but it still made me smile.

Left, right.

Front, back.

Left–

"Ow!" Myles grimaced. "Babe, you just stomped on my feet."

I looked down, and flinched when I saw that my left boot was pressed over one of his sneakers.

Sorry, I signed.

He shook his head. "You're lucky I have resilient feet," he said, then twirled me once, twice, before bringing me close to him again.

I didn't remind him how his *resilient feet* had been unsuccessful at handling Oxford shoes just a couple months ago, and had ended up looking like a carnival of blisters when he'd come over to my place. He may be the sweetest guy I know, but Myles is also a man, and most men have egos – whether they like to admit it or not.

And I also didn't tell him because once he starts pouting over something, he just doesn't let up. It's very cute, but also very concerning.

Myles dipped me briefly, to which I laughed, and then we continued our left-to-right and front-to-back routine.

The couples waltzing around us weren't doing an excellent job, if I were being honest, but they most certainly were *way* better than us.

Not that it mattered to me.

Myles and I stepped to the left as the piano's harmonies continued to play, and when he tilted his head to the side *just* a little bit before looking down at me, I saw a vein shift on the right side of his neck.

Pressing myself against him further, I leaned in and kissed his cheek once, followed by his jaw, then inhaled the orange-and-cedar smell of his cologne.

We stepped to the right, and I slowly ran my lips over the vein on his neck.

Myles's head fell forward at that, so I smiled and traced the vein all the way up to the space behind his ear.

When I heard a soft gasp from him in return, I placed an open-mouthed kiss on the vein, then gently sucked on the skin next to it, making Myles whisper a curse against my neck.

I pulled back, and when our eyes met, everything around me faded. He looked at me, I looked at him, and the music drifted away. I licked my lips, and his gaze immediately dropped towards it, resulting in my head to buzz.

I realized I was breathing hard – like I'd been running instead of pretending to waltz.

Myles gripped me tighter as he blinked at me, and when I knew for sure that I couldn't wait any longer, I touched my forehead to his before signing, *Take me home*.

43.

O ur naked bodies pressed together when Rina arched into my kiss. She moaned when the tip of my cock touched her clit, and I tugged at her bottom lip when her nipples brushed against my pecs.

She tasted so good – like biscuits or cookies or something, and her skin felt hot and silk-like in my hands when I squeezed her thighs and kissed her deeper. She tangled her fingers in my hair and pulled, and when I looked down at her, I couldn't resist grinning at her flushed appearance; at her messy hair spread out unevenly on my pillows.

We'd stumbled – yeah, I know it sounds cliché, but it's true – into my condo around fifteen minutes ago, and I'd dragged Rina directly into my bedroom before stripping us both and pulling her to me so that I could kiss her. I don't remember how we'd ended up in my bed, but we had, and I'm most definitely not going to complain about it. Feeling Rina's warmth against me – unabashed and undisturbed – was maddening to me. Sensing her every reaction to my actions was kinda erotic, in a way that gave me more opportunities to give her things I knew she'd want; to do things I knew would make her tick in the sexiest of ways.

Rina moaned as I began kissing my way down to her collarbone, and when I ran my tongue over one of her pebbled nipples before taking it into my mouth, she all but rose off the bed, panting, as she looked at me.

"Lie down," I told her, then sucked on her other nipple.

She let go of a shaky breath and did as I'd asked, and I slid down a bit, letting my lips rove over her stomach.

She shivered faintly as I moved down further, sucked onto the soft skin just above her navel, kissed my way over to her hipbone, the insides of her thighs, and then, once I got to where I wanted to be, I widened her legs further and glanced at her.

She was all but staring at me – in both impatience and glazed desire. Her eyes appeared so damn dark that I could barely see the sable in them.

I bent and pressed a teasing kiss on her clit, then another, because I simply couldn't help it, and felt myself get painfully harder against the duvet.

Rina tipped her head back and hissed, so I hooked my arms under her thighs and gripped the sides of her waist before finally leaning in and tasting her in earnest.

My *God*, she was wet. Wet and *so* fucking hot on my lips. And damn if it didn't make my senses go haywire. I was greedy for it – for *her*.

For every drop of what she had to offer.

I flattened my tongue as I swept it over the length of her, slipped it inside her once, twice, then sucked on her clit before eating her pussy proper because I was going crazy for it and didn't care if I seemed hasty about it.

Rina fisted my hair as she rode my face, widened her thighs further while her toes curled next to my elbows.

I pushed my tongue inside her again, curved it slightly so that I could hit that spot *just so*, and within seconds, I had her coming all over my lips.

I placed light kisses on her slightly sweaty skin as I made my way up to her again, and when she ran her long nails over my abs before giving me a smile, my stomach clenched in response to it.

I want you, she signed, and her eyes darkened further.

"Fucking take me, then; I'm yours," I said a little too eagerly, which made her laugh.

I joined her, and then watched as she stretched up before opening my nightstand drawer. She deftly pulled a condom out from inside it, unwrapped it, then grabbed my cock with her free hand.

"*Jesus,*" I hissed as I fell forward a bit, and our noses touched. "Rina, please."

She tilted her head a little to the right as she squeezed me and stroked me up and down at a steady but painfully slow pace.

I fisted the ends of the pillow under her head. "*Rina...*"

Our eyes met, and the smug upward turn of her lips told me she was enjoying this too much.

"Put the damn condom on, you torturous woman," I rasped. "I fucking want inside of you."

She swallowed at my words, then slowly slid the condom on me before lifting her hips towards mine.

I wrapped a hand around myself and stroked once, and when she looked down at it, I lowered myself and pushed into her in a single thrust.

Her moan echoed throughout the otherwise silent room, but I muffled it with a kiss, and grabbed her wrists before pinning them above her head.

Rina wrapped her legs around my waist and put pressure on my back with the heels of her feet, which made me chuckle.

"So eager," I whispered against her lips, then pulled out entirely before slamming into her again, and again. "You like teasing me, but don't like waiting when it comes to you?" I pulled out, then thrust in again. "Un-fucking-fair, don't you think?"

She made an urgent sound and tried to free her hands, but I held onto them tighter.

I felt a bead of sweat trickle down the back of my right ear as I rolled my hips and continued to move in and out of her. "Want me to go faster?" I asked her.

She nodded while breathing hard.

I bit down on her lower lip before kissing her once. "Clench that tight pussy around me, then," I all but ordered.

She did, and I pushed myself further inside her.

Fuck, she felt so good this deep.

223

"Harder," I panted as I pounded into her. "Clench harder."

She obeyed, and let out a sharp gasp when I fucked her faster.

"Clench again," I told her, because I *loved* the constraint it resulted in.

She did, and then took my lips in a kiss that was both bruising and intoxicating.

I pumped into her quicker when I felt my spine stiffen and balls tighten, and Rina kept kissing me as she moved her hips with mine.

I groaned into her mouth as my orgasm hit me in a blinding wave, and her wrists strained against my hold as she jerked under me and came all over my pulsing cock.

This feeling – one of letting everything go and trusting this woman with everything I have and was – was the peak of my existence. I didn't even think twice before handing myself over to her. I never would, and I knew for a fact that she, too, would take the leap with me whenever our hearts desired; whenever we felt like blocking out the world just so it could be the two of us.

Because really, it would *always* be just the two of us; there were no questions in my mind about it. And, even if everything around us faltered or winked out, I knew for sure that Rina and I never would.

44.

Carina

"**D**ude, that's great! She's gonna love it," came Taron's booming voice.

"Scream a little louder, why don't you?" Myles chastised him.

Taron scowled. "I wasn't screaming; I was *excited*," he fired back. "But now I just wanna kick you in the balls."

There was a pause as Myles shifted on his feet, then responded to Taron by saying, "Don't you *always* wanna do that, though?"

Paul and Greg shook their heads at the brothers, and I narrowed my right eye against the peephole as I continued to watch the four of them talking just below the stairs of my house.

I'd opened the door enough so that their voices could filter in, but not enough for them to catch me spying on them like a slightly bloated and short version of Natasha Romanoff.

I'd come running down to the living room a few minutes ago – hair still wet and dripping water down to my t-shirt – when I'd gotten the *Knock-knock* text from Myles. But, as I'd made to open the door to usher him and the others inside, I'd heard him asking Taron to keep his mouth shut because he '*didn't want me to hear anything about it yet*'. That bit had, of course, piqued my curiosity, and I'd hence decided to investigate the scenario before announcing myself to the guys.

Avô was at the shop, so I didn't have to worry about him finding me leaned over the door, and most probably coming to the conclusion that I've finally ended up losing every last one of my marbles.

225

Small mercy, if you ask me.

"It looks really cool, man," Greg told Myles. "She's going to love it."

"Yeah?" Myles shifted again, and this time, I could see a slim rectangular jewelry box in his hands.

"Yeah," Greg said, and Paul nodded in agreement.

Myles scratched the back of his head and smiled sheepishly. "I've never really given anything like this to someone, so I'm a bit worried," he admitted. "What if she's not into this kinda stuff? I mean, I've never really seen her with one, so I guess getting this for her was a gamble of sorts."

I needed to know what was in that box, *stat*.

"Worried that she'll think you're trying to keep her roped in by giving her expensive shit?" Taron quipped.

Paul laughed, Greg snorted, and Myles kicked Taron in the shin.

"Can you not be a dipshit?" Myles asked him.

Taron smirked. "I was genuinely happy about it until you all but ordered me to keep my voice down."

"You're a humanoid megaphone with grizzly bear similarities; of course I asked you to keep your damn voice down. I don't want Rina to find out about this," he waved the box in front of his face, "before I can surprise her with it."

Okay, now I *really* wanted to know what was in that box.

A watch?

A pen?

A necklace?

No, wait…

A WAND?!

"You two belong in a damn circus," Greg said to Myles and Taron, pulling me out of my dream fest. "Fucking clowns, both of you."

"Screw you," Myles said to him, and Taron flipped him off.

Myles then glanced at his watch, and my eyes landed on the box in his left hand. Whatever was inside of it was clearly for me, and because I was an impatient bitch, my brain automatically began coming up with ways to attain it.

Paul struck up a conversation about some potential client who wanted to sign *Reyes Constructions* to design their new home in Anthon Avenue, and Myles immediately got swept into it.

I knew it was now or never, so I whipped open the door at lightning speed, ran down the stairs, and tapped Myles on the shoulder. When he turned around, I grabbed the box from his hand and practically leaped back into the house. My heart was pounding; my entire body was thrumming with adrenaline.

I heard Myles curse, and it was followed by laughter from Taron and the others, and the former's hurried footsteps.

"Rina, stop!" he called out. "Stop!"

I grinned and looked back briefly, then shook my head before running further into the living room.

"I was going to surprise you with it, goddamn it!" Myles's footsteps got closer. "Don't steal my fucking thunder, Rina!"

I chuckled and swiveled in order to take a U turn of the room, then started running straight ahead.

"Stop shaking that ass!" he groaned as he continued to chase me. "It's distracting me!"

I wasn't exactly doing it on purpose, but because he'd pointed it out, I did put a sway in my hips as I bypassed the stairs and rushed further into the room.

Myles groaned again. "God, that ass will be my demise," he all but panted. "I can't wait to taste it later."

I wasn't sure whether he'd said that to throw me off, or whether he actually meant it. Either way, I didn't let that comment get to me.

My heart was thrashing against my chest when I reached the leather couch – *Avô's* couch – in the middle of the living room, before stopping behind it. My legs were burning; sweat was trickling down my temples, neck, and spine.

My breaths were icy in my throat, my nose, and when Myles stopped on the other side, just as out of breath as me, I wiggled the box at him.

"Give it back," he all but ordered.

I shook my head again, and took a step back when he marched over to me in just two long strides.

Oops.

His eyes gleamed as he looked down at me. "Give it back, Rina," he whispered.

No, I signed.

He bunched the side of my t-shirt and pulled me to him, and I stumbled against him before raising a brow at him.

"You really love working me up, don't you?" he asked slowly.

I rose on my tiptoes and brushed my lips against his. I didn't kiss him proper; merely touched his mouth faintly in a way I knew would affect him just the same.

He smirked as he shifted, then gently pressed his hips against my stomach.

"I'm going to fuck that smugness out of you tonight," he promised, his gaze dark. "And my God, I'm going to cherish every damn second of it."

I swallowed, and felt heat rise between my legs.

"You want that, don't you?" Myles asked, then ran his free hand over the side of my waist, up to my left breast, my collarbone, and then…

He snatched the box from me before I could even blink. "Gotcha," he said around a grin.

Dammit.

I scowled and shoved at his chest. *Asshole*, I signed, to which he chuckled.

"I meant every word, though," he told me sincerely, then gave me a chaste kiss. "I want that ass, and I want that pussy – so bad that it's driving me nuts right now."

I pressed my thighs together when I felt an ache between them. *Then take me*, I signed.

He shook his head. "I have to work, remember?"

I clicked my tongue. *Then show me what is in the box*, I told him.

He pursed his lips. "No?"

I glared at him, but he kept his expression neutral as he stared back at me.

I huffed in annoyance, then decided to just let it go as I made to walk away from him.

I'd only just passed by him, though, when he grabbed my wrist to stop me.

A small smile tugged at my lips. *Gotcha*, I wanted to sign to him, but instead, I maintained the anger on my face as I let him drag me back towards him.

Myles frowned at me when our eyes met. "I didn't mean to upset you," he said. "I'm sorry, babe."

I cupped the sides of his face and kissed him. *I am not upset*, I signed. Because really, I *wasn't*.

He sighed. "Good." He then playfully tapped the box he was holding, against my forehead. "I'd planned on taking you to dinner tonight before giving this to you, but..." He opened the box and turned it around so that I could see what was inside. "Here you go; I hope you like it."

I looked down, and gasped when I saw what Myles had gotten me.

It was a flat, fluorite-studded bracelet made of white gold. It was chain-like, and glinted brightly against the sunlight streaming into the house through the slightly open kitchen window.

I licked my lips and looked at Myles. *It is beautiful*, I signed. *Very beautiful.*

He smiled. "I'm so happy you like it," he said. "I was worried you'd think I was being a materialistic bastard by giving you something pricey, but I'm glad you don't. Here," he took the bracelet out of the box and handed it to me, "flip it over."

I ran my thumbs over the flat fluorite pieces etched onto the front of the bracelet, then turned it around, only to suck in a breath after reading what was carved on the smooth surface of the jewelry.

YOU ARE MY SANCTUM.

My eyes stung as I brought them back to Myles, who was still smiling at me.

I love you so much, I signed.

"And I love you," he answered, then took the bracelet from me. "Now, let's see if this even fits you." He dangled it between us and winked at me.

I gawked at him. *Seriously?* I signed, then pushed at his chest before stomping away from him.

What an asshole.

"Rina!" There was regret in his voice, but it did nothing to soothe my anger. "Baby, I'm sorry!"

I heard him following me as I raced up the stairs and into the storeroom.

"Rina, wait," he urged. "*Please.*"

I walked into the room, my back to him.

"Rina! Listen to me, you stubborn woman. The flooring in there is fucked; slow *down. Please.*"

I put my left foot forward, but then set it down so that I could turn around and face him.

And that's when it happened; that's when I realized the full scope of Myles's warning.

I swiveled, not realizing that my sneaker was pressed next to a jagged piece of tile. My body shifted, but my foot refused to, and I felt a sharp *crack* in my right ankle. The pain that shot through me right after that – it was *so* fucking blinding that I wanted to throw up.

I heard Myles calling my name, but it sounded more like an echo in my buzzing ears as my body fell forward against the debris-strewn floor. I managed to bring my hands in front of me, so my palms ended up taking the full impact, and not my face.

Scared – I was *so* scared. And hurt. And…

My God, *everything was hurting*. Every damn *inch* of me.

I looked at Myles, who was standing at the room's entrance, completely ashen-faced, his eyes wide.

I sniffed, and realized that hot tears were sliding down my cheeks and onto the harsh ground. I tried to shift again, but before I could sign something to him, or even make a gesture of some sort, something heavy fell on me from behind. Fell strongly against my back, my thighs.

My already broken ankle.

That's the moment it ripped out of me: a scream so sudden, so loud, that it not only shocked Myles further, but also threatened to pull me under against the weight of my pain, and of my fear.

How the hell had things gotten so out of hand in a matter of seconds?

Just…*how*?

45.

Her scream – it was so achingly guttural that it stunned me in place. It was a sound so foreign that I could do nothing, *feel* nothing but its echo in my ears as I looked at her.

And, when our eyes met, when her tears slid down her flushed cheeks, I saw the fear, affliction, struggle, and slight confusion on her face, that not only made me stumble forward a bit, but also made me want to tear through everything I was enduring – deep inside my clawing chest.

But it was when her lips shook as she tried to signal something to me through her trembling hands, that I snapped out of my brief numb-fest; that I actually realized what had happened.

She'd tripped on a broken tile, and the faulty bookshelf had fallen on her before I could stop it, or comprehend what the fuck was even happening.

A sob hitched out of Rina and reverberated across the low-lit room, and my stomach began to clench; my palms began to sweat.

And my heart – it might as well have stopped beating; my lungs may as well have stopped drawing in air. But it wasn't like I cared anymore, not when *she* was suffering…

46.

Myles

"**W**hat the fuck happened?" Taron asked frantically as him, Greg, and Paul rushed into the room. "We were outside and heard a scream." They stopped, though, and stared at me on my knees next to Rina, with my phone to my ear, and her stuck under the bookshelf.

"Jesus Christ," Greg whispered. All color had drained from his face.

"Can you please send them over as fast as you can," I pleaded with the 911 operator. "*Please.*" I was shaking, but I didn't give a fuck.

"Sir, our paramedics and rescue squad should reach you within two minutes. The teams closest to you have already been dispatched. Now, I can only ask you to relax and stay close to your girlfriend, but kindly do *not* touch anything. Can you do that for me?"

I nodded, then said, "Yeah. Yes, yeah." I disconnected the call and slid my phone into my back pocket before gently placing a hand over Rina's.

"Baby…" I almost choked on the word, and she turned her head before weakly twining her muddy fingers with mine.

"Myles…" Paul walked towards me. "Bro, what happened?" He looked shaken to the core, and rightfully so.

I gave the three of them a quick rundown of the accident, and felt Rina's hand twitch in mine once I was done.

Taron and Greg marched over to the fallen bookshelf, but I whipped my head at them before they could touch it. "Don't!"

They halted and looked confusingly at me.

"Her ankle is most probably broken," I said to them, then swallowed. "If you lift the bookshelf with the wrong amount of force, there's a strong chance it'll worsen the injury."

Their faces paled as they blinked at Rina, then at me, just as the sound of blaring sirens echoed in the street outside.

"I'll go get them," Paul said, then ran downstairs.

"I'm right here, okay?" I told Rina. "The rescue team will get you out, but I'm right *here*." I squeezed her hand. "I'm here, alright?"

She whimpered softly, and I felt a lump form in my throat at that weak response.

Paul rushed back in, followed by three firefighters and two paramedics.

I reluctantly let go of Rina's hand and got to my feet, and all but stumbled at the sudden heaviness in my head.

"Whoa, hey." Taron grabbed me from behind. "Myles, hey. You okay?"

I nodded. I felt like I was floating; I felt fucking weightless.

I watched helplessly as the firefighters used cables to steady the bookshelf before slowly lifting it off of Rina, while the paramedics sat on either side of her, checking her pulse first, and then her head for any possible injuries.

Taron and the guys looked at me, and I knew what they were thinking. They didn't even have to voice the words, because I knew exactly what they wanted to tell me: We should have discarded the faulty bookshelf and started working on the flooring instead of wasting time on something we knew was a huge liability, to begin with.

And it *had* proven true to its nature, hadn't it? It had ended up hurting the *one* person I didn't want getting hurt by it.

My eyes landed on Rina again. She wasn't moving…

Why the fuck wasn't she moving?

I made to go to her, heart in my clogged throat, but Taron grabbed my arm and pulled me back. "Wait."

I tried to jerk him off, but his grip on me tightened.

"Myles."

I glared at him. "Let me *go*."

His expression was crestfallen as he held my face between his hands. "Let them do their job," he said softly. "She'll be *fine*."

My jaw tingled, and my eyes stung. "It's–"

"No," he cut me off. "It's *not* your fault. I know what you're thinking; I know what's got you this rattled, but no, Myles, *none* of this is your fault."

I was shaking again. Sweating, too. "I cracked that stupid joke, and she got upset wi–"

"Don't." Taron's jaw hardened. "Don't do that right now, because you and I both know it won't help – not one bit. Carina will be just fine, and then, none of this will matter." He touched his forehead to mine. "I love you, and I want you to keep your wits about you today. Tell me you can do that."

I licked my dry lips as I nodded. "Yeah, I can do that."

"Good," came Greg's voice, and when I looked at him, he slid the jewelry box into my hoodie pocket before giving me a faint smile.

Paul placed a hand on my shoulder in silent support.

"She's lost consciousness; gone into shock," one of the paramedics announced. "We need to get her to *Med* ASAP."

The four of us turned to Rina.

She wasn't *moving…*

"We have a steady pulse, don't worry," the other paramedic said to me when I ran towards Rina. The bookshelf had been taken off her, thank God, but her ankle…

I sucked in a breath. They'd wrapped it in some sort of a cast, but still, it looked crooked and…broken.

I took half a step back when the rescue team helped the paramedics in getting Rina on a stretcher, and they then began carrying her out of the room and down the stairs.

Her eyes were closed, but she was breathing.

Thank *fuck* she was breathing.

"Hey." Taron tapped my back. "You go in with Carina. I'll call Miguel and the others."

I hadn't even remotely thought about Miguel, or any of Rina's friends, for that matter.

I swallowed and nodded to my brother. "Thanks, man."

"*Go*," he said.

With another nod at him, Paul, and Greg, I ran out and followed the emergency team to the ambulance.

47.

Carina

White lights – they were so blinding that I just couldn't open my eyes, even though I wanted to.

I inhaled, and a sharp smell of something I couldn't place, burned my nostrils.

I could barely feel my right leg; I could barely think straight against the throbbing pain in my ankle.

I was moving… No, I was *being* moved. Rushed, more like. There were noises around me, coming from every other direction. My head was hurting, and my throat was dry.

I felt a rush of warmth on my left hand, and then, all-too-familiar calluses brushed my skin. Those fingers I knew so well gripped mine.

"Rina…" I heard his voice, the ache and fear in it. "Rina…"

I tried to open my eyes, but failed, and then his touch was gone, and I felt so fucking empty without it.

I felt like I was drifting, gravitating.

And maybe I was, because I have no idea what was happening, or what happened next.

There was slumber, and there was pain. I chose the former and let it pull me under.

48.

Someone placed a firm hand on my shoulder and shook me a little. My eyelids fluttered seconds after I sensed the touch, and I yawned before opening my eyes and rubbing my hands over my face.

"Incoming," Taron whispered a warning in my ear.

My attention went to the waiting room's entrance, and I let go of a long breath when I saw Miguel and the others making their way over to me.

The few people in the room looked on in silence as Daniel and the crew all but crowded the otherwise vacant area.

"Where is she?" Miguel demanded.

I stood, feeling a little out of it despite the coffee Taron had forced me to drink a few minutes ago, and said to Miguel, "In the OR."

He paled. "She's *where*?"

"Excuse me, sir," the guy at the reception desk cut in. "Could you please keep it down a bit. You're in a hospital."

Miguel glared at him, then turned his icy gaze to me. "She's being *operated*?"

I clenched my jaw and glanced at the others behind him. Daniel, Cruz, Ash, Dave, Remi, and Simran – they were all present, and all six of them looked exactly how I felt: heartbroken and terrified.

"I'm talking to *you*, boy," Miguel hissed.

Paul and Greg walked into the room with steaming cups of coffee in their hands, but when they saw Miguel and the others, they muttered something about getting more coffee for everyone before heading back to the cafeteria downstairs.

I looked at Miguel, and felt my anger stir. "*Yes*, she's being operated," I finally said to him. "She broke a bone, so they had to perform an ORIF in order to mend it."

"With whose consent?" he asked.

"Her own," I told him curtly. "She signed the consent form a few minutes before they took her to the OR."

A nurse had come in and given me a copy of it, signed by Rina and the surgeon who'd be performing the surgery on her, and had told me that Rina's vitals were looking great, and that she was set to be out of the OR in under two hours.

"*Bullshit*," Miguel hissed, then shoved me. "Liar!" His eyes shone with unshed tears as he stared me down.

I stumbled, but Taron caught me before I could fall.

"Miguel!" Daniel pulled him back. "What the fuck is wrong with you?"

Miguel pointed a finger at me. "He's the reason things have gone downhill since the last few months." He made to shove me again, but Daniel *and* Cruz held him back. "He's the reason my Carina is hurt!"

I know I should be shocked by his audacity, but I wasn't. There was an ache in my gut that stopped me from caring about the man in front of me; about everything he'd said to me, or about me.

"Lay a hand on him again, and I'll forget my damn manners, asshole," Taron cautioned.

"*Taron*," I said his name with a bite as I found my balance. "Don't."

Miguel gritted his teeth at my brother. "How dare y–"

"*Avô*, stop," Remi urged. "You're not being rational right now."

Miguel looked at him, looked at the agony on his face, and something in him shifted.

He nodded and straightened himself.

Ash walked over to me. "Hey." She squeezed my hands. "Can you tell me what happened?" Her voice was thick with obvious emotions, and her eyes were misty.

I sighed and told her about the ridiculous fucking joke I'd made, which had ended up upsetting Rina, about the broken flooring in the storeroom, about how Rina had ended up tripping after she twisted her ankle against a broken tile, and then about how the bookshelf had fallen on her. I recollected everything loud enough so that the others could hear me as well, because I really didn't have the strength to repeat myself over and over again.

Ash's brows were pinched together by the time I was done, and she squeezed my hands again before saying, "It wasn't your fault."

"Wasn't it?"

She shook her head. "*No*, Myles."

"You couldn't have known something like this would happen," added Dave.

"But I could have stopped myself from making that comment," I argued.

"You didn't mean to offend her, Myles," Ash added. "It was a damn joke, not an intentional jab."

I wiped a hand over my jaw. "And what about the bookshelf?" I asked. "I knew it was trouble, but I still forced myself to keep working on it."

"Maybe that's true, but had you predicted that Rina would unknowingly put her foot on the tile that was severely broken?" asked Cruz. "Were you already aware that she'd end up falling, or that the bookshelf would decide to come down on her at the exact same moment she fell?"

I clenched and unclenched my hands as I glanced between the six of them.

"This shit was supposed to happen, Myles, and it did," Simran said. "Blaming yourself for it is only going to gnaw at your conscience."

"How long has she been in the OR for?" Daniel asked.

"An hour now," I told him, then dragged my fingers through my already mused hair.

"Hey." He placed his hands on my shoulders and looked me in the eyes. "You and I both know you're stronger than this," he told me, then gave me a reassuring smile before taking a step back. "So get that slouchy fucking look off your goddamn chiseled face and get your shit together, because once she's out of surgery, Carina is going to need you – now more than ever."

I gave him a grateful nod, just as Miguel hissed, "Like *hell* I'm letting him go anywhere near her ever again."

I bunched my jaw as I sneered at him. "But it's unfortunate for you, though, because it's not *you* who gets to decide that," I told him.

His face was red with anger as he took a step towards me. "You–"

"Careful." Cruz put a hand on Miguel's chest, then very gently pushed him back. "Do anything stupid, and you'll lose me as an employee." He raised a brow. "*And* as a friend."

"You're siding with *him*?"

"It's never been about sides, *Avô*," Simran said to him. "It's about what – *who* – makes Carina happy. And we all know Myles has done that in spades ever since the two of them have started dating."

I just stood there like an idiot, watching all these people who'd become my friends in the past few months, defend me without hesitation, and my chest felt…full, I guess. Filled with gratitude and respect for each one of them.

Miguel appeared flustered as everyone agreed with Simran.

Taron nudged me subtly. "How's it feel to one-up the grandpa?" he asked softly.

I managed to crack a barely-there smile. "Shut up," I whispered.

"Excuse me?"

The nine of us turned to the entrance, where the nurse from before was standing and looking around the room.

"Myles Reyes?" she asked.

I waved at her. "Here."

"Ah." She gave me a smile. "I just wanted to let you know that Carina's surgery was a success. The doctors are checking her vitals at the moment, just to be sure, and then we'll move her to the PACU."

I let go of a relieved breath, and felt my shoulders slump as an invisible pressure lifted off of them.

My Rina was okay.

"Is she awake?" Miguel asked the nurse.

"Yes, but she's had Propofol, so she's a bit woozy. It'll take her a few minutes to get a grip on everything."

"Can we meet her yet?" he pushed.

She gave him a reassuring smile. "Like I said: the doctors are doing a routine checkup on her at the moment, but once they're done and everything is up to the mark, I don't see why not."

Miguel sighed and slumped onto one of the cushioned chairs. "Thank you."

The nurse nodded at him, then looked at me. "She asked for you when she woke up just now," she said, and gave me a faint wink. "I told her you were outside waiting. I'll come get you once the doctors are done with her, but I thought I'd let you know that the surgery went well, and that she's going to make a full recovery." With that, she turned around and walked away.

Greg and Paul sauntered into the room with two trays full of Styrofoam cups brimming with coffee, and as they began passing them around to Taron and the others, I sat back down in the chair and scrubbed my hands over my face for the second time in a span of twenty minutes.

Rina was *okay*.

And thank *fuck* for that, because I sure would have lost every last shred of myself if she wasn't.

49.

Carina

There were so many of them crowded around the small, air-conditioned room. I could barely think straight; *see* straight.

I was lying on a bed, with a couple of not-so-soft pillows under my head. A couple more were placed beneath my right leg to keep it propped up in order to avoid any sort of swelling.

My mind was a dizzy mess due to the fresh bout of throbbing ache in my ankle, the pain meds I'd been given after the surgery, the beeping monitors on my left, and the suffocating smell of Iodoform clogging my nostrils.

When I'd woken up minutes after being brought to the hospital, the doctor and nurses had checked my vitals, put me on an IV, and informed me of my injuries. The orthopedic assigned to my case had then told me about the ORIF, and how they'd have to perform the procedure due to the severity of my fracture. They'd asked for my consent over the same, made me sign a form, and then whisked me into the OR. I don't remember much of anything after that, only that I'd been transferred to a PACU room, and my vitals had again been administered before I'd been asked to rest.

I blinked, but still felt a bit out of it.

"*Pequena?*" came *Avô's* voice.

I blinked a second time, and my vision finally decided to focus on him.

He smiled down at me, but his expression was one full of concern. "*Eu estava com tanto medo; tão... apavorado. Eu não sabia o que pensar, ou fazer, ou...*" I was so scared; so...terrified. I didn't know what to think, or do, or...

I'm okay now, I signed.

My right arm was slightly numb because of the IV drip that was attached on the forearm, so I had to use my left hand to Sign things. The words that required both my hands for it, though, had to be spelled out instead.

"I wouldn't say you're okay," *Avô* told me, then gave me a stern look. "You still have weeks of recovery ahead of you." He walked closer and sat in the chair next to my bed, then leaned in to place a kiss on my right brow. "The doctor said I can take you home in a couple of hours. I've decided to let Remi handle the shop while you get better. I want to be there for you when you need me."

I don't know if it were his words, or simply the idea of going back home that made my chest heavy, and not in the way that was comfortable. But still, I gave him a faint nod, and then glanced around the room until my eyes landed on Myles.

He was standing near the far corner of the room. His hands were in his jeans pockets, and as he lifted his head, our gazes met, and the look on his face broke me, fucking *shattered* me.

It seemed like he was holding something in – holding *himself* together by some invisible thread.

"You know, Cruz almost shat his pants when he got Taron's call earlier," Daniel said to me, so I diverted my attention to him instead.

Cruz grunted his disapproval at Daniel's joke, while the others all laughed.

Daniel gave me a pained smile. "I was out of my mind with worry, Carina," he told me, then bent to kiss my forehead. "But I'm so relieved you're okay." He clicked his tongue. "I'm surprised I haven't thrown a tantrum yet, despite all the stress I've been harboring for the last hour or so."

I chuckled. *I love you*, I signed.

His eyes glimmered as he nodded at me. "And I you, *pequena*." The way he said the term made me laugh a little, and as he stepped back, Cruz and the others walked over to me.

"I hope you know how strong you are, kid," Cruz told me. "You went through the first half of this shit-storm; now you just gotta win over the other half." He briefly placed a hand on the top of my head before stepping away.

"I was so fucking scared, babe," Ash said as she sat next to me on the bed, then kissed me on the cheek. "You don't ever get to do that to me again, you hear me?"

Sorry, I told her, but she shook her head.

"You don't have to apologize; just…just be careful. I'll come over to your place later, alright?"

Okay, I signed, then glanced at Myles again.

He was still standing near the damn corner, as if awaiting his turn or something. And I don't know why, but that hurt me even more.

Remi and the others squeezed my hand, gave me more kisses, and promised to check in on me, and once they were done, I looked at Daniel and gestured very subtly at the PACU door.

He smirked and inclined his head, then clapped his hands with frightening enthusiasm.

"Alright, people, let's clear the fuck out!" he hollered, and I was worried he'd get dragged out by a nurse before he could actually clear the room for me.

Avô glared at him. "I am going nowhere, thank you very much."

Daniel raised a brow. "Oh, you *are*." He looked at Cruz. "Be a dear and eliminate this fragile man from the room, please."

I choked on a laugh, even though my head was still a mush, while the rest snickered freely.

Paul, Greg, Ash, and Dave waved at me before leaving the room, just as Cruz sighed and walked over to *Avô*. "Let's go, Miguel."

Avô tapped his cane on the white floor and shifted in the chair. "No, thank you."

Cruz dragged a hand over his face. "Don't force me to lift you, man, because you know I will if you continue to behave like this."

Avô's eyes widened. "I beg your *pardon*?"

245

"Just get your ass up and *leave*, Miguel," Taron said. "Or I won't hesitate one bit in helping Cruz on his offer." He flashed his teeth at *Avô*.

"Hooligans," *Avô* muttered. "Utter nuisances."

I placed a hand over his, and when he looked at me, I signed, *Please listen to Daniel. I need a moment with Myles.*

Something flashed in his eyes at that, which pissed me off a little.

After the offer he'd made Myles, asking to pay him to break up with me, and Myles having refused him, *Avô* honestly had no right to act this way. I did understand where he was coming from, but it still didn't mean he could get so damn bossy whenever he wanted to.

He tapped his cane on the floor again as he glanced between Myles and I. Then, with a huff, he got to his feet and let Remi and Simran walk him out of the room.

Cruz and Daniel were the last to leave, and once the door clicked shut behind them, I exhaled slowly and faced Myles.

Come here, I signed.

He finally moved from where he'd been standing, and dragged himself over to me. Once he reached my bed, though, he fell on his knees, put an arm over my stomach, hid his face in the space between my breasts, and began…crying. *Sobbing*, more like. His breaths hitched every other second; his shoulders shook against me. His tears seeped through my hospital gown, and his voice was hoarse as he kept saying, "I'm so relieved, Rina. I'm *so* fucking relieved. I'm sorry…I'm so, so sorry."

I swallowed and cupped the back of his head with my left hand before running my fingers through his hair.

"Rina…" Myles cried harder, and the sound of his agony reverberated around the chilly room, making my own tears fall.

"I was *terrified*," he whispered, then held me tighter. "I was going *crazy*." His shoulders shook again.

I tried to clear my blurry vision by blinking a few times, but stopped when it didn't work.

The tip-tip-tap echo of my tears hitting the pillows merged with Myles's sniffs, and it was a shared symphony of solace that I both relished and appreciated.

He pressed a long kiss on the swell of my left breast, then moved back a bit reluctantly.

I looked at him then, at the tears splattered on his beautiful face, and at the relief in his eyes.

Sit, I signed.

He rose, settled in the chair to my left, and swiped the sleeve of his hoodie over his cheeks.

I should have listened to you when you warned me, I told him. *I should not have acted so foolishly.*

He shook his head. "No." He held my hand briefly and kissed my knuckles. "I shouldn't have made that stupid fucking comment. It was careless and cruel of me. But despite that, I failed to stop you from entering the storeroom. Hell, I all but let this happen to you because I was too bullheaded about keeping the damn bookshelf and pushing back the flooring process so that I could figure out a way to fix the shelf."

It was *my* turn to shake my head.

Stop it, I signed. *Don't do this to yourself. We could not have predicted any of this, but I'm still sorry I didn't take your warning seriously.*

I had to spell certain words very slowly, because I knew Myles still struggled to understand signed alphabets.

He sniffed and once again took my hand in his. This time, though, he held it between both of his and rubbed the pads of his thumbs over my fingers as he looked at me with slightly furrowed brows.

"Move in with me," he said out of the blue, then squeezed my hand.

I sucked in a breath as I searched his face, and the honest eagerness I found there warmed something in my chest.

"I know it's crazy of me to ask this of you," he continued, "but I want you with me 24-fucking-7, Rina. I'm tired of stealing moments with you; tired of looking over my shoulder every time I kiss you or touch you." He swallowed. "You and I both know that after today, your grandfather won't even let me step into your house, let alone *work* there. And I can't fucking have that; I can't not see you every day. It'll drive me *mad*." He sniffed again. "Also, I wanna be there for you while you heal. You guys keep telling me that what happened to you today isn't my fault, and maybe it isn't, but I still want to make sure I can help you however I can when it comes to your recovery. I wanna be there for you from now on – for everything."

I brought our joint hands close and kissed the inside of his wrists.

He was right, wasn't he? Once I went home, *Avô* would do everything in his power to keep Myles away from me. And, with my initial hesitation towards going back there, paired with the way *Avô* has been behaving with Myles ever since he's learnt about our relationship, my answer to Myles's request was pretty much obvious.

Because the idea of getting to *live* with him – yeah, that sounded absolutely *perfect* to me.

I smiled as I pulled my hand away from his, and when he looked at me in silent anticipation, I let go of a steady breath and signed, *Okay*.

He grinned, then – an action so lovely that it brought a spark to his eyes.

"Yeah?" he asked.

Yes, I signed.

"You sure, right?"

I chuckled. *Yes, silly*, I told him.

He laughed, then bent to kiss me, and I cupped his jaw before kissing him back.

"For a second there I thought you'd say no," he murmured against my lips. "That house holds so many memories, and for me to ask you to leave them all behind, to move in with me all of a sudden… It must've been–"

I stopped him with a kiss, and when he made a surprised sound against me, I moved back and signed, *I want to be with you. I want to make new memories*

248

with you. Memories that aren't tainted by a painful past full of loss and tragedy, but ones that are full of madness and love.

His expression softened. "Of course." He pushed my hair away from my forehead. "I'll give you anything you want, Rina. Everything I can give you, it's yours. All you have to do is ask."

What about that bracelet, then? I asked.

He chuckled and pulled a similar box out of his hoodie pocket. "This?" He then looked at it with a clenched jaw. "I was planning on returning it. This stupid piece of crap is what caused all of this." He waved the box in my direction. "Come to think of it, I should prolly burn it. Damn it to hell."

I clicked my tongue and wiggled my wrist in front of him, letting him know where *I* thought the bracelet should go.

He narrowed his eyes at me. "No."

Yes, I signed.

"Nope."

Yup.

He stared at me for a while, hoping I'd change my mind.

I didn't, of course.

"*Fine.*" He sighed, then opened the box before pulling the bracelet out. He glared at it for a second too long, then gently fastened it around my left wrist. "There you go."

The chain shone against the pale lights in the room, making the fluorite appear slightly muted.

Pretty, I signed, then admired the bracelet again. It complemented my skin tone quite well, and fit me just as perfectly, too.

"I'm glad you're happy with it." I was, but *he* didn't seem to match my enthusiasm. So, I decided to move to a different topic.

How will we get my things from the house without Avô going ballistic on us? I asked him.

He grinned slowly. "We're friends with a group of *very* determined and insanely intimidating individuals, remember? I think they'll do a perfectly fine job of retrieving your stuff from the clutches of your hungry-for-blood grandfather."

I laughed, and moaned softly when he leaned in and kissed me on the lips.

"That's it; keep that smile on your face – *always*," Myles said. "I never want it to dim. I never wanna see your tears; never wanna see you hurt. Once was enough to scar me, and I promise I'll never, *ever* let it happen again." He parted my lips and ran his tongue over the roof of my mouth.

I tangled my fingers in his hair and kissed him back – despite the dizziness in my head, the pulsing pain shooting through my leg, and the annoying beep-beep-beep of the monitor grating at my nerves.

Because none of it really mattered, not when it was just the two of us.

50.

I swiped my slightly cold fingers over my eyes before slowly blinking them open. The insistent hum of the air conditioner hit my ears as I yawned behind a hand, and the crisp morning light touched my face every so often as it peeked through the swaying grey curtain in front of the window to the right.

I pressed my lips together to stop myself from groaning at the burning pain in my ankle, then lifted my stiff back a little before shifting it this way and that to give it some movement.

Myles had gotten an elevation pillow for me in order to prevent my right leg from swelling while the ankle healed, and, because it'd only been 3 days since my surgery, adjusting to the comfortable yet massive pillow, even while in bed, was still a little difficult.

Avô had been livid when I'd told him that I was moving in with Myles. He'd protested, of course, but had had to give up when I'd stayed adamant on my decision.

He'd also been surprisingly less stubborn than expected when Daniel and Ash had gone over to the house to pack my things up 2 days ago, and I knew this was his way, however unconventional, of telling me that he was okay with me having moved out; that he was okay with the idea of me living with Myles. It was a small step forward, but still one I was glad for.

I knew Myles was just as shocked by *Avô's* change of behavior, but he didn't exactly react to it, or even acknowledge his confusion out loud.

But, speaking of things he *had* done…

My God, he'd been a *dream*. Nothing short of amazing, I'll say. He'd done everything to make me feel at ease; to make things simpler for me in his condo.

The squad had helped him with my stuff, sure, but it'd been *him* who'd done most of the arranging and organizing, whilst also looking after me.

He'd decided to clear out some space in his office so that he could install some racks for all my books and book merches.

He'd taken up a new housing project for a family that'd recently moved to Chicago and wanted to get their new apartment renovated, but had chosen to stay by my side instead of going to work himself. Taron and the crew were looking after the whole thing, and I knew my guy better than to argue with him over something that involved both me *and* his job.

Because I knew he'd always pick me, no matter what.

Seriously, Myles was a *dream* – perfect in every way that mattered to me.

He stirred, and then began mumbling something as he pressed himself closer to me. Even in his sleep, his arm around my waist tightened, which made me smile.

I turned my head so that I could look at him, and smiled wider as my eyes roamed over him.

His hair was a matted mess on his forehead, and his brown lashes touched the tops of his cheeks when his lids twitched a couple of times. He once more mumbled something I couldn't understand, and his bare chest brushed my left shoulder when he again moved closer to me.

This was the best part of living with him: getting to kiss him good night before bed, and then waking up next to him every morning. It was a routine I knew I'd cherish forever, and also one I'd never get tired of.

Sunlight again filtered into the room through the closed glass window, and illuminated Myles's side profile as he pressed his head further against his pillow.

I chuckled, I don't know why, then leaned in, pressed a soft kiss on his brow, and touched my nose to his before closing my eyes again.

51.

"Alright, I'm going to put you down now," I told Rina. "You good?"

She nodded.

I bent, with her in my arms, and gently set her down on my – no, *our* – bed. "You good?" I asked again.

She nodded a second time, so I slowly removed my arms from under her, and then very lightly placed both my hands under her right calf. "Straighten your left leg," I said to her, and when she did, I lifted her right leg and oh so gently placed it on the elevation pillow before looking at her. "You comfy?"

She smiled and gave me a thumbs up.

"Sure?" I confirmed.

Another thumbs up.

"Perfect." I crawled up on the bed, then lied next to her before propping my head on a fist.

It'd been 10 days since Rina had moved in with me. I'd finished adjusting her things with mine last week, and I'd even started making minor tweaks in my office for some of her other things. *Books*, mostly.

It'd been a bliss having her with me 24/7, and so far, Miguel hadn't knocked on my door and impaled me with that cane of his for stealing his granddaughter from him, so I guess I could count my blessings in that regard.

I cracked my neck and stretched my legs to relieve some of the stress there, then looked down at Rina, only to frown when I saw her staring at me with furrowed brows and a sullen expression on her face.

"What's wrong?" I asked.

She lifted a shoulder nonchalantly, but I saw the subtle purse of her lips, and silver lining her expressive eyes as if she was trying not to cry.

"Hey." I dragged a knuckle over her chin and leaned in a little more. "Tell me what's on your mind," I said to her. "Because there *is* something you're thinking about – I can see it. So don't even try to deny it."

She swallowed and grabbed her notebook and pencil from the nightstand.

Oh man, she was *writing* instead of signing. There really must be something that was bothering her.

She wrote something on a fresh page, then showed it to me.

I'm being a burden to you, aren't I?

I jerked my head back after reading that. "What? Why would you say that?"

I saw you stretching just now. You're tired. Looking after me day and night is taking a toll on you.

I shook my head at her. "Baby, no." I slid my right hand under her thin t-shirt just so I could feel her skin against mine, and then pressed my lips to hers. "I promise you it's nothing like that."

I don't know why she'd even thought of something like this, but I was ready to put her mind at ease, and also make sure she got the wrong idea out of her head.

You literally helped me take a dump right now, Myles.

"And?" I arched a brow at her. "I've been helping you with it for two weeks now, and I've never once minded it. Rina…" I sighed and ran my hand up and down her ribs. "I have never once thought of assisting you as a chore or an inconvenience. If anything, being there for you means more to me than you could imagine. All of this is obvious, *natural*. We live together now, babe, so these things are bound to be uncensored between us." I kissed the space between her brows. "Just because you're recovering from an injury, doesn't mean you won't shit or piss. I'm telling you it's okay, and *I'm* okay with helping you."

She looked at me, and it seemed as if she was studying me. Assessing me, maybe.

Promise? she signed.

I gave her an honest nod. "Yeah."

She began writing in her notebook again.

But if it ever gets too much for you over the course of the next few weeks, you'll tell me, right?

I sighed again as I glanced at her after reading that. "Seriously?" I chuckled when she elbowed me. "Fine." She elbowed me again, making me laugh. "*Fine.* Jesus, woman; reign in the assault. I'll tell you, okay? Even though I already know it won't get too much for me, but if that somehow *does* end up changing, I'll tell you for sure."

She toyed with the bracelet on her left wrist as she blinked at me.

I wanted to burn that thing, but she really liked it, so I couldn't exactly take it from her.

I was an absolute sucker for her, Lord have mercy.

I shifted and lied closer to her, careful not to bump the elevation pillow or her ankle.

"You're still thinking about something," I told her, then swiped the pad of my thumb over her forehead.

Just that I really don't deserve you, she wrote lazily.

I scoffed. "You know that's not true," I said. "If anything, it's *me* who doesn't deserve your sweet ass."

My ass is sweet?

I smirked. "And good enough to eat," I quipped.

She groaned and slapped my jaw, to which I laughed.

You're an asshole, she wrote.

"For stating an obvious fact?"

For trying to seduce me while I'm heavily dosed on pain meds.

"And it's a bad thing to be turned on while you're on pain meds because...?"

She rolled her eyes. *Because you can't act on what you say, and I can't let you act on what you say.*

I exhaled dramatically. "Sad, isn't it?" I mused.

She scowled at me, just as her phone *pinged* with a new message.

Rina placed the notebook and pencil back on the nightstand before grabbing her phone. She quickly read the text, then twisted the phone so that I, too, could read the message.

It was from Miguel, and it said: *Bom dia, pequena. Just checking in, as usual. I really enjoyed that audiobook you suggested last week. I finished it yesterday, and I'm curious to know your thoughts on it. How are you today? Did you take your medications? I love you.*

"When did he become so civil, knowing you're here with me and he can't do anything about it?" I told Rina.

It was more of a rhetorical question, but still one that I had no logical explanation or answers for.

She shrugged, then texted him back before showing me the response.

You should come over this weekend, Avô. We can discuss the audiobook, and you can have dinner with Myles and I. He's started cooking these days, and I have to admit: it's a pretty...interesting hobby.

I could *not* believe this woman.

"Did you really have to put me out like that?" I asked her.

She simply flashed her teeth at me.

I put my tongue to my cheek. "Just for the record: I make a pretty mean Greek salad. And meatballs. And beef sandwich. And a couple other things I can't name right now because you've left me too dumbfounded by your lack of belief in me."

She pressed her lips together. *Well, make something for me, then*, she signed. *I'm hungry.*

She spelled the word 'then' instead of signing it, so it took me a moment to understand it.

"What do you wanna eat?" I asked her.

She shrugged as she scratched the back of her hand. *Anything. Just feed me; I'm hungry.*

I raised my brows at her. "*Feed you*, huh?"

She looked about ready to strangle me as she glared up at me.

I laughed, then bent to place soft kisses on her eyelids, her cheeks, and her jaw. "You know I couldn't help it," I said against her skin.

I know, she signed, then rolled her eyes, but I still saw her smile a pretty little smile at me.

So, I erased the space between us and tasted it once, then tasted it again before saying, "Come on, let's go make some dinner."

52.

Carina

It was *so* not going well, and Myles looked like he was in complete shambles as he ran around our kitchen wearing his teal apron with the word '*Yummy*' written right over the crotch area. I had no doubt it was one of the few things Daniel had gotten him when he'd stopped by yesterday to check in on me. You'd think Myles would take the apron as a joke and toss it in the back of one of the drawers, but to see him actually wear it…

"Where's the parsley?" he muttered to himself as he sifted through various items in the pantry. "WHERE'S THE DAMN PARSLEY?!"

I grimaced when he yelled, then shifted in the chair he'd helped me in a few minutes ago.

He'd taken the elevation pillow out into the living room, placed it on a small pile of cushion pillows in front of a chair next to the kitchen counter, then lifted me in his arms before helping me settle into the chair. He'd then slowly, carefully, risen my injured leg, placed it on the pillow, and given me a swift kiss before putting that absurd apron on over his red Blackhawks tank top.

He was just too good to me, and even though I felt like I didn't deserve him, I still didn't wanna let go of him.

Selfish intentions and all, y'know.

"Aha! There you are!" He wiggled a plastic box full of chopped parsley, up in the air.

He was making *Coxinha* for the two of us. It was kind of a complex yet super delicious Brazilian dish made of chicken and flour, with a few spices and veggies in the mix, and was also one of my favorite fried snacks for when that craving for something *extra* hit me.

The kitchen was a mess, with bowls, knives, spices, and chicken packets strewn *everywhere*. A YouTube video of two women teaching how to make *Coxinha*, was playing on Myles's phone, whereas a Brazilian cookbook lay open to his right. He was scrolling through a food blog on his MacBook, clearly reading and comparing the recipe with the other two alternatives.

I tapped two spoons together to get his attention.

He whipped his head at me, eyes wide. "You need anything?"

I shook my head, then signed, *Let's order takeout.*

"What, why?" He blinked as if in a daze.

I loosely gestured at the messy kitchen counter, then at his disheveled appearance.

He glanced at himself, then returned his gaze to me again. "I don't get it."

I sighed. *You look crazy, and the kitchen looks chaotic. It's like a storm hit it.*

"Gee, babe; thanks," he muttered while scratching his head. "Your confidence is highly appreciated."

I clicked my tongue. *I just don't want you to tire yourself. We can simply order in.*

"But I wanna make dinner for you myself," Myles argued, and God, I all but melted in the chair at that. He was cute, wasn't he?

Okay, I signed. *Let me help, at least. Please?*

He exhaled loudly. "Well, thank fuck you offered, because I have no fucking idea what I'm doing."

I chuckled. *You should have just asked.*

"And hurt my pride in the process, especially after the text you sent to your grandfather?" He bent forward. "Hard pass, babe."

I laughed. *But still, here we are, are we not?*

He pursed his lips and narrowed his eyes at me. "Just help me with this so that we can eat. I'm hungry."

Sure, I told him, then dragged an empty bowl close to me, along with the glass jar containing all-purpose flour in it. *Chicken stock?* I asked Myles. I had to spell the word 'stock' because the meaning for it that I was going for, didn't exactly have a sign.

He looked at me for a beat too long, then nodded. "Right." He tapped a round pan. "It's in here. It's cooled down now, so I'll take the boiled chicken pieces out and hand over the stock to you."

Okay, I signed, and we then got into a rhythmic back-and-forth of working together.

I made a consistent dough by mixing the chicken stock, flour, some butter, and salt, while Myles minced the chicken in a mixer and prepped it for cooking the filling for the *Coxinha*.

The room soon began smelling of paprika and parsley, to which I smiled at him, then oiled my palms so that I could make small, flat circles from the dough.

Myles sautéed the mixture gently, careful not to make it mushy. He then switched off the gas, grabbed a chunk of the cooked filling, blew on it, and offered it to me.

I leaned in and wrapped my lips around his fingers, and his eyes momentarily went dark as he stared at me.

My heart began beating a little faster as I moved back and tasted the filling, and he brought his fingers to his mouth before sucking on them one by one.

It were these little moments that drove me nuts and made me fall further in love with this man. It didn't have to be anything grand, or anything remotely unique, even, because everything Myles did was special to me, no matter how big or small the act.

As I sat back in the chair and continued to taste the filling, a burst of flavor hit my tongue, making my jaw tingle.

"Good?" he asked, looking a little unsure.

I grinned and gave him a thumbs up, because Christ, the filling was fucking *awesome*.

He visibly relaxed before giving me a smile. "Great. So, now we've gotta put the filling into the dough circles and give them a teardrop shape, right?"

I nodded.

"Then we coat and fry them?"

I nodded again.

"Got it." He pointed a spoon at me. "You make them; I'll layer and fry them."

Okay, I signed, and we again got back to work.

It took us around forty minutes to finish making the *Coxinha*, and as Myles took the last of it out of the frying pan before placing it on a tissue-covered plate, I gently pressed more tissues over them to soak off the excess oil.

"Taste it," he said excitedly, then grabbed a chair, brought it close to me, flipped it around, and straddled it before sitting down. "Come on, do it."

I chuckled as I carefully broke a *Coxinha* into two and plopped one half into my mouth.

Myles's eyes were all but saucer-like as he stared at me in obvious anxiousness.

The *Coxinha* all but melted on my tongue, and it was the perfect balance of crispy, spicy, wholesome, and greasy.

I moaned as my shoulders slumped in bliss, then gave Myles two very enthusiastic thumbs up before signing, *This is so good*.

"Yeah?" he asked, like he couldn't believe it.

I offered him the other half, and when he tasted it, he grinned and puffed his chest out. "So...*now* what do you have to say about my cooking skills, huh?" He winked. "Although, I will say that your minor assistance in making these is recognized in high regards."

I laughed and shook my head, then looked up when he stood and walked over to me. He bent and brought our faces impossibly close, and I could smell the spice on his breath; see the oil stains on his apron, and even some flour on his neck and jaw.

"We're a pretty fucking epic team, aren't we?" he asked, and the question was so beautiful – random, yes, but still beautiful – that I couldn't help with smile.

I leaned in, cupped one side of Myles's face, and pressed a long kiss on his waiting lips. *We are*, I signed, and I don't think there's ever been words that I've signed with as much honesty as I did those two.

53.

"**T**he two of them are MATES?! Myles all but shrieked as he looked up from the paperback in his hands. "WHAT THE FUCK?!"

I pressed my lips together as I shifted a little. *They are*, I signed.

He blinked. "But he's so…he's…" He frowned. "What the shit-fuck?"

I chuckled. *Just keep reading*, I told him.

We were sitting in front of our massive fireplace, and Myles had basically sandwiched me between pillows and fluffy blankets, especially because we were on the floor and not the couch. There were blankets under my ass, one that was draped over my legs, with pillows bricked on either side of me, and, of course, my new best friend: the elevation pillow, which kept my right leg lifted.

The crackling of wood and fire was the only sound in the house, paired with Myles's occasional vocal reactions to the book he was reading.

When he'd told me he wanted to read fiction, but wanted to begin with something cool and interesting, I'd suggested he start the *A Court of Thorns and Roses* series by my favorite author, Sarah J. Maas. He'd immediately gone online and purchased all 5 paperbacks, and honestly, I've never been more in love with him than I was when he'd held the books in his hands last week and looked at them like they were something to be cherished and protected.

I've picked a keeper for myself, haven't I?

Myles began shifting toward me, in a slide-stop-slide manner that looked so adorably ridiculous that I couldn't help but give him a '*What're you up to?*' kinda look.

He'd pressed the open paperback to his chest, and when he reached me, he placed both his elbows on top of the pillow to my right. "Hey." He brought his face close to mine. "Tell me what happens in the next chapter," he whispered, as if someone might hear him. "Please."

I stared at him for a beat or two, slightly stunned by his words, then placed a hand over my mouth and laughed.

Man, I'd intoxicated him on book fumes, and now he just couldn't get enough.

I was *so* fucking proud of myself.

No, I signed. *Read it yourself.*

Myles frowned. "I said 'please', didn't I?"

I shook my head.

"Pretty please?"

No, I signed again.

He huffed. "I'll give you a Thai massage if you tell me. Hell, I'll do your laundry if you tell me."

You already do both of our laundries, I told him.

He groaned in frustration, then leaned in further and placed his chin on my shoulder. "*Baby...*" he sang. "*Pleeeeease?*"

I couldn't help but laugh again. *Just read*, I signed.

He pouted, so I pressed my teeth over his bottom lip and gave it a soft tug.

He grinned, shut the book and threw it on the couch behind us, then said, "Do it again."

I stared at the discarded book, then at him.

"Don't worry, I'd dog-eared the page already," he told me.

My mouth hung open in shock. And in horror. *Crime*, I signed.

Myles's lips twitched. "Dog-earing a page is a *crime...*?"

Yes, I signed. *A brutal one.*

He chuckled. "Alright, c'mere." He took one of my hands in his, and gently pulled me forward.

264

I ran the back of my fingers over the stubble on his jaw, to which he smiled.

Kiss me, I told him.

He smirked, and the storm in his blazing eyes all but set my veins on fire. "Fuck yeah," he said, then fisted my hair oh so delicately before pressing his lips to mine.

I sighed against him, at the familiar taste of him, and at the way his stubble brushed against my skin when he parted my lips and sucked on my tongue.

I leaned forward and kissed him harder, making him moan.

"I was going to make a joke about how I can smell your arousal," he began, then kissed me again. "You know, like how Rhysand and the other faes can in the books, but then the scent of your perfume hit me right in the nostrils, and I forgot all about it."

Good Lord...

I have created a monster.

I moved back a little so that I could look at him, and when he winked and wiggled his brows at me, I tipped my head back and laughed.

This is my life – my crazy, ridiculously perfect in every way that *matters*, life. And yeah, I did face some tough-ass shit to get to where I am, but every choice, every step I took in certain directions to make my past decisions, led me to Myles. He fought for us, made sure there *was* an us, to begin with. For years I thought that my silence was the only thing I needed in order to find comfort and peace, but I didn't realize what I was missing out on until Myles all but fox-trotted into my life and practically flipped it on its axis. He said he wanted me, and did everything to prove the same. He didn't give up; he gave me the strength to be stronger than I was. And, I have never once even *thought* about what would have happened if things had been different, or what would have happened if *Avô* had hired someone else to renovate the kitchen and build the library, because really, I don't wanna think about that; I don't wanna know what would've happened, or what other paths would have opened up for me.

I'm happy – *so fucking happy* – with my beautifully silly guy, and I wouldn't have him any other way. He was, after all, my everything; my forever.

My infinity.

EPILOGUE

Myles

I *can walk, Myles*, Rina signed, then huffed and wrapped her arms around my neck when I lifted her in my arms and kicked my van's passenger-side door shut.

"I know you can," I told her, "but I still wanna hold you and keep you swept off your feet in a literal way. You got a problem with that?"

She rolled her eyes, but smiled anyway. *Where are we going?* she asked.

I grinned at her. "You'll see." I don't know why I was being so cool about this. If anything, I should be freaking the ever-loving fuck out. Pissing my pants and breaking into a sweat, even. But I was calm; I was okay.

What the fuck was wrong with me? Where the hell was my sense of normalcy? But then again, everyone – including Rina – say I'm from another planet entirely, and maybe they're right, because any normal human being would be losing their shit if they were in a situation similar to mine. But me? I was cool as a damn polar bear's ass in the frigid Antarctic.

Rina and I'd woken up early, so we'd decided to go on our daily walk a bit prior to our usual time. But, instead of taking her to the usual park we went to every day, I drove us to *Millennium Park*, because I had something that I needed to do, and I simply couldn't do it without her.

Rina had been given the all-clear by her doctors almost a month ago. Her recovery process had been a slow one, but it'd also been hassle-free, thanks to physical therapy and our regular walks. And, of course, her medications.

The warm morning light hit the grass I was walking on, highlighting the path ahead of me.

267

I turned left, and then entered the gorgeous *Lurie Garden*, and Rina sucked in a breath as she looked around the massive expanse.

I took the first walkway, exactly as I'd planned, and glanced at the gold-and-black butterflies when they drifted past Rina and I.

It's beautiful, she signed, her eyes wide.

"You've never been in here?" I asked her.

She shook her head.

I smiled. "Well, I like this place. The bugs are an inconvenience, sure, but it's a little price we've gotta pay to witness *this*." I jerked my head to the right, at the lovely monkshoods flowing with the crisp breezes.

Rina pressed a kiss to the side of my head. *Thank you for bringing me here*, she signed.

I winked. "No worries, babe." I spotted the small wooden chair seconds before she did, and when she raised her brows at me, I shrugged casually before leading us to it.

Thank Christ Daniel had placed it exactly where I'd asked him to.

I stopped in front of the chair, helped Rina settle in it, and, before she could ask why I'd done that, I went on one knee in front of her.

She gasped, and a strong gush of wind whipped past us, resulting in the pretty queen-of-the-prairies around us to rustle wildly.

Rina's hair all but concealed the wild expression on her face as it moved with the wind, but she quickly pushed it behind her ears and blinked at me.

I'd thought Miguel would stake me in the heart when I'd asked – no, *told* – him about wanting to marry Rina, but he'd surprised me by not only giving me his permission, but also a too-long, slightly awkward and suffocating, fatherly hug.

A HUG.

"*You've saved my Carina*," he'd told me. "*From the past, from the thoughts in her head, and from the pain. I misjudged you, treated you unkindly, but you continued to prove me wrong; continued to show up for her. And that, Myles, is more than enough for me.*"

268

I'd paid him a quick visit a couple of days before Rina had gotten the all-clear, which meant that I was sitting on my question for too damn long.

Not anymore, though.

"I get that it's too soon," I said to Rina, then swallowed, "but trust me when I say that I *know* I want this, Rina." I rose a little so that I could be closer to her. "You can say no; you can ask me to wait longer. I'll do it – I swear I will. But I want you to know that I'm down to do this shit. I'm fucking ready." I touched my forehead to hers. "Because *no one* has ever made me feel what you do, and I know for a fact that no one else ever will. Baby…" Our eyes met, and my heart began thrashing in my chest. "You make me feel *alive*; you make me feel like I'm *worth* something. When I'm with you, I can be crazy, fucking insane, and you still love me. You lift me up and make me wanna soar. You *see* me, Rina, and you understand. For someone like me, that's *everything*." The stone walkway pressed against my knee as I shifted, and when Rina let go of a long breath before searching my face, I brought my right hand to the side of my head, then slashed it forward to say: *Will.* I then pointed at her, and clasped my hands together to say: *you marry.* And finally, I pointed at myself to say: *me.* It was then that I realized that my hands were shaking.

Good, at least I was capable of being nervous in the heat of the moment. At least I wasn't a damn alien from outer space or something.

I know my signing technique isn't the best, but I also know that Rina understood me perfectly fine.

She grabbed the chair's armrests, and then slowly got to her feet. When I opened my mouth to protest, she brought her left hand forward, palm down, and wiggled her fingers at me before giving me a grin.

I stood, feeling a little giddy, and grinned back at her. "Yeah?" I asked like the fucking idiot I was.

She chuckled. *Yes*, she signed. *Yes, I will marry you. There never was a question about it.*

"Thank fuck," I all but exhaled the words, and with still trembling hands, I pulled the teal box out of my joggers before flicking it open.

Rina sucked in a surprised breath, then looked at me with the kind of softness that I was so used to, and one I've always craved more and more of.

I pulled the pavé-style ring out of the box, then shoved the latter back into my pocket. I swallowed, took Rina's left hand in mine, and when she smiled at me, I smiled right back before slipping the ring onto her ring finger.

She lifted her hand to the sun, resulting in the diamonds to glint off her golden skin, and even leave prismatic reflections on her face when she turned her wrist this way and that.

Beautiful, she signed, then flung her arms around my neck before pressing her lips to mine.

"I'm so glad you like it," I said, and held her waist between my hands before pulling her to me. "*Fiancée.*"

She blushed a little at that, and my God, she legit took my breath away with how stunning she was.

"You're my sanctum, Rina. You know that, right?" I told her.

She nodded. *And you are my reason to start anew*, she signed, then searched my face. *I may not have words to give you, but I have all of me and my heart to offer you. I love you, Myles, and I swear I will never stop.*

It took me a long beat to understand what she'd said, but when I did, I felt my eyes sting, and my breaths turned heavy.

"You are everything I want," I said to her. "I don't need your words to know what you're feeling, when I can *see* you just as clearly as you can see *me*. And that, baby, is all I'll ever need. I love you so much." I leaned in and kissed her, and she held onto me tighter as she kissed me back.

This is my life – my slightly bumpy, absolutely amazing in every way that's important, life. And yeah, I did act like a complete coward towards the very beginning, but I'm so fucking glad I bounced back from it before it was too late. Rina held hope for me, made sure there was enough light at the end of the tunnel for her and I. For an *us*. I was, and always will be, mad for her, and ever since I've realized that she's my *it*, I haven't stopped fighting for us. She makes me stronger, more defiant in ways that matter. I don't spend time thinking about the various other ways in which my life could have moved forward had Miguel not asked me to renovate his kitchen and design the library, because really, it's not the kinda thought I like to entertain. I'm happy – *so fucking happy* – with my insanely incredible woman, and I wouldn't have her any other way. She was, after all, my everything; my forever.

My infinity.

The End.

ACKNOWLEDGEMENTS

A massive thank you to my ah-mazing and patient beta readers. You know who you are. I love you all so damn much. Thank you for sticking by my side and believing in Myles and Carina's story. You made a difference; please know that.

My lovely duo of Erin Lewicki and Yasmin Gallo. You two are the backbone of this story. Y'all are absolute gems, and I love y'all both to pieces. Thank you so, SO much for your expertise and advice.

My family – without whom I would still only be dreaming of writing books, of telling stories. Thank you, Mom, Dad, Qadir, and my lovely aunt.

A cuddly thank you to my bunnies: Moon, Snow (I miss you two), Velvet, and Coco. You four are my babies, and I'm beyond happy to be your momma. Thank you for the endless cuddles, kisses, and sniffs. Those got me through some of the hard times.

My lovely readers, I love you so much. You've stood by me from the beginning, have given my stories a chance, and for that, I'll forever be in your debt. Thank you – from the very bottom of my dramatic heart.

Printed in Great Britain
by Amazon

80372335R00163